The Amish Cook's

FAMILY FAVORITE RECIPES

The *Amish Cook's*
FAMILY FAVORITE RECIPES

Lovina Eicher

with Kevin Williams

The original books—*The Amish Cook at Home, The Amish Cook's Baking Book, The Amish Cook's Anniversary Book,* and *Amish Cooks Across America*—were published in 2008, 2009, 2010, and 2012, respectively, and portions are reprinted with permission by Andrews McMeel Publishing, LLC. Exclusive direct mail edition published in September 2013.

Printed in the United States of America
Rodale Inc. makes every effort to use acid-free ♾, recycled paper ♻.

Library of Congress Cataloging-in-Publication Data is on file with the publisher.

ISBN 978–1–62336–217–1   direct hardcover
8   10   9   direct hardcover

We inspire and enable people to improve their lives and the world around them.
For more of our products, visit rodalestore.com or call 800–848–4735.

For my mother, Elizabeth Coblentz,
who was the original Amish Cook
to a generation of readers and—
most of all—to me.

CONTENTS

Lovina Eicher, the Amish Cook

Lovina writes the internationally syndicated column "The Amish Cook," a role she stepped into upon the untimely death in 2002 of the original columnist—her mother, Elizabeth Coblentz. She has written hundreds of articles and is the coauthor of four previous books on traditional Amish cooking. Lovina lives in an Amish community in Michigan with her husband and eight children.

THE EICHER FAMILY

Mother and the Amish Cook: Lovina

Husband and father: Joe

Their children: Elizabeth, Susan, Verena, Benjamin, Loretta, Joseph, Lovina, Kevin

Kevin Williams

Kevin has been editing "The Amish Cook" since its inception in 1991. The column began when he, as a young journalism student, convinced Elizabeth Coblentz to try at writing about Amish recipes, traditions, and family happenings. He is also the coauthor, with Lovina Eicher, of four previous books from "The Amish Cook."

INTRODUCTION

From Lovina

I am so very pleased to welcome you to this exclusive edition of Amish family recipes. Each dish draws on the traditions of our close-knit community and the emphasis we place on gathering around a table full of well-made, hearty, and heartwarming food.

I've loved selecting recipes, cooking and baking tips, and personal stories from my life and the lives of other great cooks to create a cookbook reflecting the best of Amish kitchens and traditions. I hope you experience the same great enjoyment as you look through the more than four hundred recipes and tips in these pages.

The importance every Amish community places on family and tradition is hard to overstate. These are at the very core of what we believe, and the food we make and serve is always with that in mind.

Because of this, these recipes were created by generations of cooks who wanted nothing more (or less) than to satisfy the soul and stomach of people we love. To do that, we use everyday ingredients in continuously creative ways, knowing that the best test of that creativity lies in the happiness our families feel as they enjoy what we've made.

With this latest recipe collection, I'm also blessed to carry on another family tradition: My mother, Elizabeth Coblentz, was the original Amish Cook, a role she took on in partnership with her editor, Kevin Williams, beginning in 1991. After she passed away in 2002, Kevin asked me if I would consider continuing her column. You can tell my answer by looking down at the book in your hands.

I can never replace my beloved mother, nor would I ever want to. But I can nurture what she started. And if I'm very lucky, perhaps one of my daughters will decide to become the next generation of the Amish Cook one day.

I wish you the same joy I get from the food and stories you'll read about here. The cooks and families behind them, including me and mine, are delighted to be able to share them with you. May God bless you and your family!

From Kevin

I am very fortunate to have spent more than twenty years tasting, testing, and talking about Amish food; first with Elizabeth, and now with Lovina. Each year I've spent with these two amazing cooks has provided me with the honor of introducing the legendary experience of Amish cooking to more and more people.

Early on, I didn't know much about Amish food except that a lot of non-Amish people seemed to like it. The Amish-style restaurants my family and I would pass on US Route 42 outside Plain City, Ohio, when I was a kid always seemed to have lines of customers waiting patiently for a table.

It wasn't until I reached adulthood that I understood what those customers were waiting for—tables groaning with heaping helpings of homemade rolls, chicken and dumplings, buttered noodles, stuffed pork chops, panfried chicken, and slices of pie as big as a football. Amazing . . . my mouth is watering just thinking about that.

What's even more remarkable, at least to me, is that almost all this cooking and baking is done through intuition and experience above all else. To explain what I mean, let me tell you a story—one where I'm seated at a kitchen table, my laptop open, to help gather recipes for this book. Across from me was an Amish woman trying patiently to give me a sweet potato pie recipe for which she was known far and wide.

Her directions went something like this: Use a large cup of sweet potatoes, flour, sugar, brown sugar, eggs (best if they're from your own hens), cinnamon, vanilla. Salt, of course. Enough hot milk to make three pies.

"Um," I said, not knowing where to start. So I picked an obvious place: "About how much flour would that be?"

She expressed a bit of frustration at me wanting her to enunciate *every* step. "Oh, certainly anyone would know how much flour to add!" she told me, exasperation in her voice. I just nodded because it seemed better than admitting I had no earthly idea how much to add.

And so it came to be that one of my main tasks in helping compile this collection was to render recipes into a standard format where they'd be clearly understood by anyone else who doesn't know the stove setting of "Don't have your oven too hot."

Yet I still strive to be among those who can cook by feel, smell, sight, and taste. But even if I never get there, I can still make dishes worthy of a spot on the table of the "Plain People." All I have to do to create those wonders is page through this book, select a few recipes, and start cooking. I'm very glad you've joined us in doing the same thing.

THE AMISH: AN OVERVIEW

WHO ARE THE AMISH?

The Amish have long captivated the world around them by holding tightly to the ways of a seemingly bygone era. In most Amish settlements, horse-drawn carriages are still the standard, while electricity—and all that it powers—is not.

The Amish strive to keep life plain, hence their description as the "Plain People." Bright colors and designs are considered lacking in the humility their faith and beliefs require.

The Amish movement was founded in 1693 by a Swiss bishop named Jacob Ammon to create an order that adhered more strictly to Bible-based, family-centered, peace-dwelling rules. Unlike most other Christians of the time, the Amish believed only adults could choose their religion and, therefore, be baptized.

In many ways, an Amish approach creates a simpler life: no need for car insurance, no desire to stay up with costly fashion trends, no struggles to pay utility bills. But there is a trade-off; simpler doesn't mean easier. Days are long. On most Amish farms, chores begin before sunrise and continue until bedtime.

Good and plentiful food, however, is a priority—both for the nourishment it provides to hard workers as well as for the family bonds it strengthens around the table and in the kitchen. Meals are always wholesome and hearty, and family always comes first.

WHAT DO THEY COOK?

Most meals are much different than what most outsiders think when they hear the term "Amish cooking." Pop culture images of the Amish serving lard-laden piecrusts and thick chicken corn soup are rooted less in reality than in tourism brochures.

Amish cooking has won legions of fans for its simplicity and adherence to back-to-basics ingredients. The Amish are perhaps most legendary for their desserts, such as their scratch-made piecrusts filled with butterscotch, creamy custard, or bursts of handpicked berries. Cookies, cakes, and puddings also receive the careful attention of any Amish cook.

In reality, Amish menus are as varied and different as the many settlements scattered across the country, whether that's made evident in the huckleberry milkshakes of Montana or the barbecued venison meatballs in Illinois.

THE CARE AND KEEPING OF AMISH RECIPES

Throughout this book, recipes are in the same format, with measurements conveniently listed, recommendations noted for substitute ingredients when possible, as well as oven temperatures and baking times provided. But is this how the recipes look in an Amish kitchen? Not one bit.

The Amish typically cook and bake from generational cues, using tips, hints, and recipes passed down through generations. Recipes are written on tattered note cards, scraps of paper, and, very frequently, not at all. Take, for example, this recipe for a beef-vegetable bake: ground beef, fresh cabbage, coarsely cut potatoes, thickly sliced carrots, onions, salt, pepper.

That's pretty much it. It's not that the Amish are secretive—they're not. In fact, they're extremely generous with sharing their recipes because few things make Amish cooks happier than helping another family enjoy something they created in their kitchens and homes. But most assume you'll want—and know how—to change up the rough strokes they give to reflect your own knowledge and tastes.

The recipes in this book are meant to be seen in that light. They have all the specifics you need to re-create the dishes intended by their creators, but they also have the encouragement of generations of Amish cooks behind them—all encouraging you to tinker, tweak, and otherwise make the recipes your own.

morning meals

Breakfast has a special place in Amish homes. It's how each day begins, coming together to share a meal that will sustain our family through the day. These hearty morning meals can create that sense of togetherness at your table, too.

HOMEMADE RHUBARB JUICE

Makes 8 quarts

This recipe makes a concentrate, and then you can add it to other juices (for instance, pineapple, apple, or orange juice) to taste. The first year I made it, I used my sister Emma's rhubarb. I wanted to make more, but I wasn't sure what the children would think of it. Now that I know the kids like it, I always make as much as I can. I looked at the various recipes for rhubarb juice that people in my church gave me and then just sort of made up my own. The cooked stalks make good compost for the garden.

8 pounds rhubarb, cut into 1-inch pieces

2 gallons water

2 (12-ounce) cans frozen orange juice

3 cups pineapple juice

4 cups sugar

1 (3-ounce) box strawberry-flavored gelatin

Combine the rhubarb and water in a large kettle on the stove and cook until the rhubarb is soft. Pour through a strainer and catch the rhubarb juice. Discard the cooked stalks. Add the orange juice, pineapple juice, sugar, and gelatin to the rhubarb juice. Stir until the sugar is dissolved. If canning, pour the juice into sterilized jars and attach the seals and lids. Otherwise, put in pitchers and refrigerate for up to a week.

HOMEMADE GRAPE JUICE

Makes 4 to 6 quarts

Our children love this juice when made with green grapes (my youngest daughter, also named Lovina, calls them white). I like purple, too. None of us will drink store-bought grape juice. We all think it is too sweet. Some of the Amish process their juice for 10 to 15 minutes in boiling water—you can do that if you think you're going to can it and keep it for more than a few days. But around here it never lasts that long.

8 to 10 cups water

5 heaping cups grapes

2½ cups sugar

Boil the water and grapes in a large pot for 45 minutes. Put the contents of the pot through a strainer or juicer. Put the juice back on the stove and add the sugar. Let the juice come to a boil, stirring to dissolve the sugar. Immediately pour into sterilized jars (if using) and attach the seals and lids. The heat will seal the jars. Otherwise, pour into pitchers and refrigerate for up to a week.

BLUEBERRY-LEMON BUTTERMILK MUFFINS

Makes 24 muffins

The lemon adds a tang to the sweetness of the blueberries, making for a burst of flavors. Using locally grown and harvested blueberries gives these muffins a very fresh taste.

3 cups all-purpose flour

2 teaspoons baking powder

1 teaspoon baking soda

$\frac{1}{2}$ teaspoon salt

1 cup (2 sticks) butter, softened

$1\frac{1}{2}$ cups sugar

4 large eggs

$2\frac{1}{2}$ tablespoons fresh lemon juice

2 tablespoons lemon zest (see Note)

1 teaspoon vanilla extract

1 cup buttermilk

2 cups fresh blueberries

GLAZE

$1\frac{1}{2}$ cups powdered sugar

3 tablespoons fresh lemon juice

1 tablespoon lemon zest (see Note)

Preheat the oven to 350°F. Lightly grease two standard muffin pans or line with paper baking cups.

In a large mixing bowl, combine the flour, baking powder, baking soda, and salt. Set aside.

In a medium mixing bowl, cream the butter and sugar. Beat in the eggs, one at a time. Add the lemon juice, lemon zest, and vanilla and combine until smooth. Beat in the flour mixture and buttermilk, alternating the two, using about one-third of each for each addition. The mixture should be smooth and creamy. Fold in the blueberries, and mix until they are evenly distributed throughout the batter. Pour the batter into the muffin tins, filling each cup about halfway.

Bake until the muffin tops are golden, 20 to 25 minutes. Allow to cool for about 5 minutes.

Make the glaze: Stir the powdered sugar, lemon juice, and lemon zest until smooth. Brush the glaze over the muffin tops while the muffins are still warm.

Note: *Both the batter and the glaze use the juice and zest of lemons, so be sure to zest the lemons before extracting the juice.*

HOMEMADE BANANA MUFFINS

Makes 12 muffins

My children like bananas sliced with home-canned peaches. I make a mixture of bananas and peaches that tastes delicious served over these muffins.

2 teaspoons baking powder

1 teaspoon salt

½ teaspoon baking soda

½ teaspoon ground nutmeg

2 cups all-purpose flour

¼ cup vegetable oil

1 large egg, slightly beaten

⅓ cup skim milk

1 cup mashed ripe bananas

½ cup granulated sugar

¼ cup packed brown sugar

Preheat the oven to 375°F. Grease and lightly flour 12 muffin cups or line with paper baking cups.

In a large bowl, stir together the baking powder, salt, baking soda, and nutmeg until evenly blended. Add all the remaining ingredients, mixing only until the dry particles are moistened. Fill the prepared muffin cups two-thirds full and bake until golden brown, 20 to 25 minutes.

OATMEAL MUFFINS

Makes 12 muffins

I buy my oatmeal in bulk-food stores, because I can get the large amounts that I need to feed our family. This is a good recipe to use up some of the excess oats. This muffin would taste good even using other things besides raisins. For example, one could add ½ cup well-drained pineapple, shredded carrots, or chopped apples instead. Nuts could also be added.

1 cup all-purpose flour

¼ cup sugar

1 teaspoon ground cinnamon

1 tablespoon baking powder

½ teaspoon salt

1 cup quick-cooking rolled oats

½ cup chopped raisins

1 large egg, beaten lightly

¾ cup milk

1 teaspoon vanilla extract

3 tablespoons vegetable oil

TOPPING

2 tablespoons sugar

2 teaspoons all-purpose flour

1 teaspoon ground cinnamon

1 teaspoon margarine, melted

Preheat the oven to 375°F. Grease 12 muffin cups or line with paper baking cups. Set aside.

Sift the flour, sugar, cinnamon, baking powder, and salt into a large bowl. Stir in the oatmeal and raisins. In another bowl, combine the beaten egg, milk, vanilla, and oil. Add this gently to the flour mixture, stirring just until moistened. Spoon the batter into the prepared muffin cups, filling each two-thirds full.

Make the topping: Combine the topping ingredients in a small bowl and sprinkle evenly over the muffin batter in the cups. Bake until a toothpick inserted in the muffin centers comes out clean, about 20 minutes. Remove to a wire rack to cool.

SOURDOUGH CINNAMON ROLLS

Makes 24 large rolls

I didn't realize until recently that you could make cinnamon rolls with sourdough. The Sourdough Cinnamon Rolls are a lot easier if you mix up an extra batch of Sourdough Bread dough (page 159) when you're making the bread. My family all loves cinnamon rolls and can hardly wait to eat them. Sometimes I put a limit on how many cinnamon rolls the family can eat, or they'll just keep eating them!

Sourdough Bread dough, prepared through first rise (page 159)

6 tablespoons margarine or butter, softened

1 cup packed brown sugar

3 teaspoons ground cinnamon

ICING

⅓ cup margarine or butter, softened

1 teaspoon vanilla extract

4 cups sifted powdered sugar

½ cup milk

After the dough has risen overnight, punch it down, divide it in half, and form two balls of dough. Take a ball of dough and roll it out as thin as possible on a floured surface. Brush the dough with half of the softened margarine. Sprinkle half of the brown sugar evenly over the dough, then sprinkle with half of the cinnamon.

Roll up the dough like a jelly roll. Cut each roll into slices ½- to ¾-inch thick. Place the slices ½ inch apart in a buttered jelly-roll pan, and cover with waxed paper. Repeat with the remaining ball of dough and remaining margarine, brown sugar, and cinnamon. Let rise 4 hours.

Preheat the oven to 350°F. Bake the rolls until golden brown, about 20 minutes. Remove from the oven and let cool slightly.

Make the icing: Cream the margarine with the vanilla and 1 cup of the powdered sugar in a medium bowl. Gradually add the milk and the remaining powdered sugar and stir until smooth. Drizzle over the warm cinnamon rolls and serve immediately.

SWEET BREAKFAST ROLLS

Makes 2 dozen rolls

We don't often have sweets in the morning, but when we do this recipe is a good one to make. Our children like their sweet snacks in the afternoon when they come home from school. My husband, Joe, likes a cinnamon roll or sweet roll in the morning with his hot chocolate or coffee.

1 cup milk, scalded

$\frac{1}{2}$ cup (1 stick) butter

2 teaspoons salt

$\frac{1}{2}$ cup sugar

2 packages active dry yeast

$\frac{1}{2}$ cup warm water

4 large eggs, beaten

6 cups bread flour

4 tablespoons ($\frac{1}{2}$ stick) butter, softened

$\frac{1}{2}$ cup sugar

1 tablespoon ground cinnamon

Grease a jelly-roll pan or a large cookie sheet with a 1-inch rim.

In a large bowl, mix the milk, butter, salt, and sugar. Set the bowl aside until the mixture cools to lukewarm. While the mixture is cooling, dissolve the yeast in the warm water for about 10 minutes or until bubbles form. Then add the yeast mixture, eggs, and flour gradually to the lukewarm milk mixture. Knead with your hands until an elastic dough forms. Remove the dough from the bowl and place on a lightly floured surface. Knead the dough for five or six strokes, and then roll into a 12 by 20-inch rectangle. In a small bowl, mix the butter, sugar, and cinnamon until well blended. Spread the mixture over the dough. Roll the dough up from the 20-inch side. Cut the 20-inch-long roll into ¾-inch pieces and place on the prepared pan. Let the dough rise uncovered for about 30 minutes.

While the dough is rising, preheat the oven to 350°F. Bake the rolls until golden brown, 20 minutes. Add frosting (see Basic Frosting, page 348).

SPEEDY CINNAMON ROLLS

Makes approximately 2 dozen rolls

Cinnamon rolls are made from many different recipes passed around Amish settlements. From slow, let-rise-all-day yeasty cinnamon confections to quicker but no less delicious concoctions, cinnamon rolls are a staple of Amish baking. This is a favorite, fast cinnamon roll recipe.

2 cups plus 4½ cups bread flour

2 cups warm water (105° to 115°F)

½ cup granulated sugar

1 tablespoon salt

2 packages active dry yeast

2 eggs

⅓ cup lard

6 tablespoons margarine or butter, softened

1 cup packed brown sugar

1 tablespoon ground cinnamon

In a large bowl, combine 2 cups of the bread flour with the water, sugar, salt, and yeast. Beat the mixture for 2 minutes with a wooden spoon, then add the eggs and the lard. Stir until well blended. Gradually add the remaining 4½ cups of bread flour to the mixture and stir until a firm dough is formed. Cover the bowl and set it in a warm area to rest for 20 minutes.

After resting, punch the dough down, divide it in half, and form it into two balls. On a floured surface, roll one ball of the dough out as thinly as possible. Brush half of the softened margarine evenly over the dough, then sprinkle with half of the brown sugar and half of the cinnamon. Roll the dough up like a jelly roll. Cut each roll into slices that are ½- to ¾-inch thick. Place the slices ½ inch apart in a buttered jelly-roll pan. Repeat with the remaining ball of dough and the remaining margarine, brown sugar, and cinnamon. Place the rolls in a warm area and allow to rise for about 45 minutes, or until doubled in size.

While the rolls are rising, preheat the oven to 350°F. Bake the rolls for 15 to 20 minutes, until they are golden brown. Allow the rolls to cool on wire racks for 15 minutes. If desired, you may spread the rolls with your favorite frosting before serving.

MAPLE CINNAMON STICKY BUNS

Makes 12 rolls

These cinnamon rolls, infused with the fresh taste of maple, are a favorite among the Old Order Amish of the Conewango Valley in Upstate New York. The end-of-season, dark, Grade B maple syrup gives the strongest maple taste, but any grade of pure maple syrup can be used in these rolls if you can't find it.

DOUGH

1½ cups warm water (115°F)

1 tablespoon plus 2 teaspoons (0.65 ounce) active dry yeast

⅓ cup granulated sugar

4½ to 5 cups all-purpose flour

⅓ cup vegetable oil

½ teaspoon salt

1 large egg, beaten

2 tablespoons maple syrup

SYRUP

4½ tablespoons unsalted butter, plus some for greasing a pan

½ cup maple syrup

½ cup firmly packed light brown sugar

FILLING

3 tablespoons butter, softened

½ cup firmly packed light brown sugar

2 teaspoons ground cinnamon

2 tablespoons maple syrup

Make the dough: Pour the warm water into a large mixing bowl. Sprinkle the yeast and sugar into the water. Stir and let it stand until foamy, at least 3 minutes. When the yeast is foamy, mix in 1 cup of the flour until incorporated. Add the oil, salt, egg, and maple syrup. Add just enough flour that the dough is no longer sticky. It should take about 3½ more cups, but you may need more or less. Mix with a dough hook attached to a mixer on medium speed for 2 to 3 minutes, or knead by hand for 3 to 5 minutes. Place in a greased bowl, cover with plastic wrap, and let rise in a warm place for about 1 hour.

   Make the syrup: Grease a 19 by 13-inch baking pan. Combine the butter and maple syrup in a small saucepan over medium heat and stir until the butter melts. Remove the saucepan from the heat. Mix in the brown sugar. Pour the syrup into the prepared baking dish and tilt the dish to evenly coat the bottom. After an hour, punch down the dough, and roll it on a well-floured surface into a 13 by 18-inch rectangle about ¼ inch thick.

   Make the filling: Spread the softened butter all over the rectangle, except for a narrow butter-free strip along one of the long edges. In a medium bowl, combine the brown sugar and cinnamon. Spread the cinnamon-sugar mixture over the dough, gently pressing, until evenly distributed. Drizzle the maple syrup over the filling. Starting with the buttered long edge, roll up the dough and pinch the edges to secure. Cut the dough with a sharp, serrated knife into twelve equal pieces. Place in the prepared baking pan and cover. Let the rolls rise for 30 to 45 minutes, until puffy. Preheat the oven to 350°F.

Bake for 20 to 25 minutes, or until light golden brown. Remove from the oven, immediately invert onto a baking sheet, and let cool for 5 minutes. Serve warm.

PUMPKIN BREAD

Makes 2 loaves

Pumpkin, like watermelon and squash, is a vine that really spreads out. So it depends if we grow pumpkins in a particular year largely on how much space we have. I like having fresh pumpkin because it really can be used in a lot of different baked goods. This moist bread is a crowd favorite!

$3\frac{1}{2}$ cups all-purpose flour

3 cups sugar

2 teaspoons baking soda

$1\frac{1}{2}$ teaspoons salt

1 teaspoon ground cinnamon

2 cups homemade pumpkin puree, or 1 (15-ounce) can pumpkin puree

4 large eggs, beaten

$\frac{2}{3}$ cup water

$\frac{1}{3}$ cup vegetable oil

1 cup pecans, chopped

Preheat the oven to 350°F. Grease and flour two 9 by 5-inch loaf pans. Knock out the excess flour.

Combine the flour, sugar, baking soda, salt, and cinnamon in a large bowl. Whisk until blended. Stir in the pumpkin, eggs, water, oil, and pecans. Divide the batter evenly between the prepared pans. Bake until a toothpick inserted in the center of a loaf comes out clean, about 1 hour.

RAISIN BREAD

Makes 2 loaves

My father liked raisins and prunes. This bread has a lot of raisins and a thick texture from the surprise ingredient—mashed potatoes. Try this warm and spread with butter for a great breakfast! The raisins will have much more flavor if chopped before being added to the dough.

1½ cups milk

¼ cup sugar

2 teaspoons salt

½ cup (1 stick) butter, softened

1 cup unseasoned mashed potatoes

2 packages active dry yeast

½ cup warm water

1½ cups raisins

7½ cups bread flour

FILLING

½ cup sugar

2 teaspoons ground cinnamon

½ cup (1 stick) butter, softened

In a heavy saucepan, scald the milk over medium heat. Remove from the heat just before the milk reaches the boiling point, then add the sugar, salt, butter, and mashed potatoes and stir. Let cool. In a large bowl, dissolve the yeast in the warm water. Then mix with the milk mixture. Add the raisins and flour. Stir. Let rise in a warm place for 1½ hours, until double in size. Divide the dough into two balls.

Make the filling: In a separate bowl, mix the filling ingredients until crumbly in texture.

Preheat the oven to 350°F. Grease two 5 by 9-inch loaf pans.

Roll each ball of dough out on a lightly floured surface. Spread half of the filling mixture on the rolled-out dough. Starting with a short side, roll up as for a jelly roll and pinch the edges together at the ends. Place into a loaf pan, making sure all the edges remain sealed. Repeat with the second ball of dough. Place both loaf pans on a baking sheet and bake until golden brown, about 45 minutes.

Remove the bread from the pan and cool on a wire rack or windowsill. Serve warm. After the bread cools completely, it can be stored in a sealed plastic freezer bag and frozen for up to 6 months. If the bread is stored in a sealed plastic bag at room temperature, it should be consumed within 4 days.

RHUBARB BREAD

Makes 1 loaf

This is a nice bread just to slice and eat, similar to pumpkin bread. It is wonderful as a breakfast bread and goes great with a glass of cold Homemade Rhubarb Juice, page 3. Store leftover bread in a sealed bag. Leftover bread also freezes well.

½ cup (1 stick) butter, softened

1 cup sugar

2 large eggs, beaten

2 tablespoons milk

2 cups all-purpose flour

½ teaspoon salt

1 teaspoon baking soda

1 teaspoon vanilla extract

1 cup hot cooked rhubarb

TOPPING

1 tablespoon butter, melted

1 tablespoon all-purpose flour

1 teaspoon hot water

1 tablespoon sugar

1 teaspoon ground cinnamon

Preheat the oven to 375°F. Lightly grease and flour a 5 by 9-inch loaf pan and set aside.

In a medium mixing bowl, cream the butter and sugar together until it becomes light and creamy. Add the eggs and milk, and mix well. In a small mixing bowl, sift together the flour, salt, and baking soda. Add this to the butter mixture, and stir until all ingredients are thoroughly combined. Stir in the vanilla and hot rhubarb and mix until well combined. Pour the batter into the prepared pan.

Make the topping: In a small mixing bowl, combine the butter, flour, water, sugar, and cinnamon. Use a pastry blender to mix the ingredients thoroughly. Pour the mixture over the bread batter. Bake for 1 hour, or until a toothpick inserted into the center comes out clean. Let cool for 10 minutes in the loaf pan, then place the loaf on a wire rack. Slice, and eat either warm or cool.

APPLE BREAD

Makes 1 large loaf

We bake a lot of apple bread in my community, and this bread goes fast around here. I usually use Jonathan apples, which are plentiful here in Michigan.

½ cup (1 stick) butter or shortening

1¼ cups sugar

2 large eggs

2 teaspoons baking powder

½ teaspoon ground cinnamon

2 cups all-purpose flour

1 teaspoon salt

¼ teaspoon ground nutmeg

1½ cups finely grated apples

Preheat the oven to 350°F.

Cream together the butter and sugar in a large mixing bowl. Add the eggs one at a time, beating well after each addition. In a separate bowl, sift together the baking powder, cinnamon, flour, salt, and nutmeg. Add the sifted ingredients to the creamed mixture, and stir until well combined. Fold in the grated apples. Pour the batter into a greased 5 by 9-inch loaf pan and bake 1 hour, until golden.

PINEAPPLE BREAD

Makes 1 loaf

This bread is a bit lighter than denser zucchini or pumpkin breads. It tastes great with cream cheese on top.

2 cups all-purpose flour

2 teaspoons baking powder

¼ teaspoon baking soda

¾ cup packed brown sugar

3 tablespoons butter, softened

2 large eggs

1 (8-ounce) can crushed pineapple, undrained

2 teaspoons ground cinnamon

2 teaspoons sugar

Preheat the oven to 350°F. Grease a 5 by 9-inch loaf pan and set aside.

In a bowl, whisk together the flour, baking powder, and baking soda. In a large bowl, combine the brown sugar, butter, and eggs and stir well; then mix in the pineapple and its juices. Gradually begin adding the flour mixture to the pineapple mixture, and stir until completely combined. Pour the batter into the prepared loaf pan, and sprinkle the top with the cinnamon and sugar. Bake for 40 minutes, or until a toothpick inserted in the center of the bread comes out clean. Cool the bread on a wire rack or windowsill. The bread can be stored in a sealed plastic bag and remain fresh for 3 to 4 days. This bread does not freeze well.

BANANA NUT BREAD

Makes 1 loaf

I don't care for bananas when they are mushy, but in a bread they taste really good. It seems our whole family likes bananas. I can remember one night when we were in a grocery store and we had four-year-old Kevin along, and he saw some bananas. I wasn't planning to buy any that night, but he just really wanted them, so I got a bunch. As soon as we got home, he started eating them up. My mom would wait for the bananas to get as ripe as they could before eating them, but for me, as soon as they turn brown, I don't like them. If I didn't take them over to Mom's, I would use them up in bread.

1 cup sugar

2 tablespoons margarine

1 large egg

3 teaspoons thick sour milk

1 teaspoon baking soda

2 cups all-purpose flour

½ cup walnut pieces

1 cup mashed very ripe bananas

Preheat the oven to 350°F. Lightly grease a 5 by 9-inch loaf pan and set aside.

In a large bowl, combine the sugar, margarine, egg, milk, and baking soda. Then sift in the flour, and add the walnuts and bananas. Mix very well. Pour into the prepared pan and bake for 1 hour. A butter knife inserted into the center of the bread will come out clean when the bread is done.

Remove the bread from the pan and cool on a wire rack or windowsill. The bread can be stored in a sealed plastic bag and remain fresh for 3 to 4 days. This bread does not freeze well.

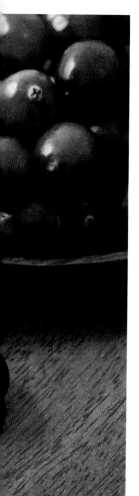

CRANBERRY NUT BREAD

Makes 1 loaf

When I think of cranberries, it always makes me think of Thanksgiving. When I was in school, in the second or third grade, we had a Thanksgiving feast. Among the things I remember eating at the feast are cranberry salad and cornbread. That gave me a taste for cranberries, which to me makes this bread delicious!

2 cups all-purpose flour

1 cup sugar

1½ teaspoons baking powder

½ teaspoon baking soda

1 teaspoon salt

1 large egg, beaten

¾ cup orange juice

1 tablespoon orange zest

1 cup vegetable oil

1 cup chopped cranberries

½ cup chopped nuts of your choice

Preheat the oven to 350°F. Grease a 5 by 9-inch pan and set aside.

Sift together the flour, sugar, baking powder, baking soda, and salt. Mix together thoroughly. In a separate large bowl, combine the egg, orange juice, orange zest, oil, cranberries, and nuts until well blended. Then gradually add in the flour mixture and stir until everything is moistened. Pour into the prepared pan and bake for 45 to 50 minutes, until golden brown.

Remove the bread from the pan and cool on a wire rack or windowsill. The bread can be stored in a sealed plastic bag and remain fresh for 3 to 4 days. This bread does not freeze well.

STRAWBERRY BREAD

Serves 6 to 8

When I was a child, my first job was picking strawberries. I started when I was in sixth or seventh grade and did it on until I was around sixteen or seventeen. My sisters and I would go pick berries with some other Amish children in the morning until the sun got too hot. Each of us would have two buckets: One would be to pick for our job, and the other would be for "seconds," those strawberries not good enough to pick and sell but still good enough to take home and eat. We had to fill the 4-quart buckets and take them to the end of the row, and they'd give us a token for each full bucket. We'd then cash in the tokens for our pay. If you were a fast picker, you could earn a lot. We would take home our seconds and make things out of them, or just eat them fresh.

2 large eggs

½ cup vegetable oil

1 cup sugar

½ teaspoon vanilla extract

½ teaspoon almond extract

1⅔ cups all-purpose flour

½ teaspoon baking powder

½ teaspoon baking soda

½ teaspoon salt

1½ cups chopped strawberries (fresh or lightly drained frozen)

½ cup chopped nuts of your choice

Preheat the oven to 350°F. Grease a 5 by 9-inch pan and set aside.

In a large bowl, beat the eggs until foamy. Add the oil, sugar, vanilla, and almond extract to the eggs and mix well. In another bowl, sift together the flour, baking powder, baking soda, and salt. Add to the oil mixture and stir until just barely moistened. Add the strawberries and nuts and lightly mix, being careful not to overmix. Pour into the prepared pan and bake until nicely browned and a toothpick inserted in the center comes out clean, 50 minutes to 1 hour. If it begins to brown too quickly, place aluminum foil over the top of the bread. This bread freezes well for long-term storage, or will keep unfrozen for 3 or 4 days in a sealed container.

DOUBLE-RISE CINNAMON BREAD

Makes 1 loaf

When I make something with cinnamon, I have a habit of putting in twice as much as the recipe calls for because I like the taste so much. This cinnamon bread is great as cinnamon toast!

2 cups milk

2 tablespoons active dry yeast

½ cup warm water

1 cup sugar

2 teaspoons salt

½ cup shortening, softened

2 large eggs, beaten

2 tablespoons ground cinnamon

7 to 8 cups bread flour

½ cup (1 stick) butter, melted

¼ cup sugar

2 tablespoons ground cinnamon

In a small saucepan, scald the milk over low heat. Remove from the heat and set aside to cool. Dissolve the yeast in the warm water and let sit until bubbles form, about 10 minutes. In a large bowl, mix the milk, yeast mixture, sugar, salt, shortening, eggs, cinnamon, and flour, until you get a smooth, elastic dough. Put the bowl in a warm place and allow to rise uncovered for 10 minutes. Knead. Let rise loosely covered in a warm place until double in size, about 1 hour.

Punch the dough down and let rise again, this time for about 30 minutes. On a lightly floured surface, roll the dough out, spread it with the melted butter, and then sprinkle on the sugar and cinnamon. Roll up and put into a 5 by 9-inch loaf pan. Let rise again for about 30 minutes.

While the dough is rising, preheat the oven to 350°F.

Bake the bread until golden, 30 to 35 minutes. Remove the bread from the pan and cool on a wire rack or windowsill. After the bread cools completely, it can be stored in a sealed plastic bag and frozen for up to 6 months. If the bread is stored in a sealed plastic bag at room temperature, it should be consumed within 4 days.

CORNBREAD

Serves 12

This is a Southern classic. Amish in more northern communities have not traditionally made cornbread, but are quickly adopting it. One taste and you'll see why!

2 cups cornmeal

2 cups all-purpose flour

1/2 cup sugar

8 teaspoons baking powder

1 teaspoon salt

3 large eggs

2 cups milk

1/2 cup melted lard or oil

Preheat the oven to 400°F. Grease a 9 by 13-inch baking pan.

Sift together the cornmeal, flour, sugar, baking powder, and salt in a large mixing bowl. Add the eggs, milk, and melted lard, and stir the mixture until all ingredients are thoroughly combined. Pour into the prepared pan and bake until the edges are golden brown, 20 to 25 minutes.

MAPLE NUT TWIST BREAD

Serves 6 to 8

The nuts in this bread remind me of our two big English walnut trees in Indiana. Mom would sit under the walnut tree and the children would bring her nuts to crack and eat, or she would save them for baking. I miss the tree now because I have to go out and buy them at the bulk-food store. Wild walnuts have such a very hard shell. I know one Amish lady who said she'd put them on the driveway so that when the milkman came he'd drive over them and partially crack them, and then she wouldn't have to do so much work.

1 tablespoon active dry yeast dissolved in ¼ cup warm water

¾ cup milk

4 tablespoons (½ stick) butter, melted

1 large egg

½ teaspoon salt

3 tablespoons granulated sugar

1 teaspoon maple flavoring

3 cups bread flour

FILLING

4 tablespoons (½ stick) butter, softened

½ cup packed brown sugar

⅓ cup walnuts, chopped

1 teaspoon maple flavoring

1 teaspoon ground cinnamon

Preheat the oven to 350°F. Lightly butter a round 9-inch pizza pan and set aside.

Combine the yeast mixture, milk, and melted butter. Beat in the egg, salt, sugar, and maple flavoring. Gradually stir in the flour. Place in an ungreased bowl and cover with a damp dish towel. Let rise in a warm place until double in bulk, about 1 hour.

Punch down and divide the dough in half. Press and stretch the first half of the dough into the prepared pan.

Make the filling: In a large bowl, stir the butter, brown sugar, nuts, maple flavoring, and cinnamon until creamy. Spread the filling over the dough. With buttered hands, stretch the remaining dough large enough to fit over the filling. Place it on top of the filling and lightly press the edges together to seal. Bake until golden brown, 20 minutes. Remove the bread from the pan and cool on a wire rack or windowsill. The bread can be stored in a sealed plastic bag and remain fresh for 3 to 4 days. This bread does not freeze well.

THE BENEFIT OF FRY PIES

My church holds baking benefits for families needing help with emergencies, such as hospital bills. Surgery and other treatments can cost a lot, but everyone pitches in to help.

The benefit is held at the home of a church member. Fry pies (some call them fried pies) are a very popular baked item to offer in exchange for a donation because everyone loves them so much. At one benefit we held, cooks and volunteers from our church made and distributed four or five thousand fry pies!

Even some Amish garage sales will have fry pies on hand, with a sign saying that a donation in exchange for a fry pie would be appreciated. I have seen fry pies in many different flavors, among them cherry, blueberry, strawberry, raspberry, and peach. A fry pie is shaped like a half-moon. I had never seen fry pies when we lived in Indiana, but they seem quite popular among the Amish here where we live now in Michigan.

A lot of preparation goes into a baking benefit. Announcements are made at churches weeks ahead of time that a fry-pie drive is coming up shortly. The day before, there is a lot of preparation with getting everything organized. The women try to start really early in the morning of the benefit day so that the same day the fry pies are made, they can be delivered.

At a baking benefit, the ladies—in assembly-line fashion—roll out the dough, put the filling in, crimp the edges, and then deep-fry them. A lot of drivers are lined up ready to take other delivery volunteers from house to house to drop off pies that have been ordered.

The ladies plan ahead as to who will take what church district. There are several people who work in teams to deliver to the whole community and then to the surrounding churches. The volunteers also go up to houses in the area and ask if the residents want any fry pies. They carry an ice-cream bucket with a slot cut through the lid, and people just put their donations into that. Benefit drives are also listed in local church bulletins, so you keep an eye out to see when one is coming up so that you'll know when to expect someone knocking at the door!

Here is a recipe for fry pies, in case you'd like to organize your own drive, or simply need a few dozen delicious treats for any special event!

FRY PIES

Makes 36 pies

This is the recipe that is most commonly used for a benefit. The pies can be made in almost any assortment of fruit flavor!

5 cups all-purpose flour

1 teaspoon baking powder

1 teaspoon salt

1 teaspoon sugar

1 cup shortening, softened

2 large eggs, slightly beaten

1 (13-ounce) can evaporated milk

2½ cups fruit filling of your choice (page 322, or use store-bought)

Shortening, for frying

In a large bowl, combine the flour, baking powder, salt, and sugar. Cut the shortening into the dry ingredients.

In a separate bowl, mix the eggs and evaporated milk together, and then add to the shortening-flour mixture. Mix with a fork just until it holds together and no more. Roll out rather thin, to about ⅛-inch thickness. Cut out rounds using a 7-inch saucer or circle as a pattern, rerolling the dough as needed. Put ½ cup fruit pie filling on one-half of the circle, leaving a bit of space clear around the edge. Be sure your filling is fairly thick and cold or it will run. Fold over the circle and seal the edges well.

Heat shortening in a deep pan to a depth of about 2 inches until very hot. Deep-fry the pies until golden brown on both sides, 2 minutes per side. Put onto a baking sheet or cooling rack to cool before serving.

OVERNIGHT OATMEAL COOKIES

Makes 5 dozen cookies

Some people refer to these as Gay's Icebox Oatmeal Cookies, but we always just call them Overnight Cookies. I'm not sure who Gay was, but I do know it is a very old recipe for oatmeal cookies that my mother often made. This cookie is great for breakfast because it acts like handheld oatmeal! Mom could mix them up the night before, and then slice and bake them in the morning. She would take her big cutting board out of the cabinet and shape a rectangular loaf so that the cookies would be elongated. They bake into a harder, crunchier cookie when made into that shape.

1 cup shortening, softened

1 cup packed brown sugar

1 cup granulated sugar

2 large eggs, beaten

1 teaspoon vanilla extract

1 teaspoon baking soda

1 teaspoon salt

1½ cups all-purpose flour

3 cups quick-cooking rolled oats

½ cup sweetened shredded coconut

½ cup walnut pieces

In a large bowl, cream together the shortening and sugars. Then add the eggs and vanilla and mix.

In a separate bowl, stir together the baking soda, salt, and flour. Combine the dry ingredients with the sugar mixture. Stir in the oatmeal, coconut, and nuts. Mix well.

Divide the dough into thirds. On a lightly floured board or waxed paper, roll each third into a log about 2 inches in diameter and 10 to 12 inches long. Refrigerate uncovered for at least 2 hours or overnight.

When ready to bake, preheat the oven to 350°F. Slice the rolled dough logs into pieces about ¾ inch thick and bake on ungreased baking sheets until golden brown, about 14 minutes. Let cool on the pans for 1 to 2 minutes before removing to a cooling rack. Cool the cookies on a wire rack or a plate and then put into sealed containers. These cookies will stay fresh for up to 5 days.

RHUBARB STREUSEL COFFEECAKE

Serves 14 to 16

This is a lovely, bright coffeecake, and it's great at breakfast with a steaming cup of coffee.

¾ cup sugar

4 tablespoons (½ stick) butter

1 large egg, beaten

1 cup milk

2 cups all-purpose flour

1 teaspoon salt

2 teaspoons baking powder

4 cups rhubarb, sliced in ¼-inch pieces

3 tablespoons strawberry-flavored gelatin, such as Jell-O

TOPPING

¾ cup sugar

½ cup all-purpose flour

½ cup quick-cooking rolled oats

4 tablespoons (½ stick) butter

Whipped cream, for topping (optional)

Preheat the oven to 350°F. Lightly grease a 9 by 13-inch pan and set aside.

In a large mixing bowl, combine the sugar and butter. Beat until the mixture is creamy, then stir in the egg and milk, and mix until smooth. In a small bowl, sift together the flour, salt, and baking powder. Add this to the butter mixture, and beat until smooth. Pour the batter into the prepared pan and spread evenly. Top the batter with the sliced rhubarb, and sprinkle with the gelatin.

Make the topping: Combine the sugar, flour, oats, and butter in a small bowl. Cut with a pastry blender until crumbly. Sprinkle the topping mixture over the batter, and bake for 35 to 40 minutes, or until the top is golden brown. Serve warm or cool. Top with whipped cream or Homemade Whipped Topping (page 47), if desired.

CHERRY COFFEECAKE

Serves 6 to 8

I remember that Mother would always can quart after quart of cherries. She would order a big batch of cherries and make cherry pie filling and can the rest. When she would open a quart, we would eat them just like we would canned peaches. But the cherries she would can wouldn't be pitted, so when we ate them we would have to make sure we didn't swallow the pits.

1 cup (2 sticks) butter or margarine,
  softened

1½ cups granulated sugar

4 large eggs, beaten

1 teaspoon vanilla extract

3 cups all-purpose flour

1½ teaspoons baking powder

½ teaspoon salt

21 ounces cherry pie filling

GLAZE

3 tablespoons butter

2½ cups powdered sugar

1 teaspoon vanilla extract

6 tablespoons milk

Preheat the oven to 350°F.

In a medium bowl, cream the butter until smooth (about 1 minute). Gradually add the sugar and continue stirring until the mixture is a creamy, pale yellow. Add the beaten eggs into the sugar mixture in four additions, stirring vigorously for about 1 minute after each addition. Stir in the vanilla. In a separate medium bowl, sift the flour, baking powder, and salt. Gradually add the dry ingredients to the egg-sugar mixture, stirring after each addition. Scrape the sides of the bowl whenever necessary to make sure the batter is being thoroughly mixed.

Spoon the batter into a 10 by 15 by 1-inch jelly-roll pan, reserving ⅔ cup of the batter. Spread the batter evenly in the pan with a spatula. Then pour the cherry pie filling over the batter, spooning it smoothly all the way to the edges. Then drop teaspoonfuls of the reserved batter over the cherry layer in four even rows of four dollops each (for a total of sixteen spoonfuls on top of the cherry layer).

Bake until the edges are slightly brown and begin to pull away from the edge of the pan, about 30 minutes. Remove from the oven and let cool.

Make the glaze: Melt the butter over low heat in a small saucepan, and then pour into a bowl. Gradually add the powdered sugar, beating well after each addition and scraping

down the sides frequently. Add the vanilla. Then add the milk, 1 tablespoon at a time, until the glaze is smooth. Drizzle over the warm coffeecake.

Let the cake cool completely and store in a sealed container or cake safe. This cake will stay fresh for 3 to 4 days.

YODER COFFEECAKE

Serves 4 to 6

This coffeecake is famous at the Sunflower Inn, an Amish restaurant in Yoder, Kansas. It's especially good if it's made with homemade butter and real vanilla extract.

½ cup sugar

1 large egg, beaten

4 tablespoons (½ stick) butter

1½ cups all-purpose flour

3 tablespoons baking powder

¼ teaspoon salt

1 teaspoon vanilla extract

¾ cup whole milk

TOPPING

1 cup firmly packed brown sugar

2 tablespoons all-purpose flour

2 tablespoons ground cinnamon

6 tablespoons melted butter

½ cup chopped walnut pieces

Preheat the oven to 375°F. Grease a 9 by 13-inch baking dish and set aside. Combine the sugar, egg, butter, flour, baking powder, salt, vanilla, and milk in a large mixing bowl. When the mixture has a creamy consistency, spread it into the prepared pan.

Make the topping: Mix all the topping ingredients in a small bowl. Sprinkle over the cake batter. Bake for 20 minutes, or until a toothpick inserted into the center comes out clean.

HONEY NUT SWIRL COFFEECAKE

Serves 6 to 8

This recipe is perfect for people who love nuts. This coffeecake tastes kind of like a sweet roll with nuts. This recipe can be challenging and requires a bit of effort, but it is well worth the work.

1 cup milk	FILLING
½ cup shortening	2 large eggs
½ cup sugar	½ cup honey
2 teaspoons salt	4 tablespoons (½ stick) butter, melted
2 packages active dry yeast	3 cups chopped nuts of your choice
1 cup warm water	2 teaspoons ground cinnamon
2 large eggs	1 teaspoon vanilla extract
6 cups all-purpose flour	

In a small saucepan, scald the milk over low heat, about 3 minutes. Remove the milk from the heat. Add the shortening, sugar, and salt to the saucepan and stir. In a large bowl, dissolve the yeast in the warm water, about 5 minutes. Add the milk mixture, eggs, and 2 cups of the flour to the yeast. Beat until smooth. Gradually add the rest of the flour to make the dough soft. Turn out the dough onto a lightly floured cutting board. Let rise for 10 minutes, uncovered, on the cutting board. Place in a greased bowl. Cover and let rise in a warm place until double in size, about 2 hours.

Punch the dough down and let it rise again for about 1 hour.

Make the filling: While the dough is rising again, mix the eggs, honey, butter, nuts, cinnamon, and vanilla until smooth and creamy. Divide the dough in half. Roll each half into 12 by 18-inch rectangles. Spread each half with the filling. Starting with the short side, roll up each sheet as for a jelly roll. Put the rolled-up dough lengthwise on a 10 by 15-inch jelly-roll pan. Let rise a third time for 30 minutes.

While the dough is rising again, preheat the oven to 350°F. Bake until the top turns golden brown, about 45 minutes. Let the cake cool completely and store in a sealed container or cake safe. This cake will stay fresh for 3 to 4 days.

BLUEBERRY STREUSEL COFFEECAKE

Serves 12

Nuts, especially pecans, make a nice addition to the streusel. Our family especially enjoys a warm coffeecake on a cold winter's morning.

STREUSEL

½ cup graham cracker crumbs

2 tablespoons sugar

½ teaspoon ground cinnamon

4 tablespoons (½ stick) butter or margarine, softened

COFFEECAKE

2 cups all-purpose flour

3 teaspoons baking powder

1 teaspoon salt

¼ cup sugar

4 tablespoons (½ stick) butter or margarine, softened

½ cup milk

1 large egg, beaten

1½ cups fresh blueberries (or thawed and drained frozen)

Preheat the oven to 400°F. Grease and flour a 9-inch round layer cake pan and set aside.

Make the streusel: In a medium bowl, mix the graham cracker crumbs, sugar, and cinnamon. Cut in the butter as for a pie dough until it is the texture of small peas. Set the streusel aside.

Make the coffeecake: In a large bowl, mix the flour, baking powder, salt, and sugar. Cut in the butter until the mixture is the consistency of coarse cornmeal. Make a well in the center and pour in the milk. Add the egg and stir quickly with a fork just until the dry ingredients are moistened. Spread the batter in the prepared pan. Arrange the berries over the batter, leaving a 1-inch margin around the edge of the pan. Sprinkle the streusel over the berries. Bake until the top is nicely browned, about 30 minutes.

Let the cake cool completely and store in a sealed container. This cake will stay fresh for 3 to 4 days.

BLUEBERRY-FILLED COFFEECAKE

Serves 8 to 12

This classic coffeecake is a favorite during blueberry season. Other fruits can be substituted if blueberries are not available.

BATTER

½ cup (1 stick) butter, softened

½ cup sugar

1 large egg

1½ cups all-purpose flour

½ teaspoon salt

½ tablespoon baking powder

½ teaspoon vanilla extract

½ cup milk

1 (16-ounce) can blueberry pie filling

TOPPING

¼ cup firmly packed brown sugar

¼ cup all-purpose flour

2 tablespoons butter, softened

¼ cup chopped walnuts

Preheat the oven to 350°F. Grease an 8 by 8-inch baking pan.

Make the batter: Cream the butter and sugar together in a small mixing bowl until smooth. Add the egg and beat until well combined. Add the flour, salt, baking powder, vanilla, and milk and mix until smooth. The batter will be thick—the consistency of cookie dough. Spread half the batter into the prepared pan. Spoon the pie filling over the batter, then cover with the remaining batter.

Make the topping: Thoroughly mix the topping ingredients in a small mixing bowl until they form the consistency of coarse sand. Sprinkle the topping crumbs over the batter and bake for 40 minutes, or until the top is golden brown.

MELT-IN-YOUR-MOUTH BLUEBERRY BREAKFAST CAKE

Serves 8 to 12

As the name implies, this is a soft cake for breakfast! A favorite way for the Amish in my area to enjoy the cake is to crumble it into a bowl and pour milk over it.

1½ cups fresh blueberries, rinsed and picked clean

1½ cups sifted all-purpose flour

2 large eggs, separated

1¼ cups sugar

½ cup shortening

¼ teaspoon salt

1 teaspoon vanilla extract

1 teaspoon baking powder

⅓ cup milk

Preheat the oven to 350°F. Grease an 8 by 8-inch baking pan and set aside.

Gently shake the blueberries in a small amount of the flour in a large bowl, and set aside. This will help prevent their sinking in the finished cake.

Beat the egg whites in a large bowl, slowly adding ¼ cup of the sugar, until stiff peaks form. Set aside.

In a separate bowl, cream the shortening, and add the salt and vanilla. Add the remaining 1 cup of sugar (reserve 1 tablespoon) and the egg yolks, and beat until light and creamy. Sift together the remaining sifted flour and the baking powder into another bowl. Add the dry ingredients, alternately with the milk, to the creamed mixture until evenly incorporated.

Fold in the beaten whites, then fold in the blueberries. Pour the batter into the prepared baking pan, and sprinkle the top with the remaining tablespoon of granulated sugar. Bake for 1 hour, or until a toothpick inserted into the center comes out clean.

APPLE FRITTERS

Makes 10 to 12 fritters

Fritters are a bit like doughnuts, and are a favorite around here in the fall. We usually eat them for breakfast.

1 cup all-purpose flour

2 teaspoons baking powder

2 tablespoons sugar

¼ teaspoon salt

1 large egg, beaten

¼ cup milk

3 apples, peeled, cored, and chopped

Vegetable oil, for deep-frying

Combine the flour, baking powder, sugar, and salt in a large bowl. Stir with a whisk to blend. Make a hole in the mixture and stir in the egg, milk, and apples.

Fill a deep fryer or Dutch oven half full of oil and heat to 375°F. Drop the batter by the tablespoonful into hot oil and fry until golden brown, just a few seconds on each side. Using a slotted spoon, transfer to paper towels to drain.

AMISH DOUGHNUTS

Makes 2 dozen doughnuts

I always liked homemade doughnuts dipped in milk when I was a child. As I grew older, I would dip them in my coffee. Doughnuts, even if they are a couple of days old, are good dunked in either milk or coffee, which will soften them. I like them best if they have glaze on them.

½ cup granulated sugar

1 teaspoon salt

1 teaspoon ground nutmeg

6½ cups bread flour

½ cup shortening, softened

3 large eggs

½ cup unseasoned mashed potatoes

2 packages active dry yeast

2 cups milk, scalded and cooled

Lard or vegetable oil, for frying

GLAZE

3 tablespoons water

1 cup powdered sugar

In a large bowl, sift together the sugar, salt, nutmeg, and flour. Blend the shortening into the dry ingredients.

Combine the eggs with the potatoes. Add to the dry ingredients. Add the yeast to the cooled milk. Gradually blend into the flour mixture. Let rise for 40 minutes.

Roll the dough ⅜ inch thick. Cut the dough into 4-inch rounds (a juice glass works great). Repeat until you've used all the dough. Let the doughnuts rise again on a baking sheet, about 45 minutes. Heat the lard in a deep pan to a depth of 2 to 3 inches until very hot. Fry the doughnuts in batches until golden, about 30 seconds on each side.

Make the glaze: Mix together the water and sugar. Dip the doughnuts into the mixture.

LARD CAKES

Makes 2 dozen lard cakes

Lard cakes actually don't contain any lard: They are just called that because they are tradition-ally deep-fried in melted lard. You can use vegetable shortening, though, too, but I don't think "vegetable shortening cakes" sounds any better than "lard cakes."

1½ cups heavy cream

2¼ cups sour milk

2 heaping teaspoons baking soda

3 large eggs

3 to 4 cups all-purpose flour

½ teaspoon salt

3 teaspoons sugar, plus sugar for rolling

Lard or vegetable shortening, for frying

In a large bowl, combine the cream, sour milk, baking soda, eggs, and flour. The consistency should be similar to that of a pie dough, so add a little more flour if needed. Add the salt and sugar. Roll out to a ¼-inch thickness and cut up into any shapes as big as you wish, or into 2 by 4-inch pieces. Cut a 2½-inch slit in the center of each cake. Make sure the slit goes completely through the cake.

Heat the lard in a deep kettle or pan to a depth of about 2 inches until very hot. Fry the cakes in batches until golden, about 1 minute on each side. Roll the cakes in a pan of sugar while still warm. Eat fresh and warm, because they get stale quickly.

HOMEMADE YOGURT

Serves 16

This is an easy, from-scratch homemade yogurt. Yogurt is great served with Homemade Granola Bars (see page 62). Whole milk should be used because lower-fat milks cause a runnier yogurt. Also, the sugar can be omitted for a less sweet variation. Finally, the Amish use leftover yogurt from a previous batch for the active culture. If this is your first batch, you can use plain store-bought yogurt as long as it doesn't have any added ingredients and includes live, active cultures.

1 gallon whole milk

2 cups active culture yogurt

½ cup sugar

Flavorings and additions, such as vanilla, fruit, or honey, as desired

Heat the milk to between 170° and 180°F. Do not allow the milk to boil. Add the active culture yogurt and the sugar, and stir with a wire whisk until the sugar is dissolved. You may also add any desired flavorings at this point. Allow the milk to cool to 120°F.

Preheat the oven to 100°F. If your oven cannot be set that low, set it to its lowest setting for 10 minutes, then turn it off. It should stay warm for 12 hours if left closed. If you open the oven door, reheat the oven for about 30 seconds to maintain temperature.

Pour the milk into a jug or a glass container and wrap the container with a bath towel to maintain temperature. Place it in the preheated oven and let it sit overnight.

Remove the container from the oven and save 2 cups of the yogurt for use in your next batch. You can serve the remaining yogurt warm or chilled. Leftover yogurt can be frozen in tightly sealed containers. Just give it a day to thaw to let the bacteria reactivate.

HOMEMADE WHIPPED TOPPING

Makes about 2 cups

In the heat of the South, a cool topping is a refreshing accompaniment to fruit salad or pancakes. Any extra can also go on pie!

½ cup boiling water

½ teaspoon cream of tartar

1 teaspoon vanilla extract

¾ cup sugar

1 large egg white

Combine all the ingredients in a small mixing bowl. Beat with a whisk or an electric mixer until the topping stands up in peaks.

SAUSAGE GRAVY

Serves 4 to 6

When I fix this recipe, I like to use my fresh sausage, but home-cured or store-bought is still good. Leftover portions can be refrigerated, but I don't think it's as good the second time around. We like to eat sausage gravy on biscuits.

1 pound bulk sausage

¼ cup all-purpose flour

4 cups milk

Salt and black pepper

In a cast-iron skillet, brown the sausage over medium heat. Drain off the grease. Sprinkle in the flour and brown lightly. Gradually add the milk and mix until very smooth. Bring the gravy to a boil, stirring frequently. Reduce the heat and cook until the desired thickness is reached. If the gravy becomes too thick, additional milk may be added. Season with salt and pepper to taste and serve over biscuits.

BUTTERMILK BISCUITS

Makes 12 biscuits

Buttermilk isn't something I buy very often. But I do substitute sour milk for the buttermilk, and it is almost the same. One cup of thick, sour milk equals 1 cup of buttermilk. Mom never worried about sour milk. She would always say that it's things like spoiled meat that will affect someone, but she never heard of anyone getting sick over sour milk. We'd use milk that was just starting to sour for sour cream and lots of baked goods. I don't think many people would try this recipe if it were called "sour milk biscuits"! These are good with gravy or with butter or jelly.

2 cups all-purpose flour

¼ cup vegetable oil

¾ teaspoon salt

3 teaspoons baking powder

1 cup buttermilk or sour milk

1 teaspoon baking soda

Preheat the oven to 400°F. Lightly grease a baking sheet and set aside.

In a large bowl, combine the flour, vegetable oil, salt, baking powder, milk, and baking soda. Stir with a wooden spoon until the mixture forms a smooth batter. Drop the dough by the teaspoon onto the prepared baking sheet. Bake until golden brown, 10 to 15 minutes.

SOUTHERN GAL BISCUITS

Makes 12 biscuits

These are easy biscuits to make. Like many Amish recipes, the name is lost to history, but the suggestion is that when Amish visited their northern brethren, they brought along this biscuit variation. So the baker's biscuits were hung with the name "Southern Gal."

2 cups sifted all-purpose flour

4 teaspoons baking powder

½ teaspoon salt

½ teaspoon cream of tartar

2 tablespoons sugar

½ cup shortening

⅔ cup milk

1 large egg

Preheat the oven to 450°F.

Sift together the flour, baking powder, salt, cream of tartar, and sugar in a large mixing bowl. Add the shortening, and blend until the mixture has the consistency of cornmeal. Slowly pour the milk into the mixture. Add the egg and stir until a stiff dough is formed. Add more flour if needed.

Drop the dough by tablespoons onto a baking sheet. Bake for 10 to 15 minutes, or until the tops begin to turn golden.

MYSTERY BISCUITS

Makes 12 biscuits

The mayonnaise and milk give this biscuit a very moist flavor. I think that is why they are so popular among the children in my house.

2 cups all-purpose flour

1 tablespoon baking powder

1 teaspoon salt

¼ cup mayonnaise

1 cup milk

1 teaspoon sugar

Preheat the oven to 375°F. Grease a baking sheet or twelve muffin cups and set aside.

In a large bowl, combine the flour, baking powder, and salt. Blend in the mayonnaise, milk, and sugar until the mixture is creamy. Drop the dough by the tablespoon onto the prepared pan or fill the muffin cups two-thirds full. Bake until golden brown, 18 to 20 minutes.

PANCAKES

Serves 8 to 10

The Amish often rely on easy, go-to recipes that can be whipped up from scratch. And no Amish cook is without a simple pancake recipe. This one is a favorite among the Amish in Colorado.

3 large eggs, beaten	3 cups all-purpose flour
3 cups milk	1½ teaspoons salt
¼ cup vegetable oil	7 teaspoons baking powder

Combine the eggs, milk, and oil in a large mixing bowl. Add the flour, salt, and baking powder. Mix until all the ingredients are thoroughly combined to form a batter. Drop the batter by quarter-cupfuls onto a hot, greased griddle. Cook until the edges are set and bubbles break the surface, about 1 minute. Flip the pancakes and continue cooking until golden brown and cooked through.

PANCAKES WITH FRESH STRAWBERRIES

Serves 4 to 6

This is a recipe that the kids like on a spring morning. It is easy to go out and pick the strawberries from the garden patch and bring them in for a pancake breakfast. Delicious!

2 cups all-purpose flour

1 tablespoon plus ½ teaspoon baking powder

½ teaspoon salt

1⅓ cups milk

2 tablespoons vegetable oil, plus more for cooking the pancakes

1 tablespoon vanilla extract

1 egg, beaten

Strawberries

Sweetened whipped cream for garnish

Combine the flour, baking powder, and salt in a medium bowl. Stir with a whisk to blend. In another bowl, whisk the milk, oil, vanilla, and egg together. Stir the wet ingredients into the dry ingredients just until combined; do not overmix.

Put a little oil on a griddle or in a large skillet and heat over medium-high heat. Drop the batter by tablespoons onto the griddle or in the pan to form several small pancakes. Cook until golden on each side, 2 to 3 minutes. Transfer the pancakes to plates. Top the pancakes with a few strawberries and some whipped cream.

HUCKLEBERRY PANCAKES

Makes about 2 dozen pancakes

These pancakes are favorites around the breakfast campfire during the annual outings that many Western Amish families make into the mountains. The recipe uses cornmeal, which gives great balance to the sweet huckleberries.

1½ cups milk

2 eggs, beaten

¼ cup vegetable oil

2 cups all-purpose flour

½ cup cornmeal

1 tablespoon sugar

½ teaspoon salt

4 teaspoons baking powder

1 cup huckleberries

Place the milk, eggs, and vegetable oil in a large mixing bowl, and whisk them until they are thoroughly combined. Add the flour, cornmeal, sugar, salt, and baking powder, and stir until all the ingredients are thoroughly combined. Gently fold the huckleberries into the batter. Drop the batter by quarter-cupfuls onto a hot, greased griddle. Cook the pancakes on the first side until the edges are set and bubbles break the surface, about 1 minute. Flip the pancakes and continue cooking until golden brown and cooked through.

BAKED FRENCH TOAST

Serves 4 to 6

Breakfast is a very important meal in any Amish home. The meal provides sustenance for the day ahead, but it also needs to be quick and easy amid the bustle of the morning. French toast fits the bill.

1 cup brown sugar, packed

½ cup butter

2 tablespoons light corn syrup

12 bread slices

½ cup granulated sugar

1 teaspoon ground cinnamon

6 eggs

1½ cups milk

1 teaspoon vanilla extract

Preheat the oven to 350°F.

In a heavy-bottomed saucepan, combine the brown sugar, butter, and corn syrup. Heat the ingredients over medium-high heat, stirring frequently. When the mixture reaches a boil, remove it from the heat and pour it into the bottom of a 9 by 13-inch glass pan. Layer the bread slices into the glass pan and sprinkle with the sugar and the cinnamon. In a large bowl, whisk the eggs, milk, and vanilla together until smooth and evenly combined. Pour the egg mixture over the bread. Bake 30 to 35 minutes, until puffed and golden.

HOMEMADE CEREAL

Makes about 24 cups

Even the most conservative Amish will go to a bulk-food store to stock up on tasty treats they can't really make, such as marshmallows, graham crackers, and some store-bought cereals. But this delicious homemade breakfast cereal keeps those trips to a minimum. Store the cereal in large airtight containers to keep it dry and fresh so it can be enjoyed for weeks. This recipe can be halved for a more manageable amount.

14 cups quick-cooking rolled oats

1 cup honey

1¼ cups vegetable oil

4 cups crisped-rice cereal, such as Rice Krispies

1 pound shredded sweetened coconut

1 sleeve graham crackers (8 to 10 crackers), crumbled but not crushed

1½ teaspoons salt

1 tablespoon vanilla extract

Preheat the oven to 350°F.

Combine all the ingredients in a large bowl or stockpot until well blended. Spread in a thin layer on five baking sheets and bake until the coconut begins to turn golden brown, 20 to 25 minutes, stirring occasionally.

VIOLA'S GRAPE NUTS

Serves 6 to 8

Uriel and Viola Miller were one of the first Amish families in Union Grove, North Carolina. Church members always enjoyed Viola's delicious grape nuts. This cereal is great served in a bowl with milk, or just by the handful for snacking. Like most Amish cooks, Viola makes this in a large batch and stores it in tightly sealed containers, where it will keep fresh for weeks.

4 pounds whole wheat flour

1¼ pounds brown sugar

1½ teaspoons salt

5 cups buttermilk

2½ teaspoons baking soda

1 tablespoon imitation maple flavoring

1½ teaspoons vanilla extract

¾ cup (1½ sticks) butter, melted

Preheat the oven to 350°F.

Mix the flour, brown sugar, and salt in a very large bowl or container until the ingredients are thoroughly combined. In a large mixing bowl, combine the buttermilk and baking soda until smooth. Add the buttermilk mixture to the flour mixture, and stir until the flour mixture is evenly coated. Add the maple flavoring, vanilla, and butter, and stir to evenly incorporate. Spread the mixture evenly on baking sheets.

Bake until nicely browned, about 2 hours. Let cool completely, and place the grape nuts in large bags overnight to firm up. The next day, crumble into fine pieces and toast in a warm (250°F) oven.

CHOKECHERRY MUSH

Serves 10

This is a favorite in the Amish community in Fertile, Minnesota, where it's a local twist on a classic dish. The mush is livened up even more by adding a splash of lemon juice or vanilla. It tastes good with cornbread or milk. Therm-Flo is a thickener available at most bulk-food stores.

3 quarts prepared chokecherry juice

1 cup Therm-Flo thickener

1 cup sugar

¼ cup water

Combine the chokecherry juice, Therm-Flo, sugar, and water in a saucepan over medium heat. Cook for 5 minutes, stirring constantly, until thickened. Remove from the heat and serve hot.

CORNMEAL PIE

Makes one 9-inch pie

This is a very moist pie that tastes like sweet cornbread in a piecrust. Be sure not to bake it too long or the top will develop cracks. People who like soft and sweet cornbread will really enjoy this pie.

2 large eggs

1½ cups packed brown sugar

3 tablespoons butter, softened

¼ cup heavy whipping cream

2 tablespoons cornmeal

1 disk My Homemade Pie Dough (page 296) or Pat-a-Pan Piecrust (page 298)

Preheat the oven to 300°F.

In a small bowl, beat the eggs and set aside. In a large bowl, stir the brown sugar, butter, cream, and cornmeal together until evenly blended. Then stir in the eggs, mixing vigorously until the mixture is smooth. Pour into the unbaked piecrust and bake until the center is set, 35 to 40 minutes. Cool on a wire rack or windowsill until the pie is firm, about 45 minutes. Store any leftovers in a sealed container.

ZUCCHINI PIE

Makes one 9-inch pie

This is an easy recipe that my daughter's teacher gave us for cooking class. It's fun to make during the summer when we have plenty of zucchini in our garden. If you like pumpkin pie, you'll like this one, too.

3 cups peeled, shredded zucchini

1½ teaspoons ground cinnamon

1 tablespoon fresh lemon juice

½ teaspoon ground allspice

1¼ cups sugar

¼ cup all-purpose flour

1 tablespoon butter

Pinch of salt

2 disks My Homemade Pie Dough (page 296)

Preheat the oven to 375°F.

In a large bowl, combine the zucchini, cinnamon, lemon juice, and allspice. Stir until the zucchini is evenly coated, and then add the sugar, flour, butter, and salt. Continue to stir until the mixture is well blended. Spoon into the prepared piecrust. Use some water to wet the rim of the bottom crust, which will help both crusts adhere together. Cover the pie with the top crust, crimping the crusts together all the way around. Bake for 30 to 45 minutes, or until golden brown. Cool on a wire rack or windowsill until the pie is firm, about 45 minutes. Store any leftovers in a sealed container. The pie will keep for about 2 days.

HOMEMADE GRANOLA BARS

Makes 28 to 32 bars

Long before grocery stores starting selling prepackaged, processed granola bars, the Amish were making their own—just like these.

5 cups quick-cooking rolled oats

4½ cups crisped-rice cereal, such as Rice Krispies

2 cups chocolate chips

1 sleeve graham crackers (8 to 10 crackers), crushed

12 tablespoons unsalted butter

¼ cup peanut butter

¼ cup vegetable oil

¼ cup honey

2 (10-ounce) packages mini-marshmallows

Lightly grease a 10 by 15-inch pan and set aside.

Combine the oats, rice cereal, chocolate chips, and graham cracker crumbs in a large bowl until well blended. Set aside. Melt the butter, peanut butter, oil, honey, and marshmallows in a large saucepan. Stir well until the mixture is evenly melted and smooth, then add to the dry ingredients and mix until thoroughly combined. Spread the mixture into the prepared pan, let cool, then cut into bars.

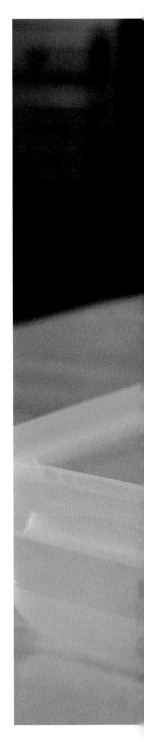

PON HOSS

Serves 12

This breakfast meat is usually made in large quantities when butchering a hog once or twice a year. Some people know this dish by its more common name: scrapple. The Amish in Indiana and points west call it Pon Hoss. The Amish of Pennsylvania and other eastern states still write it by its more familiar German spelling: Pon Haus. This dish does require setting overnight, so start the day before you want to eat it.

3 to 4 pounds pork shanks or hocks

About 4 cups of cornmeal or flour for every gallon of broth

2 tablespoons salt for every gallon of broth

1 tablespoon black pepper for every gallon of broth

Cook the pork in a large pot over medium heat until tender, about 30 minutes. As the meat cooks, it will make its own broth. Transfer the meat to a plate to cool. Once cool enough to handle, remove the bones from the meat and skim the fat from the broth. Return the meat to the broth and add just enough cornmeal or flour to thicken the liquid to a thin paste. The exact amount will vary, depending on the meat used and the amount of broth, so add the flour 1 cup at a time. Season with salt and pepper.

Pour the mixture into loaf pans. Cover and chill overnight. To serve, slice the chilled meat and fry in a large skillet over medium-high heat until golden brown on each side.

FLORIDA ORANGE RICE

Serves 5

This recipe combines citrus and rice to create something that tastes creamy and bright. This is another easy, flavorful breakfast dish that is something different from what might be enjoyed in a traditional Midwestern Amish community.

2 cups cooked white rice

2 tablespoons sugar

1½ oranges, cut into pieces

1 cup prepared Dream Whip

Place all the ingredients in a medium mixing bowl and stir until thoroughly combined. Refrigerate until chilled, at least 1 hour, before serving.

FARMER'S BREAKFAST

Serves 4 to 6

This turns out more like an omelette. We often like to enjoy "breakfast" for supper, since mornings are often so rushed around here. There is no better way to enjoy fresh pork than with eggs. This is a favorite way to serve fresh ham!

6 large eggs

2 tablespoons milk

Dash of salt

$\frac{1}{4}$ teaspoon black pepper

1 cup diced cooked ham

$\frac{1}{3}$ cup margarine or butter

2 potatoes, peeled and finely chopped

$\frac{1}{4}$ cup sliced green onion, including green tops

Combine the eggs, milk, salt, and pepper in a large bowl and beat until smooth. Stir in the ham and set aside.

Melt the margarine or butter in a large skillet over medium heat and sauté the potatoes and onion, stirring frequently, until tender, about 8 to 10 minutes. Pour the egg mixture over the potato mixture in the skillet. Cook without stirring until the mixture begins to set around the bottom and edges, about 3 or 4 minutes. Push back the edges to let the liquid run under and cook if you want to make an omelette, then fold it when cooked through, or just scramble the eggs.

DELICIOUS OMELETTE

Serves 1 to 2

With fresh eggs so plentiful in my household, omelettes often find their way onto our breakfast menus.

2 teaspoons butter

2 tablespoons chopped onion

¼ cup chopped bell pepper

¼ cup chopped bacon or ham

2 eggs

2 tablespoons water

Pinch of salt and black pepper

¼ cup shredded cheese

In a small nonstick skillet, melt 1 teaspoon of the butter over medium heat. Add the onion and bell peppers and cook for 2 minutes, stirring frequently. Add the chopped meat and cook for 2 more minutes. Transfer the cooked filling to a plate and set aside. Wipe the skillet clean with a paper towel.

In a small bowl, beat the eggs, water, and salt and pepper with a fork until well blended. Melt the remaining teaspoon of butter in the skillet over medium heat. Pour the egg mixture into the skillet and use a spatula to pull the cooked egg toward the center of the pan. Continue to cook the egg, pulling the edges inward, until it is barely moist on top. Sprinkle the shredded cheese over half of the omelette. Top the cheese with the filling mixture. Using a spatula, carefully flip the unfilled half of the omelette over the filled half. When the cheese has melted, run the spatula completely around the edge of the omelette and slide it onto a plate.

OVEN OMELETTE

Serves 4 to 6

My hens are really active egg layers, so recipes for what they produce continue to find a way into my home and into the column.

2 medium onions, diced

2 cups cheese of your choice, shredded

1 (3-ounce) package dried beef, diced

8 eggs

1 cup milk

Salt and black pepper

Preheat the oven to 325°F.

In a buttered 9 by 13-inch pan, layer the onion, cheese, and dried beef. In a large bowl, beat the eggs and the milk together until well combined. Season with the salt and pepper, then pour the egg mixture over the layered ingredients. Bake about 30 minutes, or until the eggs are set.

BREAKFAST CASSEROLE

Serves 12

Most Amish cooks have a ready supply of fresh eggs on hand, thanks to the free-range hens that usually roam the property. A breakfast casserole is an excellent—and delicious—way to use some of the supply. This recipe needs overnight refrigeration.

6 slices bread, cubed

3 cups cooked breakfast meat (sausage, bacon, and/or ham)

6 large eggs, beaten

3 tablespoons melted butter

3 cups milk

1 teaspoon dry mustard

1 teaspoon baking powder

8 ounces shredded Colby cheese

Combine the bread cubes and cooked meat. Place the mixture in a greased 9 by 13-inch pan. Place the eggs, butter, milk, mustard, and baking powder in a mixing bowl, and beat until well combined. Pour the egg mixture into the pan over the bread and meat. Cover the dish, and refrigerate the casserole overnight.

Preheat the oven to 325°F.

Bake the casserole for 45 minutes, or until it has firmed and the top is golden brown. Sprinkle the cheese on top and return to the oven for 3 minutes, to allow the cheese to melt.

EGGS LA GOLDEN

Serves 4

Many Amish and non-Amish in the St. Ignatius area of Montana enjoy raising their own free-range hens to provide a steady supply of fresh eggs. In St. Ignatius, though, grizzly bears occasionally wander down from the mountains, and they find hens to be a delicious snack. This causes the occasional confrontation between a grizzly bear and a homeowner. Bears or not, this recipe is a local favorite for breakfast.

3 tablespoons shortening

2 tablespoons all-purpose flour

1 teaspoon salt

2 cups milk

6 hard-boiled eggs, whites separated and finely chopped, yolks reserved

Salt and black pepper

8 slices toast

Melt the shortening in a heavy saucepan over medium heat. Add the flour and salt, and stir until well blended. Slowly add the milk to the flour mixture, stirring constantly until a smooth paste is formed.

Stir the chopped egg whites into the white sauce until evenly combined. Season the sauce with the salt and pepper to taste. Arrange the toast slices on a platter and pour the white sauce over them. Mash the egg yolks through a sieve and sprinkle lightly over the sauce.

BREAKFAST BURRITOS

Serves 10

I like to make this breakfast for my brothers and sisters on the first warm spring mornings when we can eat outside on our porch You can use either sausage or bacon with this recipe, but we usually use bacon. The burritos can be put into freezer bags and frozen.

2 pounds bacon

½ cup diced green bell pepper

½ cup chopped mushrooms

¼ cup chopped onion

½ cup margarine or butter

15 large eggs, lightly beaten

1 teaspoon salt

1 teaspoon black pepper

10 (8½-inch) flour tortillas

10 slices Cheddar cheese

Preheat the oven to 350°F. Fry the bacon until crisp in a large, heavy skillet. Transfer the bacon to paper towels to drain and cool slightly, then crumble and set aside. Pour away all but 2 teaspoons of the bacon grease out of the skillet, then add the bell pepper, mushrooms, and onion and fry until tender. Drain, then stir in the crumbled bacon.

In a large skillet over low heat, melt the margarine and scramble the eggs, adding the salt and black pepper. Lay each tortilla in the center of a square of aluminum foil. Place a slice of cheese in the center of each tortilla, then divide the meat mixture equally among the tortillas, followed by the scrambled eggs. Fold the bottom of each tortilla over the filling, then fold in the sides and finish rolling up the tortillas. Wrap the burritos in the foil, then place them on a baking sheet and bake until heated through, 10 to 15 minutes. Serve with sour cream and salsa.

FLORIDA AVOCADO EGG SCRAMBLE

Serves 4 to 6

Although avocados are not a food that most Amish eat in the Midwest, that's not so in Florida, where avocados are so commonplace that many families eat them sliced or mixed in with their scrambled eggs.

1 Florida avocado, halved lengthwise, skin and pit discarded, cut into medium dice

Salt

8 large eggs

½ cup sour cream

1 teaspoon black pepper

1 tablespoon butter

Sprinkle the diced avocado with the salt and set aside.

In a medium mixing bowl, beat the eggs with the sour cream until thick and creamy; season with additional salt and the pepper. Melt the butter in a medium skillet over medium-low heat. Add the egg mixture and cook, stirring occasionally.

When almost set, gently fold in the avocado. Serve immediately.

midday meals

In Amish homes, lunch is a working meal for a busy day, so you may be surprised at how simple many of these selections are to prepare. You'll also find plenty of "think big" options since I often have to feed large numbers of hungry people. These make for ideal choices for Sunday gatherings, luncheons with guests, and other midday celebrations around your table.

LONG JOHN ROLLS

Makes 32 rolls

Long John Rolls are often passed around as a snack during quilting bees, around lunchtime. I had an aunt who would fill them with cream, and I liked those even better. Long John Rolls are best when they are freshly made, as they dry out quickly and need to be eaten within a day or two of baking.

1 cup lukewarm water

2 packages active dry yeast

1 cup milk

2 large eggs, beaten

$\frac{1}{2}$ cup margarine

$\frac{2}{3}$ cup sugar

$\frac{1}{2}$ teaspoon salt

Pinch of ground nutmeg

6 to 7 cups bread flour

Vegetable shortening, for frying

Frosting (optional; use Basic Frosting, page 348)

Pour the water into a small bowl, and then add the yeast and stir until completely dissolved. Set aside. Scald the milk and let cool to lukewarm. Add the milk to the dissolved yeast.

Blend together the eggs, margarine, sugar, salt, and nutmeg until well blended, and then add to the milk and yeast mixture. Gradually add the flour until the dough is elastic and easy to handle. Put in a warm place. Cover with waxed paper and let rise until double in size, about 2 hours. Punch down and divide the dough into two large pieces. Roll out each piece to a ¾-inch thickness and cut into 7-inch-long oblong pieces.

Let rise again. Heat vegetable shortening in a deep pan to a depth of 2 to 3 inches until very hot. Fry the rolls in batches until golden, 2 minutes on each side. Frosting may be added if desired, once the rolls have cooled. Long John Rolls cannot be frozen or stored; they should be eaten the day they are made.

TOMATO CHEESE BREAD

Makes 2 loaves

Tomatoes are a big hit in our family. We are excited in the summer when we can start using tomatoes in sandwiches, soups, and even bread. My mother would always plant about a hundred tomato plants every year. I don't plant quite that many, but I like to put out at least sixty plants of different varieties. One of my favorites is beefsteak or Big Beef tomatoes. Also, Early Girl, Big Boy, Roma, and Jet Star are kinds I've tried. My daughter Lovina likes to eat one slice of tomato after another. She would live just on tomatoes if I'd let her. She'll eat them for breakfast, for a snack, or at any meal. I do have a few children who don't care for them, so this bread isn't high on their list. I can make this bread using our own homemade tomato juice, but store-bought is okay to use also.

2 cups tomato juice

2 tablespoons butter

3 tablespoons sugar

¼ cup ketchup

¼ cup grated Cheddar cheese

1 teaspoon salt

½ teaspoon dried oregano

½ teaspoon dried basil

1 package active dried yeast dissolved in ¼ cup warm water

4 cups all-purpose flour

Grease and lightly flour two bread pans. Set aside.

Heat the tomato juice and butter until the butter is melted. Stir in the sugar, ketchup, cheese, salt, oregano, and basil. Let cool until the mixture is lukewarm. Add the yeast and 3 cups of the flour and beat well. Add the remaining 1 cup of flour and stir until well combined. Divide the batter between the pans. Cover and let rise in a warm place until double in bulk, about 1 hour.

While the dough is rising, preheat the oven to 325°F. Bake the bread until a toothpick inserted in the center comes out clean, about 35 minutes. The loaves will brown only slightly.

Remove the bread from the pan and cool on a wire rack or windowsill. The bread can be stored in a sealed plastic bag and remain fresh for 3 to 4 days. This bread does not freeze well.

TOMATO BREAD

Makes 4 loaves

This is a great bread for ham and cheese sandwiches, often served at after-church meals. When tomatoes are plentiful in the summer, this is a good way to use a lot of them. Extra loaves or leftover bread can be bagged, sealed, and kept frozen until ready to use.

4 ½ cups tomato juice

4 tablespoons (½ stick) butter

6 tablespoons sugar

2 tablespoons salt

1 tablespoon ground oregano

1 tablespoon ground basil

½ cup ketchup

3 tablespoons active dry yeast

About 12 cups all-purpose flour

Preheat the oven to 350°F. Grease four standard loaf pans and set aside.

Heat the tomato juice to lukewarm in a large saucepan. Add the butter, sugar, salt, oregano, basil, ketchup, and yeast. Let the mixture sit a few minutes to dissolve the yeast. Stir in enough flour to form a soft dough, kneading when necessary. Let the dough rise in a warm place for 20 minutes. Punch down the dough. Divide the dough among the prepared pans. Allow to rise for 20 minutes longer. Bake for 1 hour.

HOBO BREAD

Makes 2 small loaves

This is a bread full of raisins. Raisins were popular in my household when I was a child since my father really liked them, but I didn't care for them. I do remember that in church when I was a little girl, they'd pass around cookies with raisins, and I would take the cookie and pick out the raisins and eat the cookie. But I like them better now as an adult. This recipe calls for soaking the raisins in water, which helps plump them up and soften them in the bread.

2 cups raisins

4 teaspoons baking soda

1 cup boiling water

4 tablespoons vegetable oil

4 cups all-purpose flour

2 cups sugar

1 cup packed brown sugar

½ teaspoon salt

Mix the raisins, baking soda, and boiling water. Cover and let stand until cooled, about an hour. Preheat the oven to 350°F. Lightly grease two 4 by 8-inch loaf pans. In a medium bowl, mix the raisin mixture with the oil, flour, sugars, and salt. Mix well. Pour into the prepared pans and bake until browned, about 1 hour.

CHEESY BREAD

Serves 10 to 12

This is a nice, soft bread that is fun for us to eat as a family. We break off pieces and share it among all of us. This tastes best when it is warm right out of the oven. Our family can go through a whole loaf of this in a single sitting!

1 cup cornmeal

1 teaspoon salt

½ teaspoon dry mustard

¼ teaspoon black pepper

3 tablespoons sugar

3 cups milk

1 cup grated Cheddar cheese

6 large eggs

Preheat the oven to 350°F. Grease a 2-quart casserole and set aside.

Combine the cornmeal, salt, dry mustard, pepper, and sugar in a large saucepan over low heat. When the mixture begins to bubble and thicken, gradually stir in the milk. Continue to cook over low heat and stir constantly until thickened. Stir in the cheese until melted, and remove from the heat. In a separate small bowl, beat the eggs vigorously and stir a small amount (2 to 3 tablespoons) of the hot mixture into the eggs. Then add the eggs to the hot mixture, mixing thoroughly. Pour into the prepared casserole and bake until puffy and browned, about 45 minutes.

Remove the bread from the pan and cool on a wire rack or windowsill. The bread can be stored in a sealed plastic bag and remain fresh for 3 to 4 days. This bread, however, does not freeze well.

DILLY BREAD

Makes 12 rolls or 1 loaf

This is a delicious, moist bread. The dill flavor makes a nice addition to a sandwich. This recipe can also be made into dinner rolls, and the little flakes of dill add a pretty green color to the rolls. Dill can be grown in the garden. Mom's dill would come up year after year, but I haven't had as much luck with mine.

1 package active dry yeast

¼ cup warm water

2 tablespoons sugar

1 tablespoon dried onion flakes

1 tablespoon butter, softened

1 teaspoon salt

1 cup small-curd cottage cheese

1 tablespoon dry dill seed or dill weed

¼ teaspoon baking soda

1 large egg

2½ cups bread flour

Dissolve the yeast in the water in a large bowl. Add the sugar, onion flakes, butter, salt, cottage cheese, dill, baking soda, and egg. Mix well. Slowly add the flour, beating after each addition. After all the flour is added and stirred in, you may need to knead the dough with your hands to finish mixing the flour in. Cover with a damp cloth. Let rise in a warm place for 1 hour.

Punch down and shape into twelve rolls or one loaf. Grease a baking sheet for the rolls or grease and flour a 5 by 9-inch loaf pan for the loaf. Place the dough on the sheet or in the pan, cover with a damp cloth, and allow the dough rise again until light, 30 to 45 minutes.

While the dough is rising, preheat the oven to 350°F. Bake until golden brown, 14 to 16 minutes for the rolls or about 45 minutes for the loaf. Remove the pans from the oven and brush the bread or rolls with melted lard or margarine. Unused rolls or bread can be sealed and frozen, or stored in a sealed container and stay fresh for 3 to 4 days.

SOUTHERN BREEZE PUNCH

Serves 8 to 12

This thirst-quenching concoction is great for picnics and lunches on hot days. It's very refreshing and attractive, and not too sweet.

4 tablespoons blue raspberry Kool-Aid powder

1 cup sugar

7 cups water

1 (46-ounce) can pineapple juice

1 (6-ounce) can frozen lemonade concentrate

2 liters ginger ale

In a very large bowl or container, combine all the ingredients and stir to dissolve and evenly distribute them. To serve, fill a glass with ice cubes, then pour the mixture over the ice to fill the glass. Stir the mixture briskly and allow a few minutes for the cubes to thaw into the punch.

PEANUT BUTTER SPREAD

Makes 1¾ cups

This sweet favorite is served at after-church meals in most Amish communities. Readers often ask about this recipe because it has been mentioned in passing so much in my column. It's an easy recipe, and ingredient amounts can be adjusted to suit your taste.

½ cup creamy peanut butter

¼ cup marshmallow crème

1 cup light corn syrup

In a medium bowl, combine the peanut butter, marshmallow crème, and corn syrup. Stir with a rubber spatula until the mixture is smooth and evenly combined. Place the mixture in a covered container and refrigerate overnight. Allow the spread to come to room temperature before serving on bread or over ice cream.

HOMEMADE CHEESE SPREAD

Serves 110 to 130

This is a spread that is also served at a lot of meals after church. It's good on a piece of bread or served as a sandwich spread. The amounts are easily scaled back if you're not feeding more than a hundred hungry people.

6½ to 7 cups milk

2 (10-ounce) cans evaporated milk

1 pound butter, softened

8 pounds American cheese, cut into 1-inch cubes

1 (16-ounce) box Velveeta cheese, cut into 1-inch cubes

Preheat the oven to 250°F. Put all the ingredients in a roasting pan and bake, stirring every 15 minutes, until melted and smooth (use the lower amount of milk if you want a thicker spread). Remove from the oven and serve as a sandwich spread. Cover and refrigerate any leftovers.

HOMEMADE SALAD DRESSING

Serves 8 to 10

This is a creamy salad dressing that can also be used on sandwiches as a spread. With its hints of honey, maple, and garlic, it goes wonderfully on a wide variety of salads and sandwiches, and appeals to a broad range of tastes.

1¾ cups water

½ cup vinegar

⅔ cup all-purpose flour

1 large egg, beaten

¾ cup (1½ sticks) butter, softened

2 tablespoons honey

2 tablespoons pure maple syrup

2 teaspoons salt

1 teaspoon fresh lemon juice

1 teaspoon dry mustard

½ teaspoon garlic powder

1 teaspoon paprika (optional)

2 teaspoons dried basil (optional)

Combine the water, vinegar, and flour in a small saucepan and cook over medium heat until thickened, stirring constantly with a whisk. In a large bowl, thoroughly combine the egg, butter, honey, maple syrup, salt, lemon juice, dry mustard, garlic powder, paprika, and basil. Add the cooked mixture. Pour everything into a blender or food processor, and process until thick and creamy. Pour the dressing into glass jars and refrigerate until ready to use.

KENTUCKY DRESSING

Serves 4 to 6

This is a delicious homemade salad dressing that uses easy-to-find ingredients. As its name suggests, I got this from another Amish cook in a Kentucky community.

2 cups Homemade Salad Dressing (page 87)

⅓ cup vegetable oil

⅓ cup ketchup

¾ cup sugar

¼ teaspoon garlic salt or onion salt

¼ teaspoon paprika

1 tablespoon vinegar

1 teaspoon prepared mustard

1 teaspoon Worcestershire sauce

Combine all the ingredients in a large mixing bowl. Mix with a wire whisk until the dressing is smooth and glossy. Serve the dressing on lettuce salads, or use it as a dip for fresh vegetables.

BLUE CHEESE DRESSING OR DIP

Makes about 1½ cups

This dressing can be used on salad or as a dip for vegetables or hot wings. It is a creamy dip with decadent chunks of blue cheese buried in it.

¾ cup sour cream

¼ cup mayonnaise

1½ teaspoons fresh dill

2 ounces blue cheese, crumbled

Whisk together the sour cream and mayonnaise in a small mixing bowl until creamy and well blended. Add the dill and blue cheese and stir to combine. The dressing is ready to serve or may be chilled first.

OVERNIGHT SALAD

Serves 8 to 10

Salads that can incorporate many different fresh vegetables from the garden are popular with Amish cooks. This was a favorite in the Coblentz household every summer.

1 large head of lettuce, chopped

1 head of cauliflower, chopped

1 medium onion, chopped

1 pound frozen peas

3 carrots, peeled and chopped (optional)

1 cup salad dressing, such as Miracle Whip

1 cup sugar

1 cup shredded Cheddar cheese

Mix the lettuce, cauliflower, onion, peas, and carrots together in a large bowl. In a separate bowl, combine the salad dressing and the sugar. Stir the dressing mixture until it is smooth and the sugar is well incorporated. Pour the dressing over the vegetables and toss until they are evenly coated. Sprinkle the cheese on top of the salad. Cover the bowl and chill the salad overnight in the refrigerator.

AUTUMN SALAD

Serves 4

2 cups peeled and diced apples

1 cup peeled and grated carrots

½ cup raisins

½ cup mayonnaise

In a large bowl, combine the apples, carrots, and raisins. Add the mayonnaise and toss until the ingredients are evenly coated. Chill for 1 hour before serving.

FRESH PEA SALAD

Serves 4 to 6

This salad is a favorite among the children because they all seem to love raw peas so much. I wish they were in season in December so I could fix this for Verena's birthday!

1 cup green peas

½ cup sweet pickle relish

½ cup chopped onion

½ cup shredded Colby or Cheddar cheese

6 hard-boiled eggs (see page 99), chopped

¾ cup mayonnaise or Miracle Whip salad dressing

Cook the peas in salted boiling water until tender, 7 to 10 minutes. Drain and let cool. Transfer to a medium bowl and stir all the remaining ingredients into the peas. Cover and chill before serving.

GARDEN RADISH SALAD

Serves 6 to 8

I rarely buy radishes in the stores; they just don't taste as good. But since their growing season is so short and they don't keep very well, I will sometimes buy them at a supermarket if we want to have them in a salad at other times of the year.

4 cups radishes, trimmed and sliced

½ cup thinly sliced onion

1 cup diced tomatoes

1¼ teaspoons salt

1 small clove garlic, minced

⅓ teaspoon freshly ground black pepper

1 teaspoon minced fresh basil or mint

2 tablespoons fresh lemon juice

2 tablespoons olive oil

Minced fresh parsley for garnish

Combine the radishes, onion, and tomatoes in a bowl. In a separate bowl, whisk together the salt, garlic, pepper, basil, lemon juice, and oil. Toss the dressing with the salad and then garnish with the parsley.

FRUITY FLORIDA COLESLAW

Serves 8 to 10

Featuring some of Florida's best fruits, this is a popular dish for gatherings. Cortland apples go well in this salad, because their flesh is slow to brown after cutting.

1 head cabbage, shredded

2 Florida oranges (or equivalent amount of canned mandarin oranges)

2 Cortland apples, chopped

1 cup red seedless grapes

1 (16-ounce) can pineapple chunks, drained

½ cup chopped walnuts

¼ cup sweetened flaked coconut

Pinch of salt

½ cup mayonnaise

¾ cup Homemade Whipped Topping (page 47)

1 tablespoon sugar

1 tablespoon fresh lemon juice

Place the cabbage, oranges, apples, grapes, pineapple, walnuts, and coconut in a large bowl and toss to combine. Mix the salt, mayonnaise, whipped topping, sugar, and lemon juice in a small bowl. Pour the dressing over the cabbage mixture, mix well, and serve in your prettiest glass bowl.

DUTCH COLESLAW

Serves 8 to 10

A nice, cool coleslaw made from fresh vegetables directly from the garden was one of my mother, Elizabeth's, favorite summer menu items.

8 cups shredded green cabbage	2 tablespoons white vinegar
1 cup shredded red cabbage	$\frac{1}{2}$ cup sugar
5 cups shredded carrots	1 teaspoon salt
1 cup mayonnaise	$\frac{1}{4}$ teaspoon black pepper

In a large bowl, mix together the cabbage and carrots. Set aside. In a small bowl, combine the mayonnaise, vinegar, sugar, salt, and pepper and stir until smooth and well incorporated. Pour the dressing over the cabbage mixture and toss until the vegetables are evenly coated. Refrigerate the coleslaw overnight before serving.

HOMEMADE BROCCOLI SALAD

Serves 10 to 12

This salad is a crunchy collision of sweet and savory. It's perfect in a larger quantity for a party or picnic.

1 head broccoli, chopped

1 head cauliflower, chopped

1 cup mayonnaise

1 cup sour cream

½ cup sugar

½ teaspoon salt

½ pound bacon, fried and crumbled

1 cup shredded Cheddar cheese

Combine the chopped broccoli and cauliflower in a large bowl. In a separate bowl, combine the mayonnaise, sour cream, sugar, and salt to make a creamy dressing. Add the dressing to the vegetables, stirring to evenly coat. Stir in the bacon and ¾ cup of the cheese. Sprinkle the remaining ¼ cup of cheese on top and serve.

DANDELION SOUR CREAM SALAD

Serves 4 to 6

This is a recipe for dandelions smothered in our favorite homemade sour cream. You can, however, use just the sour cream part for other seasoned greens as well. This same sour cream is great when used with in-season, fresh-from-the-garden lettuce and endive. Home-cured ham also goes well with it. Any unused sour cream can be refrigerated for up to 2 days.

½ cup mayonnaise

1 cup apple cider vinegar

2½ cups whole milk

Salt

4 hard-boiled eggs (see opposite), diced

4 cups packed young dandelion greens

Combine the mayonnaise, vinegar, milk, and salt to taste in a quart jar. Shake until smooth. Put the eggs and dandelion greens in a large bowl and pour the sour cream mixture over them.

GRAPE AND PINEAPPLE SALAD

Serves 6 to 8

This is a good, light salad that is commonly served after church. It's a good colorful salad because of the pineapple, but other fruit can be added in addition or in its place.

1 cup sour cream

8 ounces cream cheese, softened

1 cup sweetened whipped cream or whipped topping

1½ cups powdered sugar, sifted

1 teaspoon fresh lemon juice

3 pounds seedless grapes

1 (13-ounce) can pineapple chunks, drained

Combine all the ingredients in a large bowl and stir until the grapes are coated evenly. Cover and refrigerate overnight before serving.

tip: hard-boiled eggs

For perfect hard-boiled eggs, put raw eggs in a saucepan and cover with cold water. Bring to a boil, uncovered, and let cook for 2 minutes. Turn the heat off, cover, and let stand for 11 minutes. Transfer the eggs to cold water and let soak until cooled. They will peel easily.

HAM AND PEA SALAD

Serves 6 to 8

This is just such an easy way to use fresh peas from the garden. This salad is very colorful and is a favorite to serve to people after church services.

2 cups green peas

1½ cups chopped cooked ham

1 cup shredded Cheddar cheese

1 cup chopped red onion

½ cup ranch salad dressing

In a serving bowl, combine the peas, ham, cheese, and onion. Pour the dressing over the top and toss to coat evenly.

HAM SALAD

Serves 8

This dish is a great way to use some of the fresh ham that we harvest during butchering day.

3 cups diced ham

½ cup sweet pickle relish

2 teaspoons minced onions

2 teaspoons prepared mustard

½ cup mayonnaise

1 cup diced celery

2 hard-boiled eggs, diced

1 tablespoon lemon juice

¼ teaspoon salt

¼ teaspoon black pepper

1 cup crushed potato chips

Preheat the oven to 425°F.

In a large bowl, combine all of the ingredients, except for the potato chips. Stir until the mixture is smooth and well combined. Pour the mixture into a 2-quart casserole dish and sprinkle the top with the crushed chips. Cover and bake 20 minutes, or until the top is bubbling and golden.

EGG SALAD

Serves 20

Here is a great way to use up those leftover Easter eggs. This recipe is served at church a lot in place of ham salad, which is also a popular dish. It makes a great sandwich! Our children love this for sandwiches; they never get tired of it. This recipe is probably a bit large for the average family, so adjust it as needed.

6 pounds hot dogs

5 dozen eggs, hard-boiled (see page 99) and diced

6 cups Miracle Whip salad dressing

2 cups mayonnaise

Salt and black pepper

Grind the hot dogs in a meat grinder. In a large bowl, stir the ground meat, eggs, salad dressing, and mayonnaise together. Season to taste with salt and pepper. Cover and store in the refrigerator for up to 3 days.

SHRIMP SALAD SANDWICH ROLLS

Makes 8 sandwiches

Fresh shrimp are plentiful in the temperate Atlantic waters off Delaware and are often used in recipes by the Amish community in nearby Dover. This is a refreshing way to enjoy these delicacies on a warm summer day.

8 ounces cream cheese, softened

¼ cup sour cream

½ teaspoon dried dill

⅛ teaspoon salt

½ pound fresh shrimp, cooked, shells removed

½ cup chopped green bell pepper

⅓ cup chopped onion

1 cup chopped tomato

1 (8-roll) tube crescent rolls

½ cup cocktail sauce

½ cup shredded Monterey Jack cheese

Cream together the cream cheese, sour cream, dill, and salt in a medium mixing bowl. Chop the cooked shrimp, and stir into the cream cheese mixture until well combined. Refrigerate until chilled, about 1 hour.

Mix the chopped vegetables together in a bowl.

Bake the crescent rolls according to the package directions. Split the baked rolls lengthwise and spread a portion of the shrimp salad inside each roll. Top each with 1 tablespoon of the cocktail sauce, a portion of the chopped vegetables, and a portion of the Monterey Jack.

SOFT PRETZELS

Makes 6 medium pretzels

1½ teaspoons active dry yeast

1½ teaspoons sugar

½ teaspoon salt

¾ cup warm water

1¾ cups bread flour

1 large egg

Coarse salt for sprinkling

Preheat the oven to 425°F. Grease a baking sheet.

Mix and dissolve the yeast, sugar, and salt in the warm water. Stir in the flour until a ball forms. Put the dough on a lightly floured surface and knead until smooth. Divide and roll the dough into six small ropes, then into pretzel shapes. Place on the baking sheet. Beat the egg and brush on the unbaked pretzels. Sprinkle with coarse salt. Bake until they are a light golden color, 10 minutes.

HOMEMADE CHEESE SOUP

Serves 4 to 6

This recipe was a favorite of my mother's on cold winter days. The recipe calls for a bag of frozen mixed vegetables. She would use a blend of fresh vegetables from the garden in this recipe, and other home cooks can try the same.

¼ cup (½ stick) butter

¼ cup minced onion

¼ cup all-purpose flour

4 cups milk

1 (10-ounce) bag frozen mixed vegetables

1 cup shredded Cheddar cheese

Salt

In a 2-quart pot, melt the butter over medium heat. Add the onion and sauté, stirring frequently, until translucent. Remove the pot from the heat and sprinkle the flour over the cooked onion. Gradually add the milk, whisking constantly, until no lumps remain. Add the vegetables. Cook the mixture over medium heat, stirring constantly, until the soup thickens and coats the back of a spoon. Stir in the cheese. Continue heating until the cheese is melted and well combined. Season the soup with salt to taste.

ASPARAGUS-POTATO SOUP

Serves 4 to 6

This is a thick soup. The color is light, like a cream sauce. I usually serve a fresh salad with it.

1¾ cups chicken broth

3 potatoes, peeled and cubed

⅓ cup chopped onion

1 teaspoon salt

½ pound asparagus, trimmed and cut into ½-inch pieces

1½ cups milk

2 tablespoons all-purpose flour

1 cup Velveeta or Colby cheese (cubed or sliced)

Combine the broth, potatoes, onion, and salt in a large saucepan. Cook over medium heat until the vegetables are tender, about 20 minutes. Add the asparagus and cook for 10 minutes more.

Whisk the milk and flour together well in a small bowl and whisk into the broth mixture. Stir in the cheese until melted. Pour into warmed soup bowls and serve immediately.

Variation: *I once fried bacon strips and then crumbled them in with everything. It was very good! You could also sprinkle crumbled bacon over the top as a garnish.*

GRANDMA'S SOUP

Serves 6 to 8

We call this "Grandma's Soup" because all my children remember this delicious homemade vegetable soup. They'll always think of their grandma when I make it for them. By the way, the recipe calls for one onion. I just put it in whole for flavoring and then remove it when the soup is done cooking. Mom would always eat the onion at the end, so that is a variation on the dish that you can try. I use a pint of home-canned beef chunks instead of ground beef. The reason I like to use the beef chunks instead of ground beef is the broth from the beef chunks will give it a better flavoring.

1 pint canned beef chunks

1 medium yellow onion

2 potatoes, peeled and diced

1 cup diced carrots

1 cup diced green beans

2 cups corn kernels

2 cups green peas

4 cups tomato juice

1½ teaspoons salt

1½ teaspoons black pepper

Brown the beef chunks in a large skillet over medium heat. Put the beef chunks and the whole onion in a large pot and add the remaining ingredients. Add enough water to cover the vegetables. Cook over medium heat until the vegetables are soft, about 30 minutes.

ZUCCHINI SOUP

Serves 4 to 6

If it's September, it must be zucchini time! My mother, Elizabeth Coblentz, could find scores of ways to use this versatile vegetable. This homemade soup was just one recipe featured in our column, "The Amish Cook," during the summer of 1995.

2 tablespoons butter

½ cup sliced carrots

½ cup sliced celery

1 small onion, chopped

2 cups chicken broth

2 cups grated zucchini

2 tablespoons chopped fresh parsley

1 small potato, peeled and cubed

¼ teaspoon seasoned salt

Salt and black pepper

In a 2-quart pot, melt the butter over medium heat, then add the carrots, celery, and onion. Sauté the vegetables, stirring frequently, until the onions become translucent. Add the remaining ingredients and bring the soup to a boil. Reduce the heat and simmer for 30 to 45 minutes, until the vegetables are fork-tender.

YANKEE BEAN SOUP

Makes 4 to 6 servings

This is a thick, hearty soup that has a little bit of everything in it. Such soups are mainstays through the harsh New England winters. The sweet molasses balances out the savory for an excellent meal. A thick piece of Cheesy Bread, page 81, goes well with this soup.

1¼ cups dried navy beans, rinsed and cleaned

5 cups water

1 teaspoon molasses

½ cup salt pork, cut into ¼-inch cubes

⅓ cup finely chopped celery leaves

½ teaspoon salt, plus extra for seasoning

3 strips fresh bacon, cut into small pieces

¼ cup finely chopped onion

½ cup cooked carrots, diced

2 cups milk

Place the beans in a 4- or 5-quart saucepan or Dutch oven, add the water, and bring to a boil. Remove the pot from the heat, and let it stand, covered, for 2 to 24 hours. (The longer the beans soak, the softer the finished beans and the thicker the broth.)

Add the molasses, salt pork, celery leaves, and ½ teaspoon salt. Cover the pot and simmer for 2 hours, or until the beans are tender. Shake the pan or stir occasionally to prevent sticking.

While the soup is simmering, cook the bacon pieces and onion in a small skillet until the bacon is lightly browned. Mash the beans slightly. Add the bacon, onion, carrots, and milk to the beans. Season with additional salt. Cover and simmer the soup for 10 minutes more. The soup is then ready to serve or can be cooked longer to the desired consistency.

RIVEL SOUP

Serves 6 to 8

This is a common soup in the Berne, Indiana, Amish community, and a very typical meal scratched out of whatever is in the pantry. The title refers to the small rounds of dough that you'll find in the soup, known as rivels.

8 cups chicken broth

2 cups all-purpose flour

1 teaspoon salt

2 large eggs, beaten

1 onion, diced

2 tablespoons dried parsley

2 (14.5-ounce) cans of corn or equivalent amount of home-canned

2 cups chicken, cooked and diced (optional)

Bring the broth to a boil in a large pot over medium heat. In a large mixing bowl, mix the flour, salt, and eggs to form a crumbly mixture. Rub the mixture between your fingers over the broth, dropping in pea-size pellets, or rivels.

Add the onion, parsley, and corn, and cook until the vegetables are tender, 10 to 15 minutes. If you choose, add the chicken just before you take the soup off the stove.

CHEESY CHICKEN CHOWDER

Serves 4 to 6

This is a delicious, hearty meal for cold autumn days. Sometimes I will use 3 tablespoons of cornstarch instead of flour as a thickener for this because the cornstarch makes the soup smoother than the flour does. Sometimes as a variation I will stick it in the oven instead and bake it just like a casserole. It is even thicker when prepared that way. This is something everyone in our family really enjoys.

1 onion, chopped

1 cup chopped carrots

1 cup diced potatoes

1 cup diced celery

4 cups water

5 cups diced cooked chicken

4 tablespoons butter

6 tablespoons all-purpose flour

2 cups milk

1 cup shredded Cheddar or mozzarella cheese

1 teaspoon salt

Combine the vegetables and water in a soup pot and bring to a boil; reduce the heat to medium and cook until soft, about 20 minutes. Add the chicken and butter. Stir in the flour, then gradually stir in the milk. Add the cheese and salt and stir until the cheese is melted. Spoon into bowls and serve.

POTATO CHOWDER

Serves 4 to 6

Chowders are a staple of Maine menus, and the Amish contribute to that popularity. True to a chowder, this is a thick, creamy concoction using fresh, locally grown Maine potatoes.

2 tablespoons butter

1 small onion, chopped

3 cups chicken broth

3 medium-size potatoes, peeled and cut into medium dice

3 medium carrots, peeled and cut into medium dice

2 tablespoons dried parsley

½ teaspoon salt

½ teaspoon black pepper

¼ cup all-purpose flour

1 cup milk

8 ounces cream cheese, room temperature, or 4 ounces softened cream cheese plus
    4 ounces shredded Cheddar

2 cups cooked chicken breasts, cut into medium dice (about 2 large breast halves)

Melt the butter in a medium saucepan over low heat. Add the onion and cook until soft, about 5 minutes. Add the chicken broth, potatoes, and carrots. Bring to a boil, then reduce the heat and simmer until the potatoes and carrots are fork-tender, about 20 minutes. Add the parsley flakes, salt, and pepper.

Stir the flour and milk together in a small bowl until smooth, add the flour mixture to the soup, and bring the soup to a boil. Stir the soup until it begins to thicken. Add the cheese and mix until the cheese has melted into the soup. Stir in the chicken, and continue cooking until the chicken is heated through, but do not boil.

ONION PIE

Serves 4 to 6

This is a recipe for a savory lunch pie that even people who don't care for onions will like. It's a good way to use up those extra onions from the garden!

4 slices bacon

2 cups chopped onions

2 large eggs, beaten

1 cup sour cream

1 tablespoon all-purpose flour

½ teaspoon salt

¼ teaspoon black pepper

1 disk My Homemade Pie Dough (page 296)

Preheat the oven to 400°F. Fry the bacon in a skillet until crisp. Transfer the bacon to paper towels to drain. Drain most of the fat from the pan, leaving just enough to coat the bottom of the skillet. Add the onions and sauté until translucent, about 3 minutes. Remove from the heat and let cool.

Whisk the eggs and sour cream together in a small bowl. Whisk in the flour, then the salt and pepper.

Roll out the disk of dough to a ⅛-inch thickness on a floured surface. Fit into a 9-inch pie pan and trim to a 1-inch overhang. Fold the dough under and crimp the edges. Using a fork, prick several holes in the bottom of the crust. Spread the onion and bacon over the bottom of the pie shell. Pour in the filling. Bake for 15 minutes. Lower the oven temperature to 350°F and bake for another 15 minutes, or until nicely browned. Remove from the oven. Cut into wedges and serve hot.

DELICIOUS GREEN BEANS

Serves 4 to 6

3 tablespoons butter

2 pounds green beans

½ pound bacon, cooked to desired crispness and cut into small pieces

Salt and black pepper

Seasoning salt

Melt the butter in a large saucepan over medium heat and cook until browned. Add the green beans to the butter, and stir to coat. Continue to heat until the green beans are steaming hot. Add the cooked bacon, along with the salt, pepper, and seasoning salt, and serve.

ZUCCHINI PATTIES

Serves 4 to 6

This is a great way to get rid of excess zucchini. In addition to just eating these as patties, we also like to eat them in a sandwich, with lettuce, tomato, and onions piled on. Some people add oats or breadcrumbs to the mixture, but I've found that everything holds together very well the way I have it. During zucchini season, this recipe will often be our main supper dish. We might serve some fresh corn on the side or perhaps some beets and sliced bread.

3 tablespoons olive oil

3 cups peeled and shredded zucchini

3 large eggs

1 cup shredded Cheddar cheese

Salt

8 to 10 slices Velveeta cheese (optional)

Heat the oil in a large skillet over medium-high heat. Stir the zucchini, eggs, Cheddar, and salt to taste together in a large bowl. Drop the batter by tablespoons into the skillet pan. As the batter begins to thicken, shape it into patties using a metal spatula and fry until golden brown, about 3 minutes on each side.

Top with a slice of Velveeta and serve.

TOMATO PANCAKES

Makes 2 dozen 4-inch pancakes

You wouldn't want to use maple syrup on these "pancakes"! This is a good way to get rid of some of those extra tomatoes during the height of the season. Like Zucchini Patties (opposite), this is a quick dish that goes over well around here with the children.

4 large eggs, lightly beaten

2 cups diced tomatoes with their juice

40 saltine crackers, crushed

Salt

2 tablespoons butter

Combine the eggs, tomatoes, crackers, and salt to taste in a bowl. Stir to blend, then shape the mixture into 4-inch pancakes.

Melt the butter in a large skillet over medium heat. Add the pancakes and fry for about 2 minutes on each side until lightly browned. Serve warm.

SCALLOPED CORN

Serves 4 to 6

Illinois is corn country, and during the height of summer, fields are filled with rows of towering stalks. Corn is used in casseroles and enjoyed on the cob, slathered with butter. This scalloped corn recipe is also a favorite and is extra tasty when it's made with fresh Silver Queen or sweet corn during the summer.

2 cups fresh or frozen corn kernels

2 large eggs, beaten

1 cup milk

$\frac{2}{3}$ cup bread or saltine cracker crumbs

1 tablespoon minced onion

3 tablespoons melted butter

$\frac{1}{2}$ teaspoon salt

$\frac{1}{4}$ teaspoon black pepper

1 tablespoon sugar

Preheat the oven to 350°F. Lightly grease a 2-quart casserole and set it aside.

Combine all the ingredients in a large mixing bowl and mix until well distributed. Spoon the mixture into the prepared pan. Bake for 40 minutes, until bubbly and golden.

BAKED STUFFED TOMATOES

Serves 4

This is a great main dish during tomato season. For a heartier version, you can cook some ground beef and stuff it into the tomatoes with the rest of the mixture, but we think it tastes good just like this!

4 large tomatoes

Salt for sprinkling, plus ½ teaspoon

1 cup fresh breadcrumbs

2 tablespoons butter, melted

1 egg, beaten

1 tablespoon minced onion

1 teaspoon minced fresh parsley

Few grains of ground black pepper

Preheat the oven to 350°F. Grease a shallow baking dish.

Cut a slice from the top of each tomato. Scoop out the pulp with a spoon. Sprinkle the insides of the tomatoes with salt. Place the tomato shells in the prepared dish.

Put the breadcrumbs in a small bowl and drizzle the melted butter over them; toss lightly to coat. Lightly mix in the egg, onion, parsley, the ½ teaspoon salt, and the pepper. Spoon the mixture into the tomatoes and bake until firm, about 30 minutes. Remove from the oven and serve hot.

BACON-WRAPPED JALAPEÑOS

Serves 4 to 6

This is sort of a different way to fix jalapeños. We enjoy this as a change of pace during the summer when Joe does a lot of our cooking on the outdoor grill.

¼ cup cream cheese, softened	8 jalapeño peppers, halved and seeded
½ cup (or more) shredded Cheddar cheese	8 slices bacon, cut in half crosswise

Preheat the oven to 400°F. Line a jelly-roll pan with aluminum foil.

Put the cream cheese and Cheddar cheese in a small resealable plastic bag. Seal the bag and knead until the cheeses are well combined. Cut off a bottom corner of the bag and use it to pipe a generous portion of the cheese mixture into each of the jalapeño halves.

Wrap a piece of bacon around each jalapeño half. (If you prefer to cook them on a grill, use a toothpick to hold the bacon in place.) Place the peppers on a rack in the jelly-roll pan, cheese side up. Bake for 20 minutes, or until the bacon is crisp.

FLORIDA VEGETABLE MEDLEY

Serves 4 to 6

The Amish in Pinecraft, Florida, make use of the lovely fresh produce that surrounds them to make bright, refreshing dishes like this one.

6 to 8 small Florida squash, sliced	Salt and lemon pepper
6 ripe Florida tomatoes, cut into wedges	½ cup water
6 Florida onions (the sweetest variety you can find), sliced	Grated sharp Cheddar cheese, for garnishing

Place a layer of sliced squash in a large skillet, then add a layer of tomato wedges and a layer of sliced onions. Continue layering until all the vegetables are used. Sprinkle with salt and lemon pepper as desired. Add the water and steam over medium heat for 12 to 15 minutes, or until the vegetables are tender. Serve in a pretty dish with the cheese sprinkled on top.

ASPARAGUS WITH BACON-CHEESE SAUCE

Serves 4 to 6

This recipe is where I got the idea to add bacon to the Asparagus-Potato Soup (page 108). This is a favorite dish on our spring supper table.

2 tablespoons butter

2 tablespoons all-purpose flour

1 cup milk

¼ teaspoon salt

1 cup shredded American or mild Cheddar cheese

1½ pounds asparagus, trimmed

4 to 6 slices bacon, cooked crisp and drained

Melt the butter in a medium saucepan over medium heat. Stir in the flour and cook until smooth and bubbly, about 3 minutes. Gradually whisk in the milk. Cook, whisking constantly, until the sauce has thickened. Stir in the salt and cheese until the cheese is melted. Set aside and keep warm.

Meanwhile, cook the asparagus in 1 inch of salted boiling water in a large skillet until crisp-tender, 3 to 5 minutes. Immediately drain and rinse under cold water.

Pour the sauce over the drained hot asparagus. Sprinkle with the crumbled bacon. Serve right away.

DEEP-FRIED MORELS

Serves 6 to 8

This is probably the favorite mushroom dish in our household. I know some people like to dip them in ranch dressing, but we just like to eat them plain.

¾ cup all-purpose flour

½ cup milk

1 egg, beaten

½ teaspoon salt

Olive oil, for panfrying

12 to 15 large morel mushrooms

Stir the flour, milk, egg, and salt together in a large bowl. Heat 1 inch of oil in a large skillet until sizzling. Dip the mushrooms in the batter and put them in the skillet. Fry each side until golden brown. Using a slotted spoon, transfer to paper towels to drain.

STUFFED MUSHROOMS

Serves 4 to 6

Some years Joe doesn't have much luck finding mushrooms; it just depends on the conditions. So, even though they don't taste as good, I will buy them in the store if we don't have freshly picked ones. One simple way we like to eat fresh mushrooms is to wrap a piece of bacon around each one, put a toothpick in to hold the bacon on, and then place on a skewer and grill it. They are good like that, but stuffed mushrooms are another favorite way to eat them around here.

¼ pound bulk sausage

¼ cup diced green onion, including green parts

¼ cup mayonnaise

12 large white mushrooms, stems separated and finely chopped

½ cup shredded Cheddar cheese

Preheat the oven to 350°F. Combine the sausage and the green onion in a large skillet and brown over medium heat. Remove from the heat and stir in the mayonnaise and chopped mushroom stems. Spoon the sausage mixture into the mushroom caps. Sprinkle the cheese over the mushrooms. Place the mushrooms on a baking sheet and bake until they are heated through and the cheese is melted, about 20 minutes.

EASY HOMEMADE BARBECUE SAUCE

Makes 3 cups

It seems like every family has its own secret recipe or slightly different concoction for barbecue sauce. This formula is an Amish family favorite.

1 cup ketchup

Small dash of Worcestershire sauce

¼ teaspoon soy sauce

½ teaspoon dry mustard

½ cup firmly packed brown sugar

½ cup vinegar

½ teaspoon ground ginger

½ teaspoon chili powder

2 tablespoons chopped onion

½ cup sugar

¼ cup tomato sauce

Place all the ingredients in a large bowl and stir until they are thoroughly combined. Use the sauce fresh in your favorite recipes, or refrigerate for later use.

BARBECUED BEEF SANDWICHES

Makes 8 sandwiches

This is great with potato salad, baked beans, and cold lemonade. Many Amish cooks use home-canned beef in this recipe. A leftover roast works well, too.

2 pounds chunked, cooked beef

1 cup barbecue sauce, or as desired

¼ cup firmly packed brown sugar

Salt and black pepper

8 hamburger buns

Combine the meat, sauce, brown sugar, salt, and pepper in a large saucepan. Cook over medium heat until the meat shreds easily and the sauce is bubbling. Serve on hamburger buns. Top with your favorite barbecue sauce. You could also make your own, using the Easy Homemade Barbecue Sauce on page 127.

PORK 'N' BEANS

Serves 12

The Amish have heartily adopted this Southern staple. One common Southern variation is to add a couple of tablespoons of homemade sorghum molasses to give it a bit of sweetness.

1 pound dried navy beans or great northern beans

2 tablespoons salt

8 cups water

1 pound boneless pork, cut into very small pieces

SAUCE

1 cup brown sugar

½ cup granulated sugar

½ teaspoon black pepper

1 teaspoon dry mustard

1 teaspoon salt

1 quart tomato juice

2 cups water

1½ cups ketchup

¼ cup cornstarch

Remove any debris from the beans, then rinse them and cover them with water in a large bowl. Add the salt and let soak for 8 hours or overnight. Drain and rinse the beans three times, then cover them with the 8 cups of water. Bring the water to a boil, add the pork, and then reduce the heat to low. Simmer until the beans are soft and the pork is cooked through, 45 to 60 minutes. Drain the beans and pork, and set aside.

Make the sauce: While the beans are cooking, place all the sauce ingredients in a large saucepan and bring to a boil over medium-high heat. Reduce the heat to medium-low. Cook the sauce mixture, stirring occasionally, until it is reduced and thickened, about 1 hour.

About 10 minutes before the cooking is finished, preheat the oven to 375°F. Combine the pork mixture with the sauce and pour into a large casserole dish. Bake in the preheated oven, stirring occasionally, until thickened and bubbly, about 40 minutes.

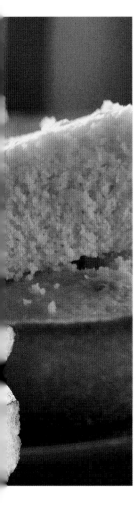

BUTTERY CORNBREAD

Serves 16

Locally milled cornmeal from the Shawnee Milling Company adds a home-state twist to this favorite from the Chouteau, Oklahoma, Amish community. When the Amish cooks aren't making items from scratch, there's a lot of support and use of locally made products. The Chouteau Baked Beans (page 132) would be a great accompaniment.

12 tablespoons (1½ sticks) butter

1 cup sugar

3 large eggs, beaten

1⅔ cups milk

1¾ cups flour

1 cup cornmeal

4½ teaspoons baking powder

1 teaspoon salt

Preheat the oven to 350°F. Lightly grease a 9 by 13-inch pan and set aside.

Cream the butter and sugar in a medium mixing bowl until light and fluffy. In a small bowl, combine the eggs and milk. In a third (medium) bowl, combine the flour, cornmeal, baking powder, and salt. Add the egg and cornmeal mixtures alternately to the butter mixture, stirring well between additions.

Pour the batter into the prepared pan and bake until a toothpick inserted into the center comes out clean, about 25 minutes.

CHOUTEAU BAKED BEANS

Serves 8 to 10

Named after the Amish community in Chouteau, Oklahoma, these popular beans are simpler and quicker than the Pork 'n' Beans version on page 129.

1 quart (2 pounds) chopped roast beef

2 teaspoons black pepper

1 onion, chopped

2 cups barbecue sauce (your favorite, or see page 127)

4 (15-ounce) cans pork and beans, drained

1 cup firmly packed brown sugar

Preheat the oven to 350°F. Grease a roasting pan and set aside.

Cook the beef, pepper, and onion together for 15 minutes, until soft. Drain off any liquid that accumulates. Mix in the barbecue sauce, pork and beans, and brown sugar. Pour the mixture into the prepared pan.

Bake, uncovered, for 30 minutes. Remove the pan from the oven and stir. Return the pan to the oven and cook for 30 minutes more, or until bubbly.

BAKED CHOCOLATE FUDGE PUDDING

Serves 14 to 16

The Swartzentruber Amish are known for their from-scratch simplicity. And even the most conservative groups get the urge for a sweet treat. This easy dessert is often the answer.

3 tablespoons shortening

¾ cup granulated sugar

1 cup all-purpose flour

1½ teaspoons baking powder

¾ teaspoon salt

½ cup milk

1 cup firmly packed brown sugar

¼ cup unsweetened cocoa powder

1¼ cups boiling water

Preheat the oven to 350°F.

Cream together the shortening and granulated sugar in a large mixing bowl. In a small bowl, combine the flour, baking powder, and ½ teaspoon of the salt. Add this mixture, alternately with the milk, to the creamed mixture. Pour into an ungreased 8 by 8-inch pan.

Mix the brown sugar, cocoa powder, and the remaining ¼ teaspoon of salt in a small bowl, sprinkle the mixture over the batter, then pour the boiling water over the batter. Bake until the cake is set, 45 to 50 minutes.

FLORIDA PUDDING

Serves 12

No one seems to know where this recipe gets its name; perhaps it was popular in Florida's Amish settlement as a cool, delicious dessert. Florida's lone Amish settlement is a melting pot of "Plain People" from various communities seeking a respite from harsh winter climes for a few weeks.

1 (4.6-ounce) box instant pudding mix, any flavor

1 cup all-purpose flour

½ cup walnut pieces

¼ cup margarine, softened

1 cup unsifted powdered sugar

1 cup cream cheese

2 cups whipped cream

Preheat the oven to 350°F. Prepare the instant pudding mix according to the package directions. Set aside.

In a large bowl, mix the flour, walnut pieces, and margarine until well combined. Press into the bottom of a 9 by 13-inch cake pan. Bake for about 10 minutes, or until lightly browned. Let cool completely.

In a separate bowl, mix the powdered sugar and the cream cheese until smooth. Gently fold 1 cup of the whipped cream into the cream cheese mixture. Spread the mixture evenly over the cooled crust, followed by an even layer of the prepared pudding. Top with the remaining whipped cream and sprinkle with additional walnut pieces, if desired. Refrigerate for at least 4 hours before serving.

SWEET POTATO PUDDING

Serves 4 to 6

Sweet potatoes are common in Southern Amish settlements, but not so much in more traditional Midwestern ones. This is a favorite recipe in Kentucky Amish communities, but is more often reserved for dessert because it is so sweet.

2 cups cooked, mashed sweet potatoes

3 tablespoons sugar

2 large eggs, well beaten

2 tablespoons butter, melted

1 teaspoon salt

1 cup milk

½ cup mini marshmallows or marshmallow creme

Preheat the oven to 350°F.

In a large mixing bowl, combine the sweet potatoes, sugar, eggs, butter, salt, and milk until thoroughly blended. Add the marshmallows and blend well.

Pour the mixture into a buttered 2-quart casserole. Bake for 45 minutes, or until the marshmallows are melted and golden.

CINNAMON PUDDING

Serves 6

I remember when I was a little girl my older sister, Leah, would make cinnamon pudding. This is special enough to fix when company comes. The pudding sort of has the taste of a cake and pudding together. We always serve it in a nice glass bowl.

SUGAR SYRUP

2 cups packed brown sugar

1½ cups water

2 tablespoons margarine or butter

PUDDING

About 3 cups all-purpose flour

1 cup granulated sugar

2 teaspoons baking powder

2 teaspoons ground cinnamon

1 cup milk

2 tablespoons margarine or butter

½ cup walnuts, chopped (optional)

2 cups sweetened whipped cream

Preheat the oven to 350°F. Grease a 9 by 13-inch pan and set aside.

Make the sugar syrup: Combine the brown sugar, water, and margarine in a small saucepan. Bring to a boil over medium heat, then remove from the heat. Set aside.

Make the pudding: Combine the flour, granulated sugar, baking powder, and cinnamon in a large bowl. Stir with a whisk to blend. Stir in the milk and margarine to make a smooth batter. Spoon into the prepared pan and smooth the top. Pour the sugar syrup over the top and sprinkle evenly with the nuts.

Bake until the center is firm when you shake the pan a little, about 45 minutes. Cut into 1-inch squares and top each with a dollop of whipped cream.

FLAT ROCK PUDDING

Serves 8 to 12

This dessert originated when someone used chocolate chip cookies instead of graham crackers in a similar recipe. It's a hit at church lunches. Everyone just loves it.

6 cups milk

¾ cup all-purpose flour

2 cups sugar

Pinch of salt

1½ teaspoons vanilla extract

4 large egg yolks

3 cups whipped topping

Peanut butter, for sandwiching the cookies

4 dozen chocolate chip cookies (store-bought, or see recipe on page 226)

Heat 4½ cups of the milk in a large saucepan over medium heat until the milk is scalded (180°F). Whisk in the flour, sugar, salt, vanilla, egg yolks, and the remaining 1½ cups of cold milk. Heat the milk mixture until thick, stirring continuously. Remove from the heat and allow to cool.

Fold in the whipped topping. Spread some peanut butter between two chocolate chip cookies to form cookie sandwiches. Repeat until all cookies have been used. Cut or crumble the cookie sandwiches into the pudding mixture, and stir until well combined.

RHUBARB TAPIOCA

Makes 4 quarts

Rhubarb adds a festive flair to this normally white-colored dessert. Some people prefer to eat this warm. It also makes a great topping for the Rhubarb Streusel Coffeecake (page 33). If you do not want to make such a large quantity, the recipe can easily be halved. Do not leave this mixture unattended or it will scorch.

5 cups rhubarb, cut into ½-inch pieces

2½ cups water

1¼ cups sugar

¼ cup granulated tapioca

Put the rhubarb and water in a large stockpot and bring to a boil over medium-high heat. Make sure that it does not boil over, and stir the rhubarb occasionally so it will not scorch. Remove the rhubarb from the heat, stir in the sugar, and very gradually add the tapioca, stirring constantly to avoid clumping. Return the mixture to medium heat and cook until the tapioca is clear, approximately 30 seconds. Remove the mixture from the heat, let it cool, then refrigerate in a sealed container.

CHOKECHERRY TAPIOCA

Serves 15 to 20

You won't see tapioca this colorful very often. The chokecherries color the dish, so if you're used to plain, pearl tapioca, this will be a change! Add lemon juice while the mixture is boiling, if you get it too sweet. Sliced apples or fresh or canned fruit may be mixed with the tapioca when it is cold, plus whipped cream if desired. Adding sugar after it is done cooking keeps it from getting stringy.

2 quarts prepared chokecherry juice

¼ teaspoon salt

1¼ cups baby pearl tapioca

½ cup sugar, or to taste

2 teaspoons vanilla or almond extract

In a large saucepan, mix the juice, salt, and tapioca. Bring to a boil over medium-high heat and cook at a boil for about 15 minutes, stirring constantly, until the tapioca is clear. Turn down the heat and simmer for another 20 minutes, then remove from the heat and let cool to room temperature. Stir in the sugar and vanilla, and refrigerate overnight before serving.

HUCKLEBERRY DELIGHT

Serves 8 to 10

Huckleberries have defied attempts at domestication. They are only found in the wild, high up in the mountains, and their scarcity can make them pricey, often selling for upward of forty dollars a gallon. In season, huckleberries are on the menu in many restaurants in Montana. Huckleberry milk shakes are a favorite, and this Huckleberry Delight is delicious.

1 (6-ounce) box blackberry or cherry gelatin mix

1 (20-ounce) can crushed pineapple

2 cups water

2 cups fresh huckleberries

8 ounces cream cheese

½ cup sugar

1 teaspoon vanilla extract

1 (8-ounce) container whipped topping, thawed

½ cup chopped walnuts (optional)

Combine the gelatin mix, pineapple, water, and huckleberries in a large mixing bowl. Stir until well combined, and spoon the mixture into a 9 by 13-inch glass baking dish.

In a separate bowl, combine the cream cheese, sugar, and vanilla. Beat with a mixer until well combined, then fold in the whipped topping. Spread this mixture evenly over the huckleberry mixture, and refrigerate until set. If desired, sprinkle with chopped walnuts before serving.

CARAMEL CORN

Makes about 2 gallons

My children really like this caramel corn. It makes a great treat to have on a brunch table when company is visiting.

1 cup (2 sticks) margarine or butter

2 cups packed brown sugar

½ cup light corn syrup

½ teaspoon salt

1 tablespoon baking soda

2 gallons popped corn (about 2 cups popcorn kernels)

Preheat the oven to 250°F.

Combine the margarine, brown sugar, corn syrup, and salt in a small saucepan. Bring to a boil over high heat and cook for 5 minutes. Add the baking soda and stir hard. Put the popcorn in a roasting pan. Pour the hot sugar mixture over the popcorn and stir well. Bake, stirring every 10 minutes, until the corn is completely coated and turns golden brown, 30 to 40 minutes.

AMISH ACROSS AMERICA

If Hollywood movies are to be believed, the Amish live only in one picturesque part of Pennsylvania. But the reality is, successful Amish communities have long been an integral part of broad swaths of the United States.

With a church doctrine that prohibits birth control, Amish have large families—eight children is average, and ten to twelve children is not unusual. When you combine a growing number of large families with an agricultural lifestyle, you end up with land shortages. As the Amish population has increased (some estimates show a doubling every generation), they have had to stake out new ground for their rural communities.

This issue has faced all older, established Amish communities, including the inarguably most-famous one—Lancaster County, Pennsylvania, which was once home to the largest population of Amish in the United States. The solution to the problem of land shortages is simple, but not easy: Find more land farther away and start a new community.

In the early to mid-1990s, waves of Amish moved away from Lancaster County to escape the increasing suburban sprawl from Philadelphia, roads crowded with commuters and tourists, and big-box stores that had snapped up large tracts of land.

One of these groups left Lancaster County to begin anew in Parke County, Indiana, a rural area with plenty of arable land, a low population density, and opportunities to make nonfarming income. There were only 16,000 residents in the county then, all living among a lovely landscape with thirty-one picturesque covered bridges, and situated alongside Interstate 70 between Indianapolis and Saint Louis.

About twenty families made the trek westward, establishing a thriving new community. Today, the farms, one-room schoolhouses, and horse-drawn buggies of more than one hundred Amish families dot the Parke County countryside. To understand how common this outmigration is, and how widespread the Amish have become, read through the descriptions on the following pages of Amish communities across America.

While doing so, bear in mind that different Amish settlements can have very different lifestyles—from minor dress code variances to significant changes in the acceptance of modern technology. And as you can tell by the recipes gathered in this cookbook, food can be wildly different due to the Amish practice of using locally grown and raised ingredients. In fact, the Amish have always been locavores, well before it became a more widespread trend.

This list doesn't cover every Amish community in the United States, but it does illustrate the interesting and exciting places where Amish cooks and their families are flavoring America.

east

Lured by William Penn's promise of religious freedom, the Amish first settled in Berks County, Pennsylvania, in 1740. Known as the Northkill settlement, this community established the Amish identity in the United States. Among the early settlers were Yoders, Troyers, Hostetlers, and Hershbergers, surnames that would become synonymous with being Amish in America over the centuries ahead. Today, Pennsylvania is home to a varied Amish population, from enclaves of the most conservative Amish to some of the most liberal.

Eastern Amish settlements are home to such classic fare as shoofly pie and chicken corn soup, and a wide variety of other foods. For example, apples are king in the lush Mohawk Valley of Upstate New York, homemade maple syrup infuses the baked goods in the Empire State's rural Conewango Valley, and blueberries and potatoes are often side by side on supper tables in rural Maine. Some Amish even partake in moose hunts in the far north, enjoying game that their Midwestern counterparts can only imagine.

Heavily populated New England states—specifically Connecticut, Vermont, Massachusetts, New Hampshire, and Rhode Island—do not have an Amish presence because of the need for large farm-based communities. Following are some tasty stops across the East.

CHERRY CREEK, NEW YORK
AT A GLANCE
Established in 1949, home to 14 church districts. Culinary highlight: homemade maple syrup

RENSSELAER FALLS, NEW YORK
AT A GLANCE
Established in 1992, home to 2 church districts. Culinary highlights: elderberries, homemade bean soup

LYNDONVILLE, NEW YORK
AT A GLANCE
Established in 1998, home to 2 church districts. Culinary highlight: apples

UNITY, MAINE
AT A GLANCE
Established in 2008, home to 1 church district. Culinary highlights: blueberries, potatoes

FREDONIA, PENNSYLVANIA
AT A GLANCE
Established in 1990, home to 2 church districts. Culinary highlight: rhubarb

DOVER, DELAWARE
AT A GLANCE
Established in 1915, home to 10 church districts. Culinary highlight: seafood

YANKEE OR ENGLISH?

The Amish sometimes refer to non-Amish as "English," a term that dates back to early American colonial times, and stems from the fact most Amish speak German as their first language. Another term used to differentiate Amish from non-Amish is "Yankee," often used by older Amish but gradually falling by the wayside among younger members.

midwest

After the Amish first settled in Pennsylvania and Delaware, they began exploring horizons to the west, an exploration that continues to this day. Ohio and Indiana saw the largest early concentrations of Amish—now Illinois, Missouri, Kansas, Iowa, Michigan, Wisconsin, and Minnesota see larger shares of incoming Amish populations.

SINKING SPRING, OHIO

AT A GLANCE

Established in 2006, home to 1 church district. Culinary highlight: traditional Amish

FLAT ROCK, ILLINOIS

AT A GLANCE

Established in 1995, home to 1 church district. Culinary highlight: venison

UTICA, MINNESOTA

AT A GLANCE

Established in 1995, home to 3 church districts. Culinary highlight: traditional

FERTILE, MINNESOTA

AT A GLANCE

Established in 2007, home to 1 church district. Culinary highlights: chokecherries, garden huckleberries

KINGSTON, WISCONSIN

AT A GLANCE

Established in 1995, home to 2 church districts. Culinary highlight: blue cheese

RICHARDS, MISSOURI

AT A GLANCE

Established in 1997, home to 1 church district. Culinary highlights: ripe tomatoes, oatmeal bologna, homemade breadsticks

YODER AND HUTCHINSON, KANSAS

AT A GLANCE

Established in 1883, home to 2 church districts. Culinary highlights: Hispanic/traditional

NAVARRE, OHIO

AT A GLANCE

Established in 1910, home to 227 church districts in surrounding Stark, Holmes, and Wayne counties. Culinary highlights: traditional, Ohio dairy, garden

south

The Amish have been slower to settle the South, choosing even far-flung Western locales over closer Dixie states. The one Southern exception has been Kentucky, which, beginning in the mid-1990s, saw thousands of Amish arrivals from Pennsylvania and Ohio, attracted to the temperate climate, fertile soil, and less touristy environment.

Because the Amish don't use electricity, air-conditioning isn't an option. This makes the swelter of the deep South unappealing for many. The clay-packed soil is difficult to farm, and cultural differences have also long acted as a deterrent to Amish settlement of the South. But that's changing—Amish families have settled from the southern bayous of Arkansas to the piney hills of northern Mississippi to rural parts of the Carolinas.

Amish cooking in this area has taken on a distinct Southern flair, with cornbread, pork and beans, pecan pie, and okra becoming staples on menus. Plants native to the South, such as muscadines and peanuts, have also been incorporated into cooking.

One Southern community is so far south that it is almost north. Pinecraft, Florida, serves as a winter way station for Amish looking to escape the brutal blizzards and cold of the Midwest, and it often has more people from Ohio and Indiana living there than full-time residents.

The most far-flung Southern settlement can be found in an area known more for its *taquerías* and javelinas than for buggies and bonnets. This settlement in Texas is far closer to Mexico than it is to any other Amish community. Let's begin there.

BEEVILLE, TEXAS

AT A GLANCE

Established in 1997, home to 1 church district. Culinary highlights: jalapeños, okra

ETHRIDGE, TENNESSEE

AT A GLANCE

Established in 1944, home to 10 church districts. Culinary highlights: molasses, cornbread, pork and beans

PONTOTOC, MISSISSIPPI

AT A GLANCE

Established in 1996, home to 1 church district. Culinary highlights: muscadines, pecans, sweet potatoes

CHOUTEAU, OKLAHOMA

AT A GLANCE

Established in 1910, home to 4 church districts. Culinary highlights: cornbread, barbecue

PINECRAFT, FLORIDA

AT A GLANCE

Established in 1925, home to 2 church districts. Culinary highlights: tropical cuisine, alligator

UNION GROVE, NORTH CAROLINA

AT A GLANCE

Established in 1995, home to 1 church district. Culinary highlights: blackberries, cereal

CROFTON, KENTUCKY

AT A GLANCE

Established in 1972, home to 2 church districts. Culinary highlight: Southern

AMISH AT WORK

Historically, the Amish were an agrarian society, earning their livelihood from the land. But several factors have made relying solely on agriculture increasingly difficult. Foremost among those are the large size of most Amish families. With land prices continuing to rise, it isn't economically feasible to buy enough of it to provide for eight to ten children.

So many Amish have turned their solid work ethic and creativity to new endeavors. They are greengrocers who sell their own produce through roadside stands and farmers' markets. They are bakers, selling bounty from their ovens. They are makers of furniture and cabinets, blacksmiths, raw milk producers, and hand-tool repairmen, to name a few sidelines. These home-based businesses allow the Amish to preserve their family life while still earning the additional income they need.

west

For most of Amish history in the United States, the American West was seen as a distant backwater, unsuitable for settlement. But as the Amish's ability to farm in the Midwest and East diminished, many have looked westward as a way to escape congestion, high land prices, and busloads of camera-toting tourists.

Montana, with its belief in natural resource conservation and its live-and-let-live culture, was the first portion of the West to appeal to the Amish. Until the 1970s, there were only sporadic attempts by the Amish to settle west of the Rockies, and most of those attempts proved unsuccessful.

But in 1974, a more determined group of Amish decided to head for Rexford, Montana, where some conservative Mennonite churches had been able to establish thriving settlements. The Amish Rexford settlement has lasted, and has since become a jumping-off point for other Amish settlements in the West.

REXFORD, MONTANA

AT A GLANCE

Established in 1974, home to 1 church district. Culinary highlights: wild game, huckleberries

ST. IGNATIUS, MONTANA

AT A GLANCE

Established in 1997, home to 2 districts. Culinary highlights: wild game and fish

SAN LUIS VALLEY, COLORADO

AT A GLANCE

Established in 2002, home to 2 church districts. Culinary highlight: Hispanic food

❧ NOT BLACK OR WHITE ❧

The term *Amish* can refer to a number of groups, all part of a much larger Protestant religious movement called Anabaptists. The Anabaptist movement also includes Mennonites, Hutterites, and Old German Baptists. A brief overview:

Old Order Amish In the Old Order, ownership of cars is prohibited, and electricity and telephones are not permitted in the home. The rare practice of "shunning" others in the community who commit grave acts against the church's beliefs originated with this group (shunning is nowhere near as common as movies have portrayed it). Worship is held in homes. An emphasis is placed on humility in all things, including wearing plain clothes of black, gray, and white to avoid undue attention.

New Order Amish This group split from the Old Order in the 1960s. Church members still dress plainly, but some modern amenities are used in the home, such as phones and electricity.

Amish Mennonites A loose confederation of churches that split from the Amish church but haven't quite joined the main Mennonite movement.

Nebraska Amish Named for the strict beliefs behind an unsuccessful attempt to develop an Amish colony in Nebraska. Widely considered the most conservative Amish culture. Nebraska Amish are now found in small enclaves in Pennsylvania and Ohio.

Old Order Mennonites Worship is held in formal churches, not in homes. Members dress plainly and some travel by horse-drawn buggy.

Mennonite Church USA The mainline Mennonite church. They embrace pacifist principles and adult baptism, but allow all forms of modern technology. They do not wear plain dress.

Old German Baptists This group wears plain dress. Members are found in Ohio, Indiana, Kansas, and California. Worship is held in meetinghouses. Men greet with a "kiss of peace" on Sundays, a brief touching of lips. Church members are allowed autos and electricity, but most choose not to own televisions or radios.

Hutterites Very much like the Old Order Amish in dress and theology. The biggest difference is this group's belief in communal living, in which all material goods are held in common. They are found mainly in prairie states and provinces, living in communities of about fifteen families each.

evening meals

Work is done. Feet are weary. Everyone needs rest and replenishing. The evening meal recipes in this chapter have all the necessary ingredients for mind, body, and soul.

HOMEMADE BAKING MIX

Makes 13 cups mix

This homemade mix from Miriam Miller—another Amish cook—has a wide variety of uses and saves many trips to the store. The mix is used in cookies, biscuits, cakes, gingerbread, and other baking treats; see opposite for Miriam's suggested uses.

9 cups sifted all-purpose flour

⅓ cup baking powder

1 tablespoon salt

2 teaspoons cream of tartar

¼ cup sugar

1 cup nonfat dry milk

2 cups shortening

Sift together the sifted flour, baking powder, salt, cream of tartar, sugar, and dry milk. Cut in the shortening until the mixture resembles coarse cornmeal. Store in an airtight container and use as you would a premeasured baking mix, such as Bisquick. Place the mix lightly in any desired measuring cup; do not pack it.

❧ THE MANY USES OF BAKING MIX ☙

This is used in several of the recipes that follow, but its uses are as limitless as your imagination. Many of your own favorite recipes can be modified to use the mix. Here are some other ideas:

* Biscuits (1 dozen): 3 cups Homemade Baking Mix, ¾ cup water. Blend only until moistened. Bake at 450°F for 8 to 10 minutes.

* Pancakes/waffles (18 medium or 6 large): 3 cups Homemade Baking Mix, 1 egg, 1½ cups water. Blend completely.

* Muffins (1 dozen): 3 cups Homemade Baking Mix, 2 tablespoons vegetable oil, 1 egg, 1 cup water. Mix the oil, water, and egg, blend with the dry ingredients, bake at 450°F for 25 minutes.

* Drop cookies: 3 cups Homemade Baking Mix, 1 cup sugar, 1 egg, ⅓ cup water, 1 teaspoon vanilla extract, ½ cup nuts, and ½ cup chocolate chips. Blend and drop the mixture on a cookie sheet. Bake at 375°F for 10 to 12 minutes.

* Coffeecake: 3 cups Homemade Baking Mix, ½ cup sugar, 1 egg, ⅔ cup water. Blend. Topping: ½ cup brown sugar, 3 tablespoons butter, ½ teaspoon ground cinnamon, ¼ cup chopped walnuts. Blend. Cover cake batter with the topping and bake at 400°F for 25 minutes.

* Yellow cake or chocolate cake (use two 8-inch cake pans): 3 cups Homemade Baking Mix, ½ cup sugar, 1 teaspoon vanilla extract, 2 eggs, 1 cup water (½ cup cocoa for chocolate cake). Blend the sugar and vanilla into the mix. If making a chocolate cake, add the cocoa here. Beat the eggs and water. Add an additional ½ cup water to the mixture. Beat for 2 minutes and bake at 325°F for 25 minutes.

HOMEMADE BREAD

Makes 2 loaves

When Mom made large batches of bread, she'd use a bread dough mixer. Her mixer had a stainless steel bucket with a handle that curves, and you'd turn a knob on top and stir. I've tried using hers, but I prefer to knead mine by hand. An unusual thing that Mom would do with bread—and I think this is just an older custom—is bake multiple loaves in the same pan. Where the loaves met would always be the best because there was no crust. I've tried many recipes for homemade white bread through the years, but I keep coming back to this one, which my mother used. It calls for lard, but also works well with shortening.

1 package active dry yeast

2½ cups lukewarm water

Lard (amount the size of an egg)

2 tablespoons sugar

1 tablespoon salt

Enough bread flour to make a soft dough

Grease two 5 by 9-inch loaf pans and set aside.

In a small bowl, dissolve the yeast in ½ cup of the warm water. In a large bowl, combine the lard, sugar, salt, and the remaining 2 cups of water. Add the yeast mixture to the bowl and stir until combined. Add the flour, ½ cup at a time, mixing until the dough is elastic and doesn't stick to the sides of the bowl. Cover the bowl loosely with plastic wrap or a damp cloth and let the dough rise until double in size, about 1½ hours in a warm, draft-free place.

Punch the dough down and form it into two loaves with your hands. Place the dough into the prepared loaf pans. Cover with a damp cloth and let rise again until the dough is level with the loaf pan, about an hour.

While the dough is rising, preheat the oven to 325°F.

Bake the bread for about 45 minutes. The bread will sound hollow when tapped. After removing the bread from the oven, brush with butter or margarine for a softer crust. Remove the bread from the pans and cool on a wire rack or windowsill. After the bread cools completely, it can be stored in a sealed plastic bag and frozen for up to 6 months. If the bread is stored in a sealed plastic bag at room temperature, it should be consumed within 4 days.

❧ MAKING GREAT BREAD ❧

* No more ineffective yeast: Freeze it for long-term keeping.

* Active dry yeast needs to be soaked in warm water for 10 to 15 minutes before adding it to any recipe. Instant yeast can be added directly in a recipe.

* The water needs to be around 100° to 115°F. Too cold and the yeast won't activate. Too hot and it kills the yeast.

* Save money by buying yeast in bulk-food stores: 1 tablespoon of loose yeast equals one package of active dry yeast.

* Remove the bread from the pans immediately after removing from the oven and cool on racks. If you don't, the bread will get soggy.

WHOLE WHEAT BATTER BREAD

Makes 1 loaf

Whole wheat is a recent addition to most Amish cooks' recipe inventory. This one is so good, you'd never know it uses healthy whole grains.

1 package active dry yeast

1½ cups warm water (105° to 115°F)

3 tablespoons honey

2 teaspoons salt

1 tablespoon shortening, softened

2 cups bread flour

1 cup whole wheat flour

In a large bowl, dissolve the yeast in the warm water. Add the honey, salt, shortening, and 1 cup of the bread flour. Mix vigorously with a wooden spoon to form a wet batter. Gradually stir in the remaining 1 cup of bread flour and the whole wheat flour until evenly combined. Cover the bowl and let the batter rise in a warm place until doubled in size, about 30 minutes. Stir the batter several times, then spread it evenly in a greased 5 by 9-inch loaf pan. Let it rise in a warm place until the batter reaches ½ inch from the top of the pan, about 40 minutes.

While the dough is rising, preheat the oven to 375°F. Bake for about 30 minutes, or until the top is golden and the bread sounds hollow when tapped. After removing the bread from the oven, brush it with butter or margarine for a softer crust. Remove the bread from the pan and cool it on a wire rack.

SOURDOUGH STARTER

If you have starter already made, just skip to the "starter feed" section of the instructions. If not, begin from scratch. Either way, this takes some time and trial and error to get it right, but once you do, it is definitely worthwhile!

STARTER

3 packages active dry yeast

1 cup warm water (105° to 115°F)

STARTER FEED

¾ cup sugar

3 tablespoons instant potatoes

1 cup warm water (105° to 115°F)

Make the starter: Mix the yeast and warm water in a small bowl. Put into a plastic container, seal, and refrigerate for 3 to 5 days.

Make the starter feed: Combine the sugar, potatoes, and water in a small bowl and stir into the starter. Cover loosely (to allow some of the pressure to escape as the gases build) and let stand at room temperature for 5 to 12 hours. The mixture will be bubbly.

Take out 1 cup to make bread and loosely cover the starter and return it to the refrigerator. Feed again after 3 to 5 days. If not making bread after feeding the starter, throw away 1 cup to avoid depleting the starter.

Note: *Do not put the lid on tight.*

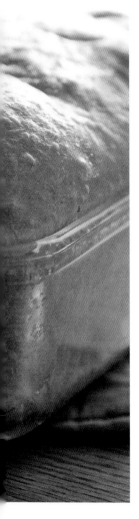

SOURDOUGH BREAD

Makes 3 loaves

Sourdough bread is something new for us. We didn't eat it growing up, but after we moved to Michigan I discovered that a lot of the Amish women in this area make sourdough breads, so it was fun to learn a new type of baking.

2 tablespoons sugar

½ cup olive oil

1 teaspoon salt

1½ cups warm water (105° to 115°F)

6 cups bread flour

1 cup Sourdough Starter (page 157)

3 teaspoons butter, melted

Combine the sugar, oil, salt, water, flour, and starter in a large bowl. Stir to make a dough. Form the dough into a ball. Grease another large bowl. Put the dough in and turn to coat. Cover with waxed paper and let stand overnight. (Do not refrigerate.)

The next morning, preheat the oven to 350°F. Punch the dough down and divide it into thirds. (If you are making Sourdough Cinnamon Rolls, page 9, punch the dough down and divide it in half.) Knead each part on a floured surface eight to ten times. Grease three 8½ by 4½-inch loaf pans and turn each loaf over in the pan to coat. Cover with waxed paper and let rise in the pans until it is just above the rims of the pans, 4 or 5 hours.

Bake the bread until the crust is nice and golden brown, 30 to 35 minutes. Remove from the oven and brush each loaf with 1 teaspoon of the butter. Unmold and let cool on wire racks.

TOP-NOTCH DINNER ROLLS

Makes 32 rolls

Occasionally the local tourism bureau would ask my mom to allow a tour into her home. She'd serve guests these homemade dinner rolls. The night before, Mom would have weighing scales on the table and waxed paper underneath each roll of dough. She'd measure each roll so that they would look and be the same size.

1 cup warm water

2 packages active dry yeast

½ cup plus 1 tablespoon sugar

1½ cups hot water

½ cup shortening, softened

2½ teaspoons salt

5 cups bread flour, plus more as needed

In a small bowl, stir together the warm water, yeast, and 1 tablespoon of the sugar and let sit until foamy, 10 to 20 minutes. Then, in a large bowl, mix the hot water, shortening, the remaining ½ cup of sugar, and the salt until the shortening is melted. Cool to lukewarm (100° to 110°F), and then add to the yeast mixture, mixing well. Gradually add the flour, beating well after each addition. Work in just enough more flour to make a soft but not sticky dough. Place in a large greased bowl and turn over once to grease the top of the dough. Cover with a dry dish towel and let rise until double in size, about 1 hour.

Punch down the dough and let it rest for 10 minutes. Divide the dough into thirty-two rolls and place onto a baking sheet. Let rise until double in size, 45 minutes to 1 hour.

While the dough is rising, preheat the oven to 350°F. Bake until lightly browned, about 25 minutes.

Remove the rolls from the pan and cool on a wire rack or windowsill. The rolls can be stored in a sealed plastic bag and remain fresh for 3 to 4 days. The rolls may also be stored in a plastic bag and frozen for up to 6 months.

DOUBLE-QUICK DINNER ROLLS

Makes 12 rolls

As the name implies, this is probably my fastest dinner roll to make. I'll prepare these in a pinch if company suddenly drops in for supper and I want to serve rolls. I like these because they are prepared using muffin tins, which makes them easy to pop into a basket to serve.

1 package active dry yeast

¾ cup warm water (115°F)

¼ cup sugar

1 teaspoon salt

2¼ cups bread flour

1 large egg

¼ cup shortening or butter (½ stick), softened

Preheat the oven to 350°F.

In a small bowl, dissolve the yeast in the warm water. Let stand for 10 minutes, or until bubbles form. In a large bowl, combine the yeast mixture with the sugar, salt, and 1 cup of the flour. Beat thoroughly for 2 minutes. Add the egg and shortening. Then gradually beat in the remaining flour until smooth. Drop the dough into twelve muffin cups. Bake until the tops of the rolls are a nice golden brown, 10 minutes. Remove the rolls from the pan and cool on a wire rack or windowsill. The rolls can be stored in a sealed plastic bag and remain fresh for 3 to 4 days. These rolls do not freeze well.

OVERNIGHT BUTTER DINNER ROLLS

Makes 24 rolls

Mom made a lot of dinner rolls. For family meals, Mom would often serve rolls for Sunday dinner, preparing them the night before. We children would cut the rolls in half, spread them with butter, and then close them again. I have several different dinner roll recipes that I like to use, especially this one.

2 packages active dry yeast

1¼ cups very warm water (150°F)

3 large eggs

5 cups bread flour

½ cup sugar

1 cup (2 sticks) melted butter

2 teaspoons salt

Sprinkle both packages of yeast into ¼ cup of the very warm water and stir with a fork. Set aside for 10 minutes, until bubbles form. In a large bowl, beat the eggs and then blend in the yeast mixture. Starting with the flour, add 2½ cups of the flour alternately with the remaining 1 cup of very warm water. Then mix in the sugar, ½ cup of the melted butter, and the salt. Mix until smooth. Beat in the remaining 2½ cups of flour to make a soft dough. Cover with a dish towel, put in a warm, draft-free place, and let rise until double in bulk, 1 to 2 hours.

Punch the dough down with vigor, cover with plastic wrap, and refrigerate overnight.

In the morning, grease twenty-four muffin-tin cups and set aside. Punch the dough down again and divide in half. On a floured board, roll out each half into a rectangle 8 by 15 inches. Spread with the remaining ½ cup of butter. Starting with the long edge, roll up each piece of dough in jelly-roll fashion. With a very sharp knife, cut each roll into twelve 1-inch slices. Place the slices in the prepared muffin cups, cut side up. Let rise until doubled in bulk, 40 minutes to 1 hour.

While the dough is rising, preheat the oven to 400°F. Bake the rolls until golden brown, 8 to 10 minutes. Immediately brush with butter. Remove the rolls from the pan and cool on a wire rack or windowsill. The rolls can be stored in a sealed plastic bag and remain fresh for 3 to 4 days. These rolls can also be sealed in a plastic bag and frozen for up to 6 months.

HOMEMADE DRESSING

Serves 6

We call this dish dressing when it is served in a serving dish, but we call it stuffing when it's stuffed into poultry. I just bake my dressing, but Mom would always fry it in a pan. I like mine better baked, because it's not as greasy. For a wonderful Sunday supper, try this dressing with the Chicken Gravy on the opposite page and Easy Baked Whole Chicken on page 172.

2 tablespoons chicken soup base

2 cups hot water

4 large eggs, beaten

¼ cup diced carrot

¼ cup diced celery

¼ cup chopped yellow onion

2 cups hot water (or use potato water for better flavor)

10 slices bread, crumbled

1 teaspoon seasoning salt

Preheat the oven to 350°F. Grease an 8-cup casserole dish or cake pan.

Dissolve the soup base in the water. Add all the remaining ingredients and mix well. Pour into the prepared dish and bake for 40 to 45 minutes.

CHICKEN GRAVY

Makes 6 cups

This is our favorite homemade gravy to use on mashed potatoes and baked chicken. Many times I don't put in the egg if I'm running short, and it always turns out fine.

4½ cups chicken broth

1½ tablespoons chicken soup base

Small pinch of garlic salt

2½ tablespoons cornstarch

2 tablespoons all-purpose flour

½ cup milk

1 large egg, slightly beaten

Combine the broth, soup base, and garlic salt in a medium saucepan. Bring to a boil.

Mix the cornstarch, flour, and ¼ cup of the milk together in a small bowl and stir into the broth mixture. Add the egg and the remaining ¼ cup of milk. Gradually whisk into the hot broth and whisk until thickened.

TOMATO GRAVY

Makes 5 cups

This is something my mother used to make a lot. It tastes great on pork chops, mashed potatoes, meat loaf, or a roast.

4 cups tomato juice

1 cup milk

2 tablespoons all-purpose flour

Salt and black pepper to taste

Bring the tomato juice to a boil in a medium nonaluminum saucepan over high heat. Stir the milk and flour together in a small bowl and whisk it into the tomato juice. Bring the mixture to a boil while whisking constantly. Remove from the heat and serve.

DANDELIONS WITH GRAVY

Serves 4 to 6

This is a popular way to prepare dandelions among Amish cooks in our community. The gravy is also good over boiled or mashed potatoes, and some even eat it with pork chops or other meats.

3 to 4 strips bacon

2 tablespoons all-purpose flour

2 tablespoons water

1 cup milk

Salt and black pepper

1 onion, chopped

1 tablespoon sugar

1 tablespoon apple cider vinegar

2 hard-boiled eggs (see page 99), chopped

4 cups packed young dandelion greens

Fry the bacon in a heavy skillet until crisp. Transfer the bacon to paper towels to drain. Stir the flour into the bacon fat and then add the water. Stir until smooth.

Add the milk and salt and pepper to taste. Continue to stir until smooth Add the onion, sugar, and the vinegar to your taste of sweet and sour. Stir in the eggs. Pour the gravy over the dandelions and toss. Serve right away.

BLUE CHEESE AND CHIVE MASHED POTATOES

Serves 6 to 8

Here's a delicious blue cheesy, chive-y potato dish that creates a wonderful array of flavors.

2 pounds russet potatoes, peeled and cut into 1½-inch chunks

½ cup crumbled blue cheese

4 tablespoons (½ stick) butter

¼ cup snipped fresh chives

½ teaspoon garlic salt

¼ teaspoon black pepper

Cook the potato chunks in boiling water in a medium saucepot until they are fork-tender, 15 to 20 minutes. Drain the potatoes well, return them to the pot, and mash them with a potato masher until smooth. Stir in the blue cheese, butter, chives, garlic salt, and pepper until thoroughly combined. Return the mashed potatoes to the stove and cook for a few minutes more, until very hot.

CORN PUDDING

Serves 4 to 6

Almost every Amish family grows corn in their garden. This recipe highlights one of the many ways it makes it onto our menus.

2 large eggs, separated

Kernels cut from 6 ears corn

¼ cup milk

½ teaspoon salt

⅛ teaspoon black pepper

Preheat the oven to 350°F. Butter a 4-cup casserole.

In a large bowl, beat the egg yolks until they are thick and pale in color. Add the corn and mix thoroughly. Stir in the milk, salt, and pepper.

Beat the egg whites in a large bowl until soft peaks form. Carefully fold them into the corn mixture. Pour the mixture into the prepared casserole.

Prepare a hot-water bath: Bring 4 quarts of water to a boil. Set the casserole in a deep pan on the oven rack. Pour boiling water into the pan until it is level with the mixture in the casserole. Bake until firm, about 30 minutes.

ASPARAGUS CASSEROLE

Serves 4 to 6

One of the first things I noticed after we moved from Pennsylvania to Michigan was an aspara-gus patch that had been planted at our new home. That asparagus shortly found its way into casseroles, such as this one.

3 tablespoons butter

1 tablespoon grated onion

¼ cup chopped red bell pepper

3 tablespoons all-purpose flour

1 cup milk

1½ teaspoons salt

¼ teaspoon black pepper

3 cups boiled asparagus

3 hard-boiled eggs, sliced

1 cup shredded mild Cheddar cheese

½ cup buttered breadcrumbs

Preheat the oven to 350°F. Grease a 9 by 9-inch baking dish and set aside.

In a heavy-bottomed saucepan, melt the butter over medium heat. Add the onion and bell pepper and sauté until soft. Sprinkle the flour over the mixture, then gradually stir in the milk. Add the salt and pepper. Continue to cook the sauce, stirring continuously, until thickened.

In the prepared baking dish, alternate layers of cooked asparagus with hard-boiled egg slices. Pour the sauce evenly over the layers. Top the casserole with the cheese and sprinkle with the breadcrumbs. Bake about 25 minutes, or until the sauce is bubbling and the crumbs are golden.

CHEESY CARROT CASSEROLE

Serves 6 to 8

During "carrot season" we'll eat this as a main dish for supper. We eat meat with many of our suppers, but sometimes it is nice to have just vegetables for a change of pace. This colorful casserole is very filling for a meatless meal.

2 pounds carrots, peeled and cut into $\frac{1}{2}$-inch slices

$5\frac{1}{2}$ tablespoons margarine or butter

$\frac{2}{3}$ cup chopped onion

$2\frac{1}{2}$ tablespoons all-purpose flour

$\frac{1}{4}$ teaspoon salt

$\frac{1}{4}$ teaspoon celery salt

$\frac{1}{4}$ teaspoon dry mustard

$\frac{1}{8}$ teaspoon black pepper

$1\frac{1}{4}$ cups milk

5 ounces Velveeta cheese

$2\frac{3}{4}$ cups cubed day-old bread

Preheat the oven to 350°F. Grease a 9 by 13-inch baking dish.

Put the carrots in a large kettle and cover with water. Bring to a boil, reduce the heat, cover, and simmer the carrots until tender, about 10 minutes. Drain and set aside.

Melt 2 tablespoons of the margarine in a large saucepan over medium heat. Add the onion and sauté until tender, about 5 minutes. Stir in the flour, salt, celery salt, mustard, and pepper. Gradually add the milk. Bring the mixture to a boil, then stir for 2 minutes. Add the cheese and stir until melted. Add the carrots and stir to coat.

Transfer the mixture to the prepared baking dish. Melt the remaining $3\frac{1}{2}$ tablespoons of margarine. Toss it with the bread cubes and sprinkle the bread over the carrots. Bake for 50 to 60 minutes, or until heated through.

CORN CASSEROLE

Serves 6 to 8

This is a good main dish during corn season; it makes a very hearty supper! To add extra color, you can add chopped red and green peppers.

1 pound bacon

½ cup (1 stick) margarine or butter

½ onion, chopped

½ cup chopped celery

5 tablespoons all-purpose flour

2 cups sour cream

Kernels cut from 6 ears corn

Salt and black pepper

1 tablespoon minced fresh parsley

Preheat the oven to 350°F. Butter a 9 by 13-inch baking dish.

Cook the bacon in a large skillet until crisp. Transfer to paper towels to drain, then crumble and set aside. Melt the margarine in a large saucepan over medium heat. Sauté the onion and celery until soft. Stir in the flour, then the sour cream, until well combined. Add the corn and most of the bacon bits and season with salt and pepper to taste. Pour into the prepared dish and sprinkle on the remaining bacon bits and the parsley. Bake until lightly browned, 30 to 45 minutes.

EASY BAKED WHOLE CHICKEN

Serves 6 to 8

Our family loves to eat chicken this way. It is one of Joe's favorite ways for it to be served. I serve it with mashed potatoes and gravy since the children don't like rice (though it's good served cooked with rice, too). I also serve dressing with it (page 164).

1 (2- to 3-pound) chicken

1 (10¾-ounce) can of condensed cream of mushroom soup

½ cup milk

1 cup shredded Cheddar cheese

Salt and black pepper

Preheat the oven to 350°F. Place the chicken in an 8-cup baking dish.

Combine the soup, milk, and ½ cup of the cheese in a medium bowl. Stir to blend. Pour over the chicken and season with salt and pepper to taste. Cover the dish and bake for 60 minutes. Sprinkle the remaining ½ cup of cheese on top. Bake until the cheese is melted, about 15 minutes longer.

PARMESAN CHICKEN

Serves 4 to 6

Here is an easy way to do chicken. This is another of Joe's favorites. There are many variations to this dish, but I'm sharing the recipe that probably makes it taste the best. I cook sometimes with just what I have on hand. For instance, if I am making this chicken and I don't have dried bread-crumbs on hand, I'll use crackers in a pinch. Another thing I'll do if I don't have crumbs is just roll the chicken in cornflakes.

1 cup all-purpose flour

2 teaspoons salt

2 teaspoons sweet paprika

¼ teaspoon black pepper

2 tablespoons garlic powder

2 large eggs

3 tablespoons milk

⅔ cup grated Parmesan cheese

⅓ cup dried breadcrumbs

1 (3- to 4-pound) chicken, cut into serving pieces

Preheat the oven to 400°F. Butter a 10 by 15-inch baking pan.

Combine the flour, salt, paprika, pepper, and garlic powder in a shallow bowl. Stir with a whisk to blend. Beat the eggs and milk in another shallow bowl. Combine the cheese and breadcrumbs in a third shallow bowl. Dredge the chicken pieces in the flour mixture, then dip them into the egg mixture, then dredge them in the crumb mixture. Place in the prepared pan.

Bake until the juices run clear when a piece of chicken is pierced with the tip of a knife, 50 to 55 minutes.

BAKED CHICKEN POTPIE

Makes two 9-inch pies

Some Amish recipes for potpie resemble a soup with bits of dough in it. This recipe, though, is more like a homemade version of the potpies found frozen in the supermarkets. Use any leftovers from the Easy Baked Whole Chicken on page 172.

2 cups peeled and diced potatoes

1¾ cups sliced carrots

⅔ cup chopped onion

1 cup (2 sticks) butter, softened

1 cup all-purpose flour

1¾ teaspoons salt

¾ teaspoon black pepper

2 tablespoons chicken soup base

3 cups chicken broth

1½ cups milk

4 cups cubed cooked chicken

1 cup fresh or frozen peas

4 disks My Homemade Pie Dough (double the recipe on page 296)

Preheat the oven to 425°F.

Boil the potatoes and carrots in a large saucepan over medium heat until almost tender, about 10 minutes. Drain and set aside. In a large skillet, sauté the onion and butter until tender. Stir in the flour, salt, pepper, and chicken soup base until blended. Gradually stir in the broth and milk. Cook, stirring, for 2 minutes, or until thick. Add the chicken, peas, potatoes, and carrots to the broth mixture. Remove from the heat.

Divide the chicken mixture evenly between two unbaked pie shells. Use some water to wet the rim of the bottom crusts, which will help both crusts adhere together. Cover the pies with the top crusts, crimping the crusts together all the way around. Bake the pies for 35 to 40 minutes, until the crust is golden brown. Cool on a wire rack or windowsill until the pie is firm, about 45 minutes. Store any leftovers covered in the refrigerator or a cool cellar. The pie will keep for about 7 days in the refrigerator.

CHICKEN AND DUMPLINGS

Serves 4 to 6

Chicken and homemade dumplings is one of my favorites. The children like to drop the dumplings into the broth, so it is a good family meal to fix together.

DUMPLINGS

2 cups all-purpose flour

1 teaspoon salt

½ teaspoon baking powder

6 tablespoons margarine or butter, melted

1 large egg, beaten

½ cup milk

2 boneless, skinless chicken breast halves

2 (10¾-ounce) cans cream of chicken soup

Make the dumplings: Combine the flour, salt, and baking powder in a large bowl. Stir with a whisk to blend. Stir in the melted margarine, egg, and milk until a smooth, soft dough forms. Roll out to a ½- to ¾-inch thickness on a floured surface and cut into 1-inch squares.

Place the chicken in a medium saucepan, add enough water to cover the chicken, and simmer over medium-high heat until the chicken is cooked through. Cool, drain the water, and cut the chicken into bite-size pieces. Combine the chicken pieces and soup in a large pot and simmer until tender, about 30 minutes. Add the dumplings one at a time. Simmer for 5 more minutes and then serve.

tip: meat pies

Pie doesn't have to always be filled with fruits or vegetables.
There are many meat pies that make filling and easy meals. Piecrusts can
be filled with chicken, pork, or beef to make a delicious dinner,
as shown on the opposite page.

EASY CHICKEN CASSEROLE

Serves 6

My children and husband, Joe, really go for this dish. If I go too long without fixing it, Joe will start asking me when I'm going to make it again. I kind of go by feel; I add a little more of this and that to make a meal. As a variation, I sometimes use canned soup instead of making the sauce. If I don't have cream of chicken soup on hand, I'll use cream of mushroom. It still tastes great!

½ cup (1 stick) margarine or butter

⅓ cup all-purpose flour

1 cup milk

2 cups chicken broth

1½ teaspoons salt

½ teaspoon black pepper

1 (3-ounce) can mushrooms, or 3 ounces fresh mushrooms

2 cups cubed cooked chicken

8 ounces noodles, cooked and drained

⅓ cup grated Parmesan cheese

Preheat the oven to 350°F. Grease an 8-cup casserole dish.

Melt the margarine in a large saucepan over low heat, then whisk in the flour until smooth. Gradually whisk in the milk, then the broth, and cook until thickened. Stir in the salt, pepper, and mushrooms. Add the chicken, cooked noodles, and cheese.

Spoon the mixture into the prepared dish. Bake until it is bubbly and golden, about 45 minutes.

BEEF AND BLUE CHEESE SUPPER

Serves 4 to 6

This is a hearty, delicious dish that melds meat, potatoes, and the flavor of blue cheese. Plentiful, homegrown tomatoes are incorporated flavorfully into this dish to make it a complete meal.

4 medium-size russet potatoes

Butter, for dressing the potatoes

Sour cream, for dressing the potatoes

Salt and black pepper, for seasoning

2 (6-ounce) beef tenderloin fillets, 1½ inches thick

1 large tomato, diced

3 green onions, sliced

3 ounces blue cheese, crumbled

Pierce the potatoes with a fork and bake for about 1 hour at 375°F, or microwave them on high for 12 minutes, or until they reach your desired doneness. Cut a slit in each potato and fluff the insides with a fork. Season each potato lightly with your preferred amount of butter, sour cream, salt, and pepper.

While the potatoes are cooking, grill the steak to your desired doneness. Cut the cooked steak into bite-size pieces and place equal amounts in each potato. Sprinkle the potatoes with the tomato, green onions, and blue cheese.

BEEF VEGETABLE CASSEROLE

Serves 4 to 6

Any fresh vegetables can be used in season for this hearty supper casserole. The ingredient amounts are approximate, so feel free to use more or less of each one or substitute something else altogether to use up whatever you have on hand.

1 head fresh cabbage, coarsely cut

8 large potatoes, thickly sliced

Bunch carrots, cut into medallions

6 large onions, thinly sliced to make rings

Salt and black pepper, to taste

1 pound fresh ground beef

6 cheese slices, such as American, Cheddar, or Swiss

Preheat the oven to 350°F.

In a roaster or baking dish, put in a thick layer of fresh cabbage, making sure to use only cabbage on the bottom layer. Then layer the potatoes, carrots, and onions on top of the cabbage. Repeat the layers until the dish is ½ inch from full. Sprinkle on salt and pepper. Put a layer of the uncooked ground beef on top and cover tightly with a lid or foil. Bake 1½ to 2 hours, or until the beef is cooked through and the vegetables are tender. Before serving, cover with the cheese slices.

BISCUITS AND BEEF CASSEROLE

Serves 6 to 8

This is such a hearty, beefy casserole to enjoy. What makes it different are the biscuits on top. The biscuits sort of sink down into the casserole and end up almost covering the top. Make sure not to bake the biscuits beforehand, just put the dough on top of the casserole.

1½ pounds ground beef

½ cup chopped onion

1 (8-ounce) package cream cheese, softened

1 (10¾-ounce) can cream of chicken or mushroom soup

¼ cup milk

1 teaspoon salt

¼ cup ketchup

1 package refrigerated biscuits

Preheat the oven to 375°F. Grease an 8-cup casserole dish.

Brown the beef with the onion in a large skillet over medium heat, about 10 minutes. Drain the grease.

Combine the cream cheese, soup, milk, salt, and ketchup in a medium bowl. Stir to blend. Add to the ground beef and stir well. Spoon into the prepared dish.

Bake for 10 minutes. Place the unbaked biscuits on top. Return the casserole to the oven and bake until the biscuits are browned and cooked through, 10 to 15 minutes.

YUMASETTI

Serves 6 to 8

My sister Elizabeth Eicher wrote about this easy supper casserole as a guest columnist for "The Amish Cook" in 2008. She was thirteen at the time and wrote that this recipe was a sparkling success.

3 pounds ground beef

1 medium onion, chopped

1 (16-ounce) package egg noodles

2 cups peas

2 (10¾-ounce) cans cream of mushroom soup

1 (10¾-ounce) can cream of chicken soup

1 cup sour cream

10 bread slices, toasted and cubed

2 cups shredded cheese of your choice

Preheat the oven to 350°F. Grease a large casserole dish and set aside.

In a large skillet, cook the beef and the onion over medium heat. Remove from the heat when the beef is browned. Drain the grease and transfer the meat mixture to a large bowl. Cook the egg noodles in salted water, according to the package directions, until tender. Drain well. Add the noodles, peas, mushroom soup, chicken soup, sour cream, and bread to the meat mixture. Stir until all the ingredients are well combined. Transfer the mixture to the prepared casserole dish and top with the shredded cheese. Bake for about 30 minutes, or until the casserole is bubbling and the cheese is melted.

ZUCCHINI BEEF CASSEROLE

Serves 4 to 6

This casserole is great as a main dish for supper. If you want a meatless dish, this one also tastes great even if you make it without the ground beef.

1 pound ground beef

1 (1¼-ounce) package taco seasoning

4 large eggs

½ cup olive oil

½ teaspoon salt

½ teaspoon black pepper

1 teaspoon minced fresh parsley (optional)

3 cups shredded zucchini

1 cup Bisquick

¼ cup shredded onion

½ cup shredded cheese, any kind

Preheat the oven to 350°F. Grease a 9 by 13-inch baking dish.

Brown the ground beef in a large skillet and stir in the taco seasoning. Drain and set aside.

Beat the eggs, oil, salt, pepper, and parsley together in a bowl until blended. Stir in the zucchini, Bisquick, and onion until smooth. Stir in the ground beef until distributed evenly in the mixture. Pour into the prepared dish. Bake for 30 minutes, then sprinkle evenly with the cheese. Continue baking until the cheese is melted, about 10 minutes. Remove from the oven and spoon onto individual plates to serve.

tip: replacing potatoes

Those who grow zucchini often complain they end up giving away or throwing out a good portion of their too-plentiful harvest. But did you know zucchini can be used in place of potatoes and you can hardly tell the difference in taste? When I make a casserole, I use zucchini in the same way I would potatoes. When a recipe calls for hash brown potatoes, I'll use grated zucchini. Try it!

POOR MAN'S STEAK

Serves 6

When my family and I moved from Pennsylvania to a new settlement in Michigan, we brought many of our favorite recipes with us, including this one.

1½ pounds lean ground beef

1 cup dry breadcrumbs

1 small onion, chopped

2 eggs

1 teaspoon salt

⅛ teaspoon black pepper

¼ teaspoon garlic powder

1 (10¾-ounce) can cream of mushroom soup

½ cup water

½ cup milk

1 (4-ounce) can sliced mushrooms, drained

Preheat the oven to 350°F. Grease a 9 by 9-inch baking dish and set aside.

In a large bowl, combine the ground beef, breadcrumbs, onion, eggs, salt, pepper, and garlic powder. Knead the mixture with your hands until it is smooth and uniformly combined. Shape the meat mixture into a loaf and cut it into nine slices. In a greased skillet, fry the meat slices until browned on each side. Drain off the excess grease and transfer the browned slices to the prepared baking dish.

In a medium bowl, combine the mushroom soup, water, and milk. Stir until smooth. Pour the soup mixture evenly over the meat slices and sprinkle with the drained mushrooms. Bake uncovered for 30 to 40 minutes, until the meat slices are cooked through and the sauce is bubbling.

GROUND BEEF SUPPER

Serves 6

With our big family, large help-yourself casseroles like this are always good. This will feed a crowd easily if you double it.

1 pound ground beef

½ cup chopped onion

1 cup chopped green bell pepper

1 pound tomatoes, diced

½ cup white long-grain rice

2 teaspoons chili powder

½ teaspoon salt

⅛ teaspoon black pepper

2 cups shredded mozzarella cheese

Preheat the oven to 350°F.

In a large skillet, brown the beef over medium-high heat. Drain the grease. Add the onion and bell pepper. Stir in the tomatoes, rice, chili powder, salt, and pepper and heat thoroughly.

Pour the mixture into an ungreased 8-cup casserole dish. Cover and bake for 50 minutes. Sprinkle the cheese evenly on top and bake, uncovered, for about 10 minutes more, or until the cheese is melted and the casserole is bubbling.

CHEESEBURGER MEAT LOAF

Serves 6 to 8

This is one of those hearty, meaty dishes that seem to go perfectly on a cold February night.

2 pounds ground beef

½ cup fresh breadcrumbs

1 (10½-ounce) can cream of mushroom soup

1 egg, slightly beaten

3 tablespoons fresh parsley, chopped

1 tablespoon Worcestershire sauce

2 tablespoons chopped onion

1 teaspoon salt

⅛ teaspoon black pepper

1 medium tomato, sliced

1 cup grated mild Cheddar cheese

Preheat the oven to 350°F.

In a large bowl, combine the beef, breadcrumbs, soup, egg, parsley, Worcestershire sauce, onion, salt, and pepper. Knead the mixture by hand until it is smooth and uniformly combined. Shape the mixture into a large loaf and place it in a shallow, rimmed baking pan. Bake for 1 hour.

Remove the loaf from the oven and top with the tomato and cheese. Return the loaf to the oven and bake until cooked through and the topping is bubbling, 10 to 15 minutes.

DELICIOUS BAKED MEATBALLS

Serves 6

Fresh ground beef makes for the best meatballs! After using beef from your own steer, eating other meatballs isn't as enjoyable. We like to add a dash of chili powder to add some spice.

MEATBALLS

1 cup milk

3 pounds ground beef

2 cups old-fashioned rolled oats

2 large eggs, beaten

1 cup chopped onion

$\frac{1}{2}$ teaspoon garlic powder

2 teaspoons salt

$\frac{1}{2}$ teaspoon black pepper

2 teaspoons chili powder

SAUCE

2 cups ketchup

$1\frac{1}{2}$ cups packed brown sugar

$\frac{1}{2}$ teaspoon garlic powder

$\frac{1}{2}$ cup chopped onion

2 tablespoons liquid hickory smoke (optional)

Preheat the oven to 350°F.

Make the meatballs: Combine the milk, ground beef, oats, and eggs in a large bowl and mix with your hands until well blended. Stir in the onion, garlic powder, and seasonings. Shape the mixture into 1½- to 2-inch balls and put them in a roasting pan. Set aside.

Make the sauce: Stir all the sauce ingredients together in a medium bowl. Pour over the meatballs. Bake until the meatballs are browned and cooked through, about 50 minutes.

PIZZA CASSEROLE

Serves 4 to 6

This is typical of the type of casserole we use green peppers in. Just chop them up and add them to it. For this recipe, I sometimes add a layer of pepperoni slices just before the cheese. This makes it taste like pizza, except without a crust. This is something we'll prepare for the evening meal on the day we have church. It's an easy casserole to prepare more of if additional guests arrive.

1 pound ground beef

⅓ cup chopped onion

½ cup diced green bell peppers

1 (4-ounce) can sliced mushrooms, or 4 ounces fresh sliced mushrooms

½ teaspoon salt

8 ounces spaghetti, cooked

2 (10-ounce) cans pizza sauce

2 cups shredded mozzarella cheese

Preheat the oven to 350°F. Grease a 9 by 13-inch baking dish.

Brown the ground beef with the onion and green pepper in a large skillet over medium heat. Drain the grease. Stir in the mushrooms, salt, and cooked spaghetti, and spoon the mixture into the baking dish. Pour the sauce over the top and sprinkle with a layer of cheese. Bake until the cheese has melted and the casserole is bubbling, about 30 minutes.

POTATO BEEF SUPREME

Serves 8 to 10

With this dish, the potatoes turn brown very quickly after peeling and/or grating. It is best to have the rest of your casserole assembled, then quickly add the peeled and grated potatoes to avoid having a gray-looking potato dish. Switch out the ground beef for sausage if you like.

SAUCE

4 tablespoons (½ stick) butter

¼ cup all-purpose flour

2 cups milk

POTATOES

1½ cups (3 sticks) melted butter

½ cup chopped onion

¼ teaspoon black pepper

4 ounces cream cheese, softened

1 teaspoon salt

2 pounds potatoes, peeled and grated

1 pound ground beef

TOPPING

2 cups cornflakes, crushed

4 tablespoons (½ stick) melted butter

1 teaspoon dried parsley (optional)

Preheat the oven to 350°F.

Make the sauce: Melt the butter in a medium saucepan over medium heat. Whisk in the flour to form a paste. Gradually add the milk, whisking constantly. Cook until the mixture thickens into a smooth sauce.

Make the potato mixture: Place the sauce in a large bowl. Add the melted butter, onion, pepper, cream cheese, and salt, and combine thoroughly. Stir in the potatoes and mix thoroughly. Brown the ground beef (or sausage), and stir the browned meat into the potato mixture. Pour the mixture into a 4-quart casserole dish.

Make the topping: Combine the cornflakes, melted butter, and parsley flakes, and sprinkle on top of the assembled casserole. Bake for 1½ hours, until the top of the casserole is golden brown and crisp.

STUFFED GREEN PEPPERS

Serves 4

A neighbor lady told me that you can hollow out the green peppers ahead of time, stuff them with waxed paper, and freeze them, and they'll keep for a long time. Ever since she gave me that advice I have done mine that way, and it really does work well. This recipe makes a very good supper!

1½ teaspoons salt

4 large green bell peppers

1 pound ground beef

1 tablespoon minced fresh parsley

½ teaspoon black pepper

⅔ cup cooked rice

1½ cups canned tomatoes, pushed through a sieve

¼ cup finely chopped white onion

¼ cup water

4 slices mozzarella cheese

Preheat the oven to 350°F. Grease an 8-cup baking dish.

Fill a large pot with water, add ½ teaspoon of the salt, and bring to a boil over medium-high heat. Cut out the stems of the peppers and rinse out the seeds, leaving the peppers whole. Put the peppers in the boiling water, cover the pot, and cook for 5 minutes. Drain the pot and set the peppers aside to cool.

Brown the ground beef in a large skillet over medium heat. Drain off any excess grease. Stir in the remaining 1 teaspoon of salt, parsley, ¼ teaspoon of the black pepper, and rice. Lightly fill the peppers with the mixture, heaping slightly. Stand the peppers upright in the prepared baking dish.

Combine the tomatoes, onion, water, and the remaining ¼ teaspoon of the black pepper in a small bowl. Mix well. Pour over the bell peppers. Place a slice of cheese on each pepper. Bake until the peppers are tender, about 25 minutes.

SAUERKRAUT SUPPER

Serves 4 to 6

Sauerkraut is something that we enjoy in December and January. The cabbage is usually ready in the fall and, after I make it into sauerkraut, I usually let it sit in sealed containers in my cellar for two months to get that perfect taste.

5 to 6 cups sauerkraut

2 to 3 cups water

1 teaspoon onion powder

1 teaspoon garlic powder

1 teaspoon sugar

1 teaspoon salt

½ teaspoon black pepper

1 (2- to 3-pound) boneless pork roast

DUMPLINGS

2 cups Bisquick

1 cup water

Preheat the oven to 250°F.

Rinse the sauerkraut and put it in a roasting pan. Add the water, then stir in the onion powder, garlic powder, sugar, salt, and pepper. Set the roast on top. Bake for 4 hours, or until tender. Remove the roast, let it cool, then cut into bite-size pieces.

Make the dumplings: Mix the Bisquick and water together in a medium bowl. Place the roasting pan with the sauerkraut on the stovetop and bring to a slow boil. Drop the dumpling batter by spoonfuls into the sauerkraut and water and cook for 8 to 10 minutes. Remove the roasting pan from the heat and put the pork pieces back in the pan with the sauerkraut for serving.

SWISS HAM BAKE

Serves 6 to 8

Mom and Dad always sugar-cured our hams and used the meat in hearty recipes like this one. This is a layered casserole that definitely goes a long way in feeding a large family or any company that might drop by.

8 tablespoons (1 stick) butter

½ cup chopped onion

½ cup chopped green bell pepper

1 (10¾-ounce) can condensed cream of mushroom soup

1 cup sour cream

8 ounces noodles, cooked and drained

2 cups shredded Swiss cheese

3 cups cubed cooked ham

1 cup fresh breadcrumbs

Preheat the oven to 350°F. Butter a 3-quart casserole.

Melt 4 tablespoons of the butter in a medium skillet over medium heat and sauté the onion and bell pepper until soft, about 5 minutes. Stir in the soup and sour cream.

In the prepared dish, layer one-third of the noodles, one-third of the cheese, one-third of the ham, and half of the soup mixture. Make a second layer the same way. Make a third layer of ham, noodles, and cheese only.

Melt the remaining 4 tablespoons of butter in a medium skillet and toss the breadcrumbs to coat. Sprinkle the buttered crumbs evenly over the casserole. Bake until the casserole is bubbling and the cheese is melted, about 40 minutes.

SAUSAGE AND NOODLE DINNER

Serves 8

You can use store-bought sausage for this recipe, but we always use fresh sausage. Although we do our butchering in the winter, recipes like this are enjoyed year-round, as I home can some and freeze some.

1 pound bulk pork sausage

1 head cabbage (about 1½ pounds, cored and thinly sliced)

1 large onion, thinly sliced

1 large carrot, peeled and shredded

2 teaspoons chicken soup base

¼ cup boiling water

2 cups sour cream

¾ teaspoon salt

½ teaspoon black pepper

8 ounces noodles, freshly cooked and drained

Minced fresh parsley for garnish

Brown the sausage in a large skillet over medium heat. Drain the grease. Leave the sausage in the skillet and add the cabbage, onion, and carrot and mix well. Dissolve the chicken soup base in the boiling water and add to the pot. Cover and cook over medium heat until the vegetables are tender, 10 to 15 minutes.

Reduce the heat under the skillet to low and stir in the sour cream, salt, and pepper. Transfer the mixture to a large serving bowl, add the hot noodles, and toss. Garnish with parsley.

OKRA GUMBO

Serves 4 to 6

This is a quick Amish adaptation of the thick, delicious, traditional Southern dish. It leaves out the time-consuming roux and the long simmering time at the end. You can substitute other meats on hand for the sausage.

1 tablespoon vegetable oil

½ pound smoked sausage, casing removed and cut in ½-inch-thick slices

4 cups sliced okra

1 green bell pepper, seeded and chopped

2 cloves garlic, minced

1 medium-size onion, chopped

3 medium-size tomatoes, peeled and chopped

Salt and black pepper

Cooked rice, for serving (optional)

Heat the vegetable oil over medium heat in a Dutch oven. Add the sausage, and cook, stirring occasionally, until browned, 3 to 4 minutes. Remove the browned sausage with a slotted spoon, and set aside.

Add the okra, green pepper, garlic, and onion to the Dutch oven, and sauté in the reserved pan drippings until tender. Add the chopped tomatoes and the reserved sausage. Reduce the heat to medium-low, and simmer for 30 minutes, stirring frequently. Season with salt and pepper to taste. The gumbo may be served over cooked rice, if desired.

BAKED FISH

Serves 4 to 6, depending on size of fish

While Joe will sometimes catch catfish or crappies, our favorite fish to eat here in Michigan is bluegill. This is a pretty easy baked fish dish to prepare, and I think it's healthier for the kids to eat than deep-fried, but we do like it that way also.

1 whole bluegill, 2 to 3 pounds, cleaned

5 cups water

Salt and black pepper

6 saltine crackers, crushed

Dash of salt

1 tablespoon minced fresh parsley

1 tablespoon minced fresh thyme

1 tablespoon butter, melted

4 thin strips salt pork

2 cups cornmeal

Preheat the oven to 300°F. Butter a baking dish big enough to hold the fish.

Remove the head and tail of the fish. Put the head and tail in a medium saucepan with the water. Simmer for 15 minutes to make a broth, adding salt and pepper to taste.

Combine the cracker crumbs, salt, parsley, thyme, and butter in a large bowl. Moisten the stuffing with 3 tablespoons of the fish broth. Stir to blend. Freeze the rest of the broth for another use. Stuff the fish with the stuffing and fasten with skewers.

Cut a few shallow slashes across both sides of the fish. Wrap the salt pork around the fish and roll it in the cornmeal. Bake until the flesh is opaque throughout, about 1 hour. Serve on a warmed platter.

FISH LOAF

Serves 4 to 6

Fishing is a favorite pastime among Amish. My husband, Joe, likes to go fishing, and even goes ice fishing on occasion when it is cold enough and he has the time. You can use most types of freshwater and saltwater fish—catfish, trout, salmon, bluegill, and bass are just a few examples.

1 pound diced, fresh fish, or 1 (15-ounce) can salmon

2 large eggs

1 teaspoon dry mustard

¾ teaspoon salt

⅛ teaspoon black pepper

½ cup milk

½ cup chopped celery

2 cups dried breadcrumbs

3 tablespoons finely chopped fresh parsley

2 tablespoons minced onion

Preheat the oven to 375°F.

If using canned fish, do not drain. If using fresh fish, remove the skin and bones. Place the fish in a large mixing bowl.

In a separate small bowl, beat the eggs with the mustard, salt, and pepper. Mix in the milk, celery, breadcrumbs, parsley, and onion with a fork. Add the egg mixture to the fish and stir to combine. Pack the mixture into a greased 9 by 12-inch or smaller pan. Bake for 45 minutes, or until the top begins to turn golden brown. Slice and serve warm.

GRILLED LIME FISH FILLETS

Serves 4 to 6

Lime and other citrus fruits are not common in Amish kitchens in the North. Traditionally, oranges are often something reserved for special occasions. But in the Pinecraft, Florida, Amish community, citrus grows in the tiny yards and finds its way into many recipes—such as this one. This recipe can be used with any white fish. Snapper is a favorite Gulf of Mexico catch.

2 pounds frozen fish fillets, thawed

About 2 tablespoons canola oil

Paprika

½ cup (1 stick) butter, melted

¼ cup fresh lime juice

Salt and black pepper

Lime wedges, for garnish

Cooked white or wild rice, for serving

Brush the fish fillets with the oil and sprinkle with the paprika. Combine the melted butter and lime juice and set aside.

Place the fish on a well-oiled grill, 3 to 4 inches from medium-hot coals. Cook for 5 to 7 minutes on each side, or until the fish flakes easily with a fork, basting frequently with the lime juice mixture. Just before serving, sprinkle with salt and pepper. Garnish with the fresh lime wedges, and serve with rice.

Variation: *Before placing the fish on the grill, place lime slices on one side of the fish, and wrap the fish and lime slices with a strip of uncooked bacon. Secure the bacon with toothpicks, then grill in the same way.*

ON THE HUNT

Autumn is hunting season in many Amish communities. The harvesting is done for the year, and it's a good time to stock up on meat for the winter.

My husband, Joe, began to hunt with his father when he was thirteen years old. He started with pheasants, but he could never hit them. He finally figured out that he was using the wrong eye to sight down the rifle! Once he got that problem sorted out, he could hit them easily.

Joe hunted more in Indiana than he does here in Michigan—back there, he could just walk into my mother and father's woods and settle down to wait. He still enjoys it, but doesn't have as much time for it anymore. Joe's favorite game to hunt is deer, but he won't pass up any rabbit or squirrel that happens by.

One time, Joe went hunting and sat on the ground beside a tree. He got so tired that he fell

asleep, and when he woke up there were deer tracks right in front of him!

Soon it will be Joe's turn to take our sons—Benjamin, Joseph, and Kevin—hunting. Before they're allowed to go with him, though, he'll insist they take hunting safety classes. The Amish around here really encourage that, and it's something Joe believes in, too. It also makes me feel a bit better, too, because I admit that the idea of hunting accidents scares me and I want them all to know how to be safe.

Joe especially loves venison steak fried with eggs and potatoes. The way I really enjoy venison is in the summer sausage recipe on the next page. I've also included some of the other most popular game recipes created by Amish cooks across the country to make use of the hunting bounty in their local communities.

VENISON SUMMER SAUSAGE

Makes 30 pounds

With Michigan having so many deer, a lot of venison can be found on the tables of the local Amish. This is a wonderful recipe that makes a very tender sausage. It makes a great snack with crackers or cheese or to give to someone as a gift.

30 pounds ground deer or elk meat

2 cups Morton's Tender Quick meat cure

2 cups firmly packed brown sugar

2 tablespoons ground coriander

5 tablespoons onion salt

3½ teaspoons garlic powder

1 teaspoon ground nutmeg

1 tablespoon black pepper

5 teaspoons liquid smoke

2 tablespoons seasoning salt

3 tablespoons Worcestershire sauce

15 cups water

In a very large bowl or container, combine all the ingredients and mix thoroughly. Refrigerate the mixture for 24 hours to allow time to cure.

Preheat the oven to 350°F. Form the meat mixture into 2 by 8-inch logs. Wrap each with aluminum foil, shiny side facing the meat. Place the sausages on rimmed baking sheets and bake for 1½ hours. Allow the sausages to cool, then remove the aluminum foil and drain off the grease. Wrap the sausages in plastic wrap, and refrigerate or freeze until ready to use.

Set out the meat to thaw the night before you're ready to use it. Freezing for storage allows the sausage to keep for a year or longer if tightly sealed.

VENISON SAUSAGE

Serves 8

Deer meat is a highlight of the fall hunting season. The children get so excited to see their dad come out of the woods after a successful hunt. Deer meat, or venison, can be used in many different ways: steaks, burgers, stews, soups, jerky, casseroles, and, one of our favorites, sausage. This recipe is a big hit in our household.

¼ teaspoon garlic powder

1 tablespoon mustard seed

¼ teaspoon onion powder

3 tablespoons salt

4 teaspoons black pepper

1 cup cold water

½ teaspoon liquid smoke

2 pounds venison, ground

In a large bowl, mix all the spices with the water and the liquid smoke. Then add the meat and mix well. Form into two loaves and wrap them in foil with the shiny side next to the meat. Place the loaves in the refrigerator for 48 hours. Remove from the refrigerator and, using a butter knife, make five small slashes in each loaf through the foil. Place the loaves in a large pot and cover with cold water. Bring to a boil. Decrease the heat and simmer uncovered for 1½ hours. Remove the loaves from the water and let cool. Rewrap in new foil and refrigerate for 12 hours, then cut and enjoy.

BARBECUED VENISON MEATBALLS

Serves 6 to 8

Even if you find venison "gamey," the barbecue sauce, which carries a hint of tang and a suggestion of sweetness, makes this Amish delicacy something worth trying. You can also substitute ground beef for the venison.

3 pounds ground venison

1¾ cups milk

1 cup quick-cooking rolled oats

1 cup saltine cracker crumbs

3 large eggs, beaten

1 teaspoon chili powder

1 teaspoon onion salt

1 teaspoon garlic salt

Salt and black pepper

BARBECUE SAUCE

2 cups ketchup

¾ cup firmly packed brown sugar

1 tablespoon prepared mustard

1 tablespoon vinegar

1½ teaspoons liquid smoke

Preheat the oven to 350°F.

Place all the meatball ingredients in a large bowl. Stir or knead until the meat mixture is well combined. Shape the meat into 1½-inch balls, place the balls on baking sheets, and bake for 15 to 20 minutes, or until the meat is no longer pink inside.

Make the barbecue sauce: While the meatballs are baking, place all the sauce ingredients in a Dutch oven and stir until they are well combined. Cook over medium heat, stirring frequently, until the mixture almost boils. Add the baked meatballs to the sauce, reduce the heat to medium-low, and simmer until ready to serve.

ELK BOLOGNA

Makes about 30 pounds

Elk is a prized catch for Amish hunters in Montana. Amish cooks there say it has a less gamey taste than venison. The meat in this recipe takes several days to cure, and it makes a large batch to freeze for later. You can also use any combination of meat to make bologna, such as beef, pork, or whatever else you have lots of.

25 pounds ground elk meat

½ pound Morton's Tender Quick meat cure

¾ cup firmly packed brown sugar

½ cup salt

½ teaspoon saltpeter

4 teaspoons black pepper

4 teaspoons garlic salt

2 tablespoons liquid smoke

2 quarts water

Mix the ground meat in a large bowl with the Tender Quick, brown sugar, salt, saltpeter, black pepper, garlic salt, and liquid smoke. Refrigerate the mixture for 4 days to allow to cure. After the allotted time, process the meat mixture through a meat grinder or in batches with a food processor. Mix the water into the ground meat mixture and combine thoroughly.

Place the meat mixture into loaf pans, and bake at 175°F for 10 hours. At that point, the meat may be sliced, and any extra should be frozen if not used within a week.

FRIED ALLIGATOR NUGGETS

Serves 4 to 6

Alligator meat is common in Florida. It has its own unique flavor, one that is easily enhanced with the same seasonings and sauces you would use for pork or chicken. You could also use your own favorite dipping sauces. Horseradish, barbecue sauce, honey mustard, hot pepper, and cocktail sauce are a few other favorites. Alligator meat has a light, fine-grained texture, not unlike some hearty fish fillets, such as shark.

1 pound alligator meat, cut into 1-inch chunks or strips

1 cup all-purpose flour, seasoned with salt and pepper

Vegetable oil, for frying

Lime wedges, for serving

Tartar sauce, for serving

Dredge the meat pieces with the seasoned flour. Heat the vegetable oil (about 1 inch deep) in a medium skillet. Add the fillets and fry for 2 to 3 minutes, until the pieces float to the top. Drain on paper towels. Serve hot with the lime wedges and tartar sauce.

CREAMY MOOSE STEAKS

Serves 6 to 8

This is another great use for moose meat. The cream of mushroom soup can hide some of the gamey taste that wild meat can have, allowing the tenderness of the meat to be enjoyed.

2 pounds moose steaks

Salt and black pepper

1 (10.75-ounce) can cream of mushroom soup

1 cup water

1 large onion, sliced

Season the moose steaks with salt and pepper. Fry the steaks over medium heat in a large skillet, until lightly browned on both sides. Combine the soup and water in a small bowl, then pour the mixture over the steaks in the skillet. Add the sliced onion to the mixture. Cover the skillet with a lid and reduce the heat to medium-low. Simmer for 10 to 15 minutes, until the steaks are cooked through and tender.

GRILLED MOOSE STEAKS

Serves 4 to 6

Moose meat is very lean. Some describe it as less stringy than beef and having a slightly sweet flavor to it. Wild game meat taste can always vary depending on what the animal's diet has consisted of. This recipe requires some overnight setting, so prepare it the night before.

2 pounds moose steaks

2 teaspoons meat tenderizer salt

1 (16-ounce) bottle Italian dressing

2 teaspoons paprika

Salt

Sprinkle both sides of the steaks with the meat tenderizer salt. Place the steaks and the dressing in a resealable plastic bag, seal tightly, and marinate in the refrigerator for at least 12 hours or up to 24 hours.

Preheat a grill to high. Remove the steaks and discard the marinade. Season the steaks on both sides with the paprika and salt, and grill for 3 to 4 minutes per side, depending on the thickness.

PHEASANT BAKED IN CREAM

Serves 4 to 6

Ring-necked pheasant is one of the most popular game birds in Kansas, which makes the flavorful fowl a favorite on Amish supper tables in that state.

¼ cup shortening

1 (2½- to 3-pound) pheasant, cut into quarters

1 cup heavy cream or half-and-half, or as needed

¼ cup chopped onion

½ clove garlic, minced

1½ teaspoons Worcestershire sauce

1 teaspoon salt

⅛ teaspoon black pepper

¼ cup cold water

1 tablespoon all-purpose flour

Preheat the oven to 325°F.

Melt the shortening over medium heat in a heavy skillet. Place the pheasant pieces in the pan, and brown the meat on all sides. Transfer the pheasant pieces to a 9 by 13-inch baking dish. Pour the cream over the pheasant, and sprinkle with the onion, garlic, Worcestershire, salt, and pepper.

Cover the pan with foil, crimping the foil to the edge of the pan. Bake for about 2 hours, adding more cream if necessary, to keep everything moist.

Transfer the pheasant pieces to a serving plate. Strain the cream gravy from the pan into a medium saucepan set over medium heat. Stir together the water and flour in a small bowl. Whisk the flour mixture into the gravy and boil for 1 minute, until thickened. Serve the pheasant pieces with the gravy.

In the mountains, an abundance of wild game means plenty of outdoor meals for Amish hunters and the family members who join them for a few days in the outdoors. Many times, others from their churches will stop by for fellowship and a delicious meal.

After an elk is caught—a prized meat for Amish hunters—this delicious stew often appears in a kettle to cook over an open fire: 5 pounds of tender elk roast, potatoes, carrots, onions, celery, whole-kernel corn, tiny precooked sausages called Smokies (sold in stores), cabbage, and green beans, all seasoned with Cajun spices, thickened with flour, and simmered for hours. It makes for an enjoyable evening and a fun meal for everyone.

The Mountain Pie, below, is another favorite campfire food, especially for the children who accompany their parents to the hunting grounds.

MOUNTAIN PIE

Serves 1

Mountain pies are basically pizza-style sandwiches. This recipe requires sandwich irons (some call them hobo irons) to cook the pies over the open flame, but you can easily make a home version with any commercially sold sandwich maker.

2 slices bread, buttered on one side

2 tablespoons pizza sauce

3 tablespoons shredded mozzarella cheese

Pizza toppings of your choice (mushrooms, beef, pepperoni, peppers, etc.)

Place one slice of the bread, buttered side down, onto an over-the-fire sandwich iron (or in a sandwich maker). Spread the pizza sauce evenly over the bread, then sprinkle the mozzarella over the sauce. Add any additional pizza toppings. Apply the second slice of bread, buttered side up, and clamp the sandwich iron closed.

Put the sandwich iron into the campfire, and cook for about 2½ minutes on each side, or follow your sandwich maker's instructions. Carefully remove the sandwich from the iron and serve.

AMISH TEX-MEX?

Jalapeños. Salsa. Tacos. These aren't the foods that typically come to mind when a person thinks of "Amish food." Amish cooking, however, is a bit like tofu: It absorbs the flavors of whatever is around it.

The Amish and their closely related Mennonite brethren have been journeying to Mexico for generations. Old Order Mennonites were lured to northern Mexico in large numbers during the 1920s. The government of Mexico, looking to revive a slumping agricultural economy in the north, promised the agrarian Mennonites that they could live without intrusion and free from compulsory military service. Canada, at the time, did not offer such assurances when it came to conscription, so Mexico had an appeal to the pacifist Mennonites. (The Amish are pacifists, too, and today, Amish and Mennonites in both the United States and Canada are permitted to claim "conscientious objector" status if faced with conscription.)

The Mennonites have isolated farming enclaves in rural Chihuahua state to this day. Intermarriage with native Mexicans is rare, so the communities are islands of German-speaking, blond-haired and blue-eyed peoples in this Hispanic country. Among the crops Mennonites in Mexico raise are jalapeños, tomatillos, and cilantro, which they sell at local produce markets and inevitably bring to their relatives back in Canada and the United States, spreading a love for traditional Hispanic flavors into other Anabaptist communities. The Amish and Mennonites are prolific recipe- and seed-sharers, so a taste for Tex-Mex spread among the Anabaptists.

Even without the Mennonites settling in Mexico, it was likely only a matter of time before the Amish "discovered" the culinary charms south of the border. Over the past twenty years, Old Order Amish have been traveling with increasing frequency to Mexico for medical treatment. Clinics catering to a largely Anabaptist clientele have sprung up in Tijuana, where the Amish seek out remedies not available in the United States, or, at the very least, less expensive medical care, since they don't carry traditional medical insurance.

And even if the Amish didn't go to Mexico for medical treatment, they probably would still be serving salsa, thanks to the growing presence of "Mexican" fast-food chains, supermarket salsas, and breakfast burritos across the United States.

Salsa is a natural dish for Amish homemakers to prepare. Tomatoes are a staple of Amish gardens, and salsa is a great way to use up those extra tomatoes. For centuries, Amish and Mennonite culinary culture has been "plain," so the spiciness of homegrown hot peppers probably has a lot of appeal. Other ethnic foods, such as Italian, Cajun, and Chinese, have not caught on as much among the Amish, although pizza enjoys popularity among the Anabaptists.

FLOUR TORTILLAS

Makes 12 to 15 tortillas

Colorado has a growing Hispanic population, and its foods are definitely making their way into Amish homes in the area. Here's one of the best. So easy and so good!

4 cups all-purpose flour

2 teaspoons baking powder

1 teaspoon salt

½ cup lard

1 cup water

Place the flour, baking powder, and salt in a large mixing bowl and stir until the ingredients are thoroughly combined. Using a pastry blender or your hands, cut the lard into the dry ingredients until the mixture is crumbly. Stir in the water, kneading as necessary, to form a dough. Allow the dough to rest for 30 minutes.

Form the dough into twelve to fifteen balls. On a lightly floured surface, roll out each ball to about ⅛-inch thickness. Cook each tortilla on a hot, ungreased griddle until browned and no longer doughy in appearance, 1 to 2 minutes per side.

CORN TORTILLAS

Makes twelve 6-inch tortillas

This recipe comes from an Amish cook, Dorcas Martin, who lived with her family in Honduras during the 1970s. That Amish community is now gone, and its residents have returned north, but its recipes live on.

2 cups corn flour (called masa harina in ethnic stores)

½ teaspoon salt

1 to 1¼ cups warm water

Combine the corn flour and salt in a small mixing bowl. Add 1 cup of the water, a little at a time, as you mix ingredients. Knead the dough, adding more water if necessary to keep the dough moist and to hold its shape. Let the dough rest for 25 to 30 minutes.

Divide the dough into twelve balls, each the size of a medium egg. Press and pat the balls into a tortilla shape, or use a tortilla press. Place each tortilla on an ungreased hot griddle, and cook until golden brown. When the bubbling stops, turn the tortilla and brown the other side. Remove from the griddle while the tortilla is pliable. Stack the finished tortillas to keep them moist and warm. Use immediately or allow to cool.

AMISH COOKS IN HONDURAS?

In the 1960s, a group of Amish led by Pathway Publishing (an Old Order Amish publishing house) founder Joseph Stoll attempted to build a community in Honduras. The attempt is chronicled in Stoll's book, *Sunshine and Shadow: Our Seven Years in Honduras*. Eventually more than a dozen Amish families called Honduras home from 1969 to 1977.

Coffee, sugarcane, and roasted ears of Central American corn were often on menus. Raising bees provided a plentiful source of homemade honey. Many of the Amish also had bananas and grapefruit growing on their property.

The community disbanded in 1977 and its members went back to various northern communities. Stoll returned to his native Canada.

FRESH GREEN CHILE SALSA

Makes 2 to 3 cups salsa

Homemade salsas are increasingly popular among the Amish because almost everything needed for a tasty version can be grown in one's garden. Amish homemakers discovered salsa was a natural fit with their menus. Some Amish now make flaming salsas with homegrown jalapeños, while others prefer milder versions. This recipe is great with tortilla chips, crackers, or quesadillas, such as those in the recipe on page 213.

3 or 4 Anaheim or poblano peppers, chopped

1½ cups chopped tomatoes

½ cup chopped onion

1 clove garlic, minced

2 tablespoons fresh lime or lemon juice

1 tablespoon snipped fresh cilantro

½ teaspoon salt

⅛ teaspoon ground cumin

Mix together all the ingredients in a medium bowl until well combined. Chill to allow time for the flavors to meld, 30 minutes to 1 hour.

SOUTH TEXAS RICE

Serves 6 to 8

This is a one-pot dish that melds some of the most powerful flavors of the Rio Grande region with such traditional Amish staples as hamburger and tomatoes.

½ pound ground beef

1 green bell pepper, seeded and cut into medium dice

1 red bell pepper, seeded and cut into medium dice

1 large onion, finely chopped

1 jalapeño pepper, seeded and chopped

2 cups uncooked white rice

4 cups tomato juice

1 to 2 teaspoons taco seasoning, to taste

1 teaspoon chili seasoning mix

2 teaspoons garlic powder

2 teaspoons salt

1 to 2 teaspoons fajita seasoning, to taste

1 tomato, chopped

1 teaspoon dried basil

In a very large skillet or Dutch oven, brown the ground beef, green and red bell peppers, and onion. Drain off the grease, then add the jalapeño, rice, tomato juice, taco seasoning, chili seasoning mix, garlic powder, salt, fajita seasoning, tomato, and basil, and stir until thoroughly mixed.

Bring the mixture to a boil over medium-high heat, reduce the heat to low, and cover the skillet. Allow the mixture to simmer until the rice is tender and has absorbed most of the liquid, about 30 minutes.

QUESADILLAS

Serves 4 to 6

This is a favorite in a central Kansas Amish settlement, where the Hispanic influence has surged in recent years. Taquerías and Mexican groceries are mainstays in small towns there, and they have influenced traditional Amish cooking.

1 medium onion, finely chopped

¼ cup jalapeño peppers, finely chopped and seeded, or 2 (4-ounce) cans diced green chiles, drained

2 cups grated sharp Cheddar cheese

2 cups browned beef

10 (8-inch) Flour Tortillas (page 209)

Fresh Green Chile Salsa (page 211)

Sour cream, for serving

Combine the onion, peppers, cheese, and beef in a medium mixing bowl.

Spray a large skillet or griddle with nonstick spray, and heat over medium-high heat. Place one tortilla in the skillet. Top with ⅔ cup of the cheese mixture, spreading evenly. Top with another tortilla, then cook until the tortilla is lightly browned and the cheese begins to melt, about 1 minute. Carefully flip the tortilla "sandwich" and brown the other side. Reduce the heat slightly, if necessary, to avoid overbrowning. Transfer to a platter and keep warm while you repeat with the remaining tortillas and cheese mixture.

Cut the quesadillas into wedges and spoon the salsa and sour cream on top.

WET BURRITOS

Serves 4 to 6

As the name implies, wet burritos need to be eaten with a fork, not with your hand. The dish is a cheesy, melty mess, which makes the experience all the more enjoyable!

1 pound ground beef

1 tablespoon taco seasoning

1 (16-ounce) can pinto beans

2 tablespoons onion, chopped

1 (10.75-ounce) can cream of mushroom soup

1/3 cup salad dressing, such as Miracle Whip, or 1/2 cup sour cream

6 Flour Tortillas (page 209)

1 cup shredded Cheddar cheese

Salsa, for serving (see Note)

Preheat the oven to 325°F.

Brown the ground meat in a medium skillet over medium heat. Drain off the grease, then add the taco seasoning, beans, and onion. In a medium bowl, mix the mushroom soup and salad dressing until the mixture is smooth. Pour the soup mixture over the meat mixture, and combine thoroughly.

Place two tortillas on the bottom of a 2-quart casserole dish, followed by a layer of one-third of the meat mixture. Continue layering until all the ingredients have been used, ending with the meat mixture on top. Sprinkle the shredded cheese on top of everything. Bake until the casserole is bubbling and the cheese is melted, about 30 minutes. Serve with salsa, if desired.

Note: *Use your favorite store-bought salsa, or make the Fresh Green Chile Salsa, page 211.*

CHEESY ENCHILADAS

Serves 6 to 8

To make your own enchilada sauce for this dish, take any amount of tomato juice and the same amount of tomato sauce, and add a powdered enchilada seasoning, a little brown sugar, and salt to taste. Pour the enchilada sauce over the filled tortillas, then the cheese sauce on top of that.

½ cup (1 stick) margarine

¼ cup all-purpose flour

3 cups milk

½ pound Velveeta cheese, cut into small cubes

2 pounds chicken or ground beef

1 medium-size onion, chopped

12 Flour Tortillas (page 209)

1 cup enchilada sauce

Salt to taste

Melt the margarine in a medium saucepan over medium heat. Whisk in the flour until a paste forms, and gradually whisk in the milk, heating until the mixture becomes thickened. Stir in the cheese until it is melted through. Remove the sauce from the heat and set aside. Preheat the oven to 350°F.

In a large skillet, sauté the chicken with the chopped onion until the meat is no longer pink. Divide the meat among the twelve tortillas, roll up, and place seam side down in a 9 by 13-inch baking dish. Pour the enchilada sauce over the top, and the cheese sauce over that. Bake until hot and bubbly, about 30 minutes.

weddings

Weddings are such a blessed, celebratory time in the Amish church, and baked goods are an important part of the day. The item I remember most from weddings when I was growing up is a special pastry called Nothings (page 219).

When I was in third grade my sister Leah was married, and that was when I saw Nothings made for the first time. I loved watching the cooks make them and put them into the deep fryer with such great care, knowing they were an important symbol of the day.

Weddings are usually held on Thursdays; a long-time tradition. Everyone is expected to pitch in, including the bride. For instance, before I got dressed for my wedding, I helped Mom and my sisters get the first skillets of chicken frying around 4:15 a.m. Mom was already dressed in her wedding clothes because she knew she wouldn't have time to change later.

By 7:00 a.m. the bride, groom, and attendants need to be seated because everyone wants to shake hands with the wedding party before the ceremony starts a couple hours later. It was exciting, but both Joe and I were really nervous!

If you are a designated cook, you don't go to the service because you need to be ready to feed all the attendees immediately afterwards.

However, cooks closely related to the bride or groom will go in to see the union of marriage. Here in Michigan the mothers of the bride and groom don't have anything to do, which is actually kind of nice because it gives the parents more time to enjoy the ceremony.

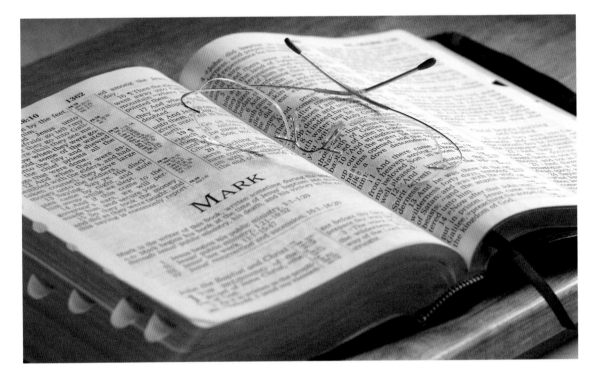

My mom never got too much enjoyment out of our weddings because she had to spend the day taking care of everything. Around here each wedding has a head cook to organize and direct all the other cooks. The head cook is usually a close family friend of the bride's side. So, unlike my mom, I won't have to do anything when my daughters get married except greet visitors, tend to my daughters, and take in the day.

At our wedding, Joe and I had around fourteen couples as table waiters, an unmarried girl and boy who worked basically as busboys, and two water boys who kept water carried to the tables. It's considered a high honor to be chosen as a table waiter, water boy, or cook.

We had about thirty cooks at our wedding. To select the cooks you gather all your aunts, married sisters, and husband's married sisters and aunts. My mother also chose several ladies who were close friends of hers to be cooks. For our wedding there was a large noon meal served after the ceremony, plus a supper for those still in attendance.

Weddings also mean baking a lot of cookies, because halfway through the service they'll take a snack out for the younger children and lemonade and coffee for the cooks. Hundreds of cookies have to be made ahead of time and brought in by family members.

Our wedding cake was four layers high. Mom decorated my wedding cake, and I had my side cakes done by a friend. We weren't allowed to have a tiered cake in the church district where we got married; all the cakes had to be the same size, and all had to have white icing. The side cakes also had white icing, but half were white inside and half were chocolate.

In the community where Joe and I got married, after all the guests were fed in the evening, the table waiters and young folks all sit around a table and sing songs. While they sing, the bride and

SAMPLE MENU FOR AN AMISH WEDDING

Green beans
Swiss and hot pepper cheeses
Lettuce salad
Carrot salad
Potato salad
Celery sticks
Bread and butter with rhubarb jam

———

300 pounds fried chicken
Mashed potatoes
Chicken and noodles
Gravy
Dressing
Corn

———

Tapioca pudding
Variety of cakes
Fruit salad
90 assorted raisin, rhubarb, oatmeal, and cherry pies
Nothings

groom cut the wedding cake and lay the pieces out on a big tray to pass around.

The bride slips a ring into a piece of the cake before passing it all out to the young folks. The girl or boy who gets the ring in the piece of cake is teased about being the next one to get married. This is all in fun, and it's a tradition passed down in that community.

This ring is the only piece of jewelry an Amish woman will ever buy, and it is always a very cheap one. It's not worn by the girl or boy who finds it; it's simply stored away among other memories.

HOMEMADE WEDDING ROLLS

Makes 24 rolls

Most of the food for weddings here in Michigan is prepared in the "wedding wagons," but one item is baked in the home: wedding rolls. In the kitchen, the tables are covered with the laid-out, rising roll dough. Women bake them and take them out of the oven. At least a few hundred have to be made for each wedding. The dinner rolls are then served nice and fresh in baskets all around the tables with butter in the baskets. After one wedding meal was over, all of us cooks were allowed to take a basket off a table as a keepsake. As far as dinner rolls go, this really is an easy one to make, but it's such a special treat.

2 cups warm water

2 packages active dry yeast

½ cup sugar

3 teaspoons salt

¼ cup vegetable oil

1 large egg

6½ to 7 cups bread flour

In a large bowl, combine the water, yeast, sugar, salt, oil, and egg until the mixture is well blended. Add 3 to 4 cups of flour and mix well. Then add the remaining flour and mix until an elastic dough forms. Cover the bowl and let the dough rise for about 2 hours.

Preheat the oven to 400°F. Shape the dough into fist-size rolls. Let them rise again until double in size, about 1 hour. Bake until golden, 13 to 15 minutes.

WHAT TO WEAR?

Joe and I were still living in Indiana when we got married, and the rules of our community required that I wear a black dress. Joe wore a black suit and white shirt.

Here where we are now in Michigan, brides can choose their wedding dress colors; hunter green, burgundy, and dark blue are frequently seen. An Amish bride also wears a black *kapp* (the German word we use for our head covering; it's the origin of the English word "cap"). After she is married, she changes into a white *kapp* and doesn't ever wear the black one again.

April through October is the traditional season for weddings in the Amish community, with June being the peak month. Many Amish weddings are held at least partially outdoors, if not entirely. This adds a layer of complexity to an already hectic day.

One service available to blissful but busy brides and grooms is a wedding wagon. The wagon—which is transported to the site by a non-Amish hauler with a sturdy vehicle that can pull its heavy weight—comes complete with everything needed for the occasion.

There are five gas stoves, plenty of cookware (spoons, knives, cutting boards), and one gigantic coffeemaker large enough to brew 160 cups of coffee at once. Another feature of the wedding wagon is plenty of workspace for such tasks as peeling the hundreds of potatoes served at any Amish wedding.

The wagon, which can easily accommodate a wedding for seven hundred guests, has front and back lattice-door entrances so cooks can come and go without crashing into each other. Wedding wagons are rented for a week at a time, so cooks have plenty of time for prewedding preparations.

NOTHINGS

Makes 8 pastries

This is a pastry commonly served as a dessert at weddings. The dish is decorative and functional. The Nothings are stacked on plates and placed on tables for guests to enjoy after a hearty meal.

1 large egg

¾ cup heavy cream

Pinch of salt

2 to 3 cups all-purpose flour

Lard or shortening, such as Crisco, for frying

Powdered sugar, for sprinkling

Place the egg in a large mixing bowl and beat until foamy. Stir in the cream, salt, and enough flour to form a stiff dough. Knead the dough until well combined, then divide the dough into eight balls.

On a floured work surface, roll out each ball of dough into a very thin circle. Cut three slits into each flat piece of dough. Place the lard in a large skillet and heat until ready for frying. One by one, fry each piece of dough, turning once, until golden on both sides. Remove from the hot oil, set on paper towels to cool, and then sprinkle the pastry with powdered sugar. Stack the finished pastries on a serving plate.

funerals

I have been been to three or four Amish funerals, including the funeral for Lovina's mother, Elizabeth Coblentz, who began "The Amish Cook." I was grief-stricken at the sudden loss of Elizabeth, since we had worked closely together for a long time and were very fond of each other.

Lovina's brothers, sisters, saw his grief, and they tried to comfort me. I was surprised by that. I told them that it should be the other way around—*I* should be the one comforting them.

It's important to understand that one of the most enduring and steadfast beliefs the Amish have is that after our death, we are born anew into a better, higher, place. All Amish share this certainty and their funerals reflect that. As such, Amish funerals pay tribute to the person who has passed on, while also celebrating the gift that was that person's life—a gift to all in the community.

After the simple graveside ceremony, during which the Amish place a wooden grave marker with only the person's initials carved in it, everyone heads back for a large meal prepared by others in the community. Sadness is then usually replaced by smiles, stories, and a sense of acceptance that the person has passed to a better beyond.

Here are some of the traditional recipes you'll see after an Amish funeral.

—by Kevin Williams

AMISH FUNERAL COOKIES

Makes 3 dozen

Funerals are sad times for family, but they are also a time when everyone pulls together. A service is held usually at the home of the deceased, followed by a large meal for all in attendance. These cookies, which don't need to be baked, are called funeral cookies because they can be made in a hurry to take to a grieving family. Be sure to use quick-cooking oats for this recipe and not the instant kind, or the cookies won't hold together well.

½ cup (1 stick) butter

½ cup milk

2 cups sugar

3 tablespoons unsweetened cocoa powder

½ cup creamy peanut butter

1 teaspoon vanilla extract

¼ teaspoon salt

3 cups quick-cooking rolled oats

½ cup chopped pecans

In a small saucepan over medium heat, bring to a boil the butter, milk, sugar, and cocoa, and cook for 1 minute. Remove from the heat and stir in the peanut butter, vanilla, and salt. Mix in the oats and pecans. Drop by the teaspoon onto waxed paper and allow the cookies to stand unrefrigerated for 1 hour. After the cookies are set, store in an airtight container with waxed paper between the layers.

These cookies will keep for up to 1 week.

FUNERAL PIE

Serves 8

This raisin pie is a funeral tradition in Pennsylvania Amish communities, where the thick pie is a comfort to the grieving family. In some other Amish communities, a raisin pie is served at more celebratory occasions, like weddings.

2 cups raisins

2 cups water

½ cup packed light brown sugar

½ cup granulated sugar

3 tablespoons cornstarch

1½ teaspoons ground cinnamon

¼ teaspoon ground allspice

Pinch of salt

1 tablespoon apple cider vinegar

3 tablespoons butter

2 disks My Homemade Pie Dough (page 296)

Preheat the oven to 400°F.

Put the raisins and ⅔ cup of the water in a medium saucepan and heat over medium heat for 5 minutes.

Combine the sugars, cornstarch, spices, and salt in a medium bowl and, stirring constantly, gradually add the remaining 1⅓ cups of water. Add this mixture to the raisins. Cook and stir until the mixture starts to bubble. Add the vinegar and butter and heat until the butter is melted. Remove from the stove and let cool until just warm.

Roll out one disk of dough to a ⅛-inch thickness on a floured surface. Line a 9-inch pie pan with the dough. Trim to a ½-inch overhang. Pour the filling into the crust. Roll out the second disk of dough, place on top of the pie, and trim to a 1-inch overhang. Fold the dough under and crimp the edge. Cut decorative slash marks into the top crust. Bake until golden brown, about 15 minutes. Remove from the oven and let cool completely.

simple snacks

Snacks have never merely been things to just grab and go between meals to quell momentary hunger. In our families, they have another important function, too: adding a smile to our day. These snacks do exactly that.

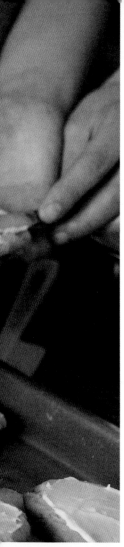

WORLD'S BEST SUGAR COOKIES

Makes 4 dozen

The original Amish Cook—my mother, Elizabeth Coblentz—called these sugar cookies "the world's best." And judging by how fast they disappear in my household, perhaps they are!

1 cup powdered sugar

1 cup granulated sugar

1 cup margarine or butter, softened

1 cup vegetable oil

2 teaspoons vanilla extract

2 large eggs

5 cups all-purpose flour

1 teaspoon salt

1 teaspoon baking soda

1 teaspoon cream of tartar

Preheat the oven to 350°F.

In a large bowl, cream together the powdered sugar, granulated sugar, margarine, oil, and vanilla until light and fluffy. Add the eggs and beat until evenly incorporated. In a second large bowl, sift together the flour, salt, baking soda, and cream of tartar. Gradually add the dry ingredients to the wet mixture, stirring until well combined.

Form the cookie dough into walnut-size balls and place 2 inches apart on ungreased baking sheets. Flatten the balls using the bottom of a glass dipped in sugar. Bake for 10 to 12 minutes, until the edges turn golden brown. Allow the cookies to cool for 2 minutes on the baking sheets before removing. Transfer the cookies to wire racks to cool completely. Cookies may then be frosted, if desired (see Basic Frosting, page 348).

OUTRAGEOUS CHOCOLATE CHIP COOKIES

Makes 4 to 5 dozen cookies

This chocolate chip cookie recipe is a favorite of my children and readers. It has appeared in my column on several occasions. It makes a superb cookie to crumble into Flat Rock Pudding, page 137.

2 cups (4 sticks) butter

2 cups granulated sugar

1½ cups firmly packed brown sugar

2 cups peanut butter

2 teaspoons vanilla extract

4 large eggs, beaten

4 cups all-purpose flour

2 cups quick-cooking rolled oats

4 teaspoons baking soda

1 teaspoon salt

1 (12-ounce) package chocolate chips

Preheat the oven to 350°F.

Melt the butter and mix with the sugars, peanut butter, vanilla, and eggs. Stir until creamy and smooth. Add the flour, oats, baking soda, and salt. Mix the dough until thoroughly blended. Stir in the chocolate chips until evenly distributed throughout the dough. Roll the dough into 1-inch balls and place on baking sheets. Bake the cookies for 10 to 15 minutes, until the edges are golden brown. Transfer to wire racks to cool completely.

PIZZA COOKIES

Makes 18 cookies

The children enjoy having snacks such as cookies, crackers, and popcorn while traveling. It was really a treat when we stopped at a Dairy Queen on the way back from Ohio and got them all a milkshake. Pizza cookies are colorful and fun for kids to eat in the car. They are less messy than other cookies because they do not crumble as easily. A round pizza pan can be used for this, or a baking sheet.

½ cup granulated sugar

⅓ cup packed brown sugar

4 tablespoons (½ stick) margarine or butter

1 large egg

½ cup smooth peanut butter

1 teaspoon vanilla extract

1½ cups all-purpose flour

1 cup chocolate chips

2 cups mini-marshmallows

2 cups mini M&Ms

Preheat the oven to 375°F.

Combine the sugars, margarine, egg, peanut butter, and vanilla in a medium bowl. Add the flour and mix until well blended. Press or roll the dough onto a 15-inch pizza pan or a baking sheet. Roll the dough to the edge of the pan. Bake for 10 minutes. Remove from the oven and top with the chocolate chips, marshmallows, and M&Ms. Return to the oven until the chips, marshmallows, and M&Ms melt, 5 to 8 minutes. Remove from the oven and let cool completely. Cut into wedges or squares.

SORGHUM MOLASSES COOKIES

Makes 3 dozen medium-size cookies

Many Amish make their own molasses, which infuses these cookies with a rich taste of locally made sorghum. They are a staple in many Amish homes. We do not have a refrigerator to chill the cookie dough, but I've added this step to the instructions for easier baking.

1 cup shortening	4 teaspoons baking soda
2 cups firmly packed brown sugar	2 teaspoons ground ginger
2 cups molasses	2 teaspoons ground cinnamon
2 large eggs	½ teaspoon ground cloves
6½ cups all-purpose flour	1 cup buttermilk
1 teaspoon salt	½ cup granulated sugar, for rolling the dough

Preheat the oven to 375°F.

In a large mixing bowl, mix the shortening, brown sugar, molasses, and eggs. In a separate bowl, sift together the flour, salt, baking soda, ginger, cinnamon, and cloves. Add the dry mixture alternately into the molasses mixture and the buttermilk. Stir until well blended.

Chill the dough for 1 hour. Remove the dough from the refrigerator and shape into walnut-size balls. Roll them in sugar and place them about 2 inches apart on a greased cookie sheet. Bake for 10 to 12 minutes, or until set. Transfer to a wire baking rack to cool.

MOLASSES

Many Amish homes have a small outbuilding similar to the sugar shacks you may have seen around maple syrup producers. But instead of being used to make maple syrup, these are our sorghum sheds, used to make molasses in the fall. The molasses is then used and enjoyed year-round in cooking, gingerbread, and bread. An equal amount of honey will perform the same in a recipe with a different, but very pleasant, taste.

PINWHEEL COOKIES

Makes 3 dozen cookies

This is a pretty cookie with the swirls of chocolate dough contrasting with the lighter colors. Children love to help make these cookies. They can help roll the dough. I always liked watching my mother when she sliced them and laid them on the baking sheet, because I liked to see the different stripes. You don't see pinwheel cookies as much anymore, probably because they take a little more time to make.

1 pound butter, softened	¼ cup milk
½ teaspoon salt	4 large egg yolks
2 cups sugar	6 teaspoons unsweetened cocoa powder
6 teaspoons baking powder	2 teaspoons vanilla extract
6 cups all-purpose flour	

In a large bowl, stir together the butter, salt, sugar, baking powder, flour, milk, and egg yolks. Stir vigorously with a wooden spoon until the dough is elastic, adding more flour if needed.

Divide the dough in half. Put one dough half in a bowl and add the cocoa. Knead the dough with your hands until the cocoa is thoroughly mixed in and the dough turns a dark color. Put the other dough half in another bowl, add the vanilla, and work it through the dough until mixed, adding more flour if needed to keep the dough elastic.

On two floured surfaces, roll each dough ball into 9 by 12-inch rectangles about ¼ inch thick. Place the white dough on top of the cocoa dough and press together. Then roll tightly lengthwise, like a jelly roll, into a roll 2 inches in diameter. Cover and set in the refrigerator, for several hours or overnight.

When ready to bake, preheat the oven to 350°F. Slice the dough into ½-inch-thick slices and arrange flat on baking sheets. Bake until the cookies are firm, about 20 minutes. Cool the cookies on a wire rack or a plate and then put into sealed containers. These cookies will stay fresh for up to 5 days.

PEANUT BUTTER COOKIES

Makes about 2 dozen cookies

This is a classic cookie enjoyed in many Amish settlements. While lard is gradually falling out of favor in some Amish kitchens, many still use it, as this cookie recipe reflects. An equal amount of shortening also works well.

1 cup lard

1¼ cups granulated sugar

1 cup firmly packed brown sugar

2 large eggs, beaten

1 cup peanut butter

½ teaspoon salt

2 teaspoons baking soda

1½ teaspoons vanilla extract

3 cups all-purpose flour

Preheat the oven to 350°F.

Cream together the lard, 1 cup of the granulated sugar, and the brown sugar in a large bowl until light and fluffy. Mix in the eggs, peanut butter, salt, baking soda, vanilla, and flour, stirring until well combined. Form the dough into 1-inch balls, then roll the balls in the reserved ¼ cup of granulated sugar. Place the balls on baking sheets, flattening slightly. Bake until the cookies are browned at the edges, 10 to 12 minutes.

SNICKERDOODLES

Makes 3 dozen cookies

Snickerdoodles have been around for as long as I can remember. They are simple—a plain cookie rolled in cinnamon and sugar right before baking—and delicious. As a child, the name would always make me think of a Snickers candy bar.

1 cup shortening, softened

1½ cups plus 2 tablespoons sugar

2 large eggs

2¾ cups all-purpose flour

1 tablespoon cream of tartar

1 teaspoon salt

1 teaspoon baking soda

2 tablespoons ground cinnamon

Preheat the oven to 350°F.

Mix together the shortening, 1½ cups of the sugar, and the eggs. Stir in the flour, cream of tartar, salt, and baking soda. Chill the dough for at least 2 hours.

In a small bowl, combine the cinnamon and the remaining 2 tablespoons of sugar. Roll the dough into 1½-inch balls and roll into the cinnamon and sugar mixture. Place them 2 inches apart on ungreased baking sheets and bake until the edges are golden brown, about 10 minutes. The cookies will spread out and flatten while they are baking. Cool the cookies on a wire rack or a plate and then put into sealed containers. These cookies will stay fresh for up to 5 days.

OLD-FASHIONED GINGER COOKIES

Makes 4 dozen cookies

I always keep ginger on hand for these cookies and other recipes that ask for ginger. The flavor of ginger mixes beautifully with the molasses while baking.

1 cup shortening

1½ cups molasses

1 cup butter, softened

1 cup sugar

2 cups buttermilk or sour milk

5½ cups all-purpose flour

½ teaspoon salt

1 tablespoon baking soda

¾ teaspoon ground ginger

1 teaspoon ground cinnamon

In a nonstick saucepan, heat the shortening, molasses, butter, and ½ cup of the sugar over medium heat until melted. Add the buttermilk, stir until smooth, and remove from the heat.

In another bowl, mix the flour, salt, baking soda, ginger, and cinnamon together. Stir in the liquid ingredients until a smooth dough forms. The dough may seem too soft, but don't add more flour. Chill the dough in the refrigerator for at least 2 hours.

Preheat the oven to 350°F. Remove the chilled dough from the refrigerator and roll into 2½-inch balls. In a small, shallow bowl, pour the remaining ½ cup of sugar. Dip and roll the dough balls into the sugar and place 2½ inches apart on baking sheets. Flatten the dough gently with the back of a spoon. Bake them until the centers begin to turn dark brown, 20 to 25 minutes.

Cool the cookies on a wire rack or a plate and then put into sealed containers. These cookies will stay fresh for up to 5 days.

GINGERBREAD COOKIES

Makes 2 to 3 dozen cookies

These are very traditional gingerbread cookies from a recipe that is older than anyone remembers. My mother, Elizabeth Coblentz—who was the first writer of "The Amish Cook" column—selected this recipe to go into a cookbook she was working on before she suddenly passed away. I'm very happy to include it here.

2 cups all-purpose flour

1 teaspoon baking powder

1 teaspoon baking soda

1 teaspoon ground cinnamon

1 teaspoon ground ginger

1/3 cup sugar

1/2 cup vegetable shortening

1/2 cup molasses

3 tablespoons hot water

Preheat the oven to 400°F.

In a large bowl, combine all of the ingredients and stir with a wooden spoon until well blended. Refrigerate the dough for at least 1 hour before handling. On a floured surface, roll the chilled dough to about 1/8-inch thickness. Use your favorite cookie cutters to cut shapes from the dough. Place the cookies on ungreased baking sheets. Bake for 8 to 10 minutes, until the edges of the cookies are golden brown. Transfer to wire racks to cool before decorating.

THIMBLE COOKIES

Makes 2 dozen cookies

If you want to have a cookie that isn't too sweet, this would be a good choice. I use strawberry jam in mine. You could even replace the jam with chocolate chips or candy. These are called thimble cookies because Amish women will use a thimble to make the tiny holes in the center for filling with jam, but if you don't have one, the back of a small spoon or your thumb could be used.

1 cup butter (2 sticks), softened

½ cup sugar

4 large eggs

1 teaspoon vanilla extract

2 cups all-purpose flour

½ cup jam, any flavor of your choice

Preheat the oven to 325°F.

In a large bowl, cream the butter and sugar until well blended. Beat in the eggs and vanilla. Work in the flour until a firm dough forms. If the dough seems too sticky, let it chill for a couple of hours in the refrigerator.

Form the dough into 1-inch balls and place 2 inches apart on ungreased baking sheets. Use a clean thimble to press a hole in each one. Fill the hole with a small amount of jam. Bake until the edges of the cookies are golden brown and the jam begins to bubble, about 25 minutes.

Cool the cookies on a wire rack or a plate and then put into sealed containers. These cookies will stay fresh for up to 5 days.

HONEY SPICE COOKIES

Makes 2 to 3 dozen cookies

My husband, Joe, used to put honey in his coffee instead of sugar. My dad used to mix lemon juice and honey together for a cold. We'd heat it and the warm mixture would soothe your throat. When I first got married and I needed a spice, I'd have to go buy it, but it seems now I am stocked up on most of them, like the ginger required for this recipe. I probably go through more cinnamon than anything else. This is a cookie I almost always have the spices on hand to make.

¾ cup (1½ sticks) butter, softened

1 cup packed brown sugar

1 large egg

¼ cup honey

2 cups all-purpose flour

2¼ teaspoons baking soda

½ teaspoon salt

1 teaspoon ground ginger

½ teaspoon ground cinnamon

¼ teaspoon ground cloves

Granulated sugar for rolling

Preheat the oven to 350°F.

Cream the butter, brown sugar, egg, and honey together in a large bowl. In a separate bowl, mix together the flour, baking soda, salt, ginger, cinnamon, and cloves. Add the flour mixture to the wet ingredients, a little at a time, until a stiff dough forms. Shape the dough into 1½-inch balls and roll in sugar to coat. Place the balls on ungreased baking sheets and bake until the cookies are golden brown and cracked on top, 10 to 15 minutes. Cool the cookies on a wire rack or a plate and then put into sealed containers. These cookies will stay fresh for up to 5 days.

BROOMSTICK COOKIES

Makes 2 dozen cookies

These cookies resemble broomsticks. They are fun for the children to prepare by rolling the dough between the palms of their hands. You can make the broomsticks different lengths for fun.

1½ cups shortening

3 cups packed brown sugar

3 large eggs, beaten

1 cup dark corn syrup

¼ cup raisins

2 teaspoons vanilla extract

½ cup walnuts, chopped

6½ to 7 cups all-purpose flour

Powdered sugar or Basic Frosting (page 348)

Preheat the oven to 375°F. Grease two baking sheets and set aside.

In a large bowl, cream together the shortening and sugar. Add the beaten eggs and corn syrup and stir.

Put the raisins in a small saucepan and add just enough water to cover. Cook over medium-low heat until all of the water is evaporated, about 10 minutes. Add the cooked raisins, vanilla, and nuts to the shortening mixture. Mix well. Add the flour a little at a time, mixing between each addition, until the mixture resembles pie dough.

Roll pieces of stiff dough between your hands to form thin, 5-inch-long "broomsticks." Place lengthwise on the prepared pans. Bake until golden, about 15 minutes. Let stand for a few minutes before removing from the baking sheets, and then top with powdered sugar or frosting.

Cool the cookies on a wire rack or a plate and then put into sealed containers. These cookies will stay fresh for up to 5 days.

CHURCH COOKIES

Makes 10 dozen cookies

Halfway through the service, cookies, crackers, and pretzels are passed around for the little children. After services, they are passed around for everyone (that's the reason these are called Church Cookies). You can even make them the weekend before—they actually get better if stored in an airtight container in a cool place for a week or so. The days before church are busy enough with preparation, so it is nice to have a cookie that can be done further in advance. This recipe easily halves if you don't need this many cookies.

3 cups lard

5 cups sugar

5 large eggs

2½ cups milk

3 teaspoons vanilla extract

2 teaspoons baking soda

5 teaspoons baking powder

1 teaspoon salt

11 to 12 cups all-purpose flour, plus more for rolling out

Preheat the oven to 375°F.

In a large bowl, combine the lard and sugar. Add the eggs, beating well. Add the milk and vanilla, and then stir in the dry ingredients until a soft dough forms. Roll the dough out on a lightly floured surface to about a ½-inch thickness. Use cookie cutters to cut into various shapes, or use a glass to make round cookies. Bake until the edges are golden, about 10 minutes.

Cool the cookies on a wire rack or a plate and then put into sealed containers. These cookies will stay fresh for up to 2 weeks.

HOMEMADE BUTTERMILK COOKIES

Makes 4 dozen cookies

Old-fashioned buttermilk is the milk left over after butter has been churned from cream. Store-bought versions are somewhat different, being a bit thicker than the homemade kind, but will still work in this recipe. Because we rarely throw anything away, Amish women have found lots of different ways to use up buttermilk, such as in cookies, pies, cakes, and biscuits. The thick, slightly sweet milk gives a nice flavor that holds up during the baking process.

1 cup (2 sticks) butter, softened

2 cups sugar, plus more for sprinkling

3 large eggs

1 teaspoon vanilla extract

2 teaspoons baking soda

2 teaspoons cream of tartar

5 cups all-purpose flour

¾ cup buttermilk

Preheat the oven to 350°F.

Cream together the butter and sugar in a large bowl. Add the eggs, beating well. Then add the vanilla. Mix together the baking soda, cream of tartar, and flour. Add the buttermilk and the dry ingredients alternately to the butter mixture. Chill the dough uncovered for several hours.

Roll out and cut out the cookies using a round glass or cookie cutter and place on ungreased baking sheets. Sprinkle with sugar and bake until golden, about 10 minutes.

Cool the cookies on a wire rack or a plate and then put into sealed containers. These cookies will stay fresh for up to 5 days.

RANGER COOKIES

Makes 4 dozen cookies

This is a really good cookie, although I'm not sure why they are named this way. If you want a crunchier cookie, bake them for 5 minutes longer. My husband, Joe, likes these as a crunchier cookie. You can taste the oatmeal and cereal in them. Personally, I prefer these over a chocolate chip cookie. In some Amish communities, these are known as Ranger Joe Cookies.

1 cup packed brown sugar

1 cup granulated sugar

1 cup shortening, softened

2 large eggs, beaten

1 tablespoon vanilla extract

$\frac{1}{2}$ teaspoon salt

$\frac{1}{2}$ teaspoon baking soda

$\frac{1}{2}$ teaspoon baking powder

2 cups all-purpose flour

2 cups puffed rice cereal

2 cups quick-cooking rolled oats

Preheat the oven to 400°F.

In a large bowl, cream the sugars and shortening. Add the beaten eggs and vanilla to the sugar mixture. Mix thoroughly.

In a separate bowl, sift together the salt, baking soda, baking powder, and flour. Add to the wet mixture. Stir in the cereal and oats. Roll the dough into walnut-size balls and place 2 inches apart on ungreased baking sheets. Bake until golden brown around the edges, about 10 minutes.

Cool the cookies on a wire rack or a plate and then put into sealed containers. These cookies will stay fresh for up to 5 days.

SPRITZ COOKIES

Makes 5 dozen cookies

This is an old favorite in many Amish communities. The cookies are small in size, but big in sweet flavor. If you don't have a cookie press as the recipe calls for, the batter can be dropped by the teaspoonful onto a baking sheet.

1 cup (2 sticks) butter, softened

⅔ cup sugar

3 large egg yolks

1 teaspoon vanilla extract

2½ cups all-purpose flour

Preheat the oven to 400°F.

Mix the butter, sugar, egg yolks, and vanilla together thoroughly in a large bowl. Add the flour and mix well. Using one-quarter of the dough at a time, shape through a cookie press onto ungreased baking sheets. Bake until set but not browned, 7 to 10 minutes. Cool the cookies on a wire rack or a plate and then put into sealed containers. These cookies will stay fresh up to 5 days.

HOMEMADE MAPLE SYRUP COOKIES

Makes about 4 dozen cookies

These cookies are faintly sweet with just a hint of maple flavor. A little additional maple syrup can be used for a stronger maple taste. This is a soft cookie that is very nice enjoyed with a cup of coffee.

1 teaspoon baking soda

1 tablespoon milk

1 large egg, beaten

½ cup shortening

1 cup pure maple syrup

3 cups all-purpose flour

1 tablespoon baking powder

½ teaspoon salt

1 teaspoon vanilla extract

Preheat the oven to 350°F.

Dissolve the baking soda in the milk in a small bowl, and set aside. In a large bowl, mix the egg, shortening, syrup, flour, baking powder, salt, and vanilla, in that order, until fully combined. The dough will be very thick and sticky. Add the soda mixture, and mix until fully incorporated.

Drop the dough by rounded teaspoonfuls 2 inches apart on an ungreased baking sheet. Bake until the cookies look set and are honey brown, 10 to 12 minutes. Let the cookies cool for a couple of minutes, then remove them from the baking sheet. The cookies will remain soft when stored in an airtight container.

MAPLE DROP COOKIES

Makes about 5 dozen cookies

Maple flavorings are available at most bulk-food stores. The Amish-run bulk-food stores carry many different kinds of extracts and flavors, from peppermint to root beer. This cookie has a great taste of maple from the liquid flavoring.

3½ cups all-purpose flour

1 teaspoon baking soda

Pinch of salt

1 cup (2 sticks) butter, softened

2 cups packed brown sugar

3 large eggs

¼ teaspoon maple flavoring

¼ cup walnut pieces

Preheat the oven to 375°F.

In a large bowl, combine the flour, baking soda, and salt. In a separate medium bowl, cream together the butter and sugar. Add the eggs one at a time, mixing well after each addition. Add the maple flavoring and walnuts. Stir vigorously until the batter is smooth and well blended. Gradually add the dry ingredients until well blended. The batter will be somewhat crumbly. Form into balls approximately 1 inch in size. Place on ungreased baking sheets. Bake until the edges are golden brown, 12 to 14 minutes. Let rest on the baking sheet for 2 to 3 minutes before transferring to a cooling rack.

Cool the cookies on a wire rack or a plate and then put into sealed containers. These cookies will stay fresh for up to 5 days.

CHOCOLATE MARSHMALLOW COOKIES

Makes 4½ dozen cookies

This is a very soft cookie with an interesting mix of textures. They are great for an after-school snack!

4 cups all-purpose flour

1 teaspoon baking soda

1 teaspoon salt

⅔ cup unsweetened cocoa powder

1 cup shortening, softened

2 cups granulated sugar

2 large eggs

2 teaspoons vanilla extract

1 cup thick sour milk

36 large marshmallows, cut in half

FROSTING

6 tablespoons butter or margarine, melted

¼ cup unsweetened cocoa powder

1 teaspoon vanilla extract

3½ cups powdered sugar

5 to 6 tablespoons milk

Preheat the oven to 350°F. Lightly grease baking sheets and set aside.

In a medium bowl, stir together the flour, baking soda, salt, and cocoa powder. In another bowl, beat together the shortening, sugar, eggs, and vanilla until fluffy. Add the flour mixture to the shortening mixture alternately with the sour milk, mixing well after each addition.

Drop the batter by the teaspoonful onto the prepared baking sheets. Bake for 8 minutes. Top each cookie with a marshmallow half, and return to the oven for another 2 minutes to soften. Remove from the oven and cool the cookies on a wire rack or a plate and then put into sealed containers. These cookies will stay fresh for 2 days.

Make the frosting: In a medium bowl, combine all the ingredients and beat together until smooth. Once the cookies are cooled, spread the frosting over the tops, covering the marshmallows.

OATMEAL COOKIES

Makes 3 dozen cookies

This is a very good oatmeal cookie. This recipe makes a softer cookie than the Overnight Oatmeal Cookies (page 32). They are easy to mix and bake, and are an ideal recipe for young bakers who are just learning to bake. These cookies don't last very long in our household because they are so good served right out of the oven! My children eat them with milk.

1 cup margarine, softened

2 cups packed brown sugar

2 large eggs

2 teaspoons vanilla extract

2½ cups all-purpose flour

1 teaspoon salt

1½ teaspoons baking soda

3 cups quick-cooking rolled oats

2 cups granulated sugar

In a large bowl, cream together the margarine and brown sugar. Mix well, and then add the eggs and vanilla. Stir until the eggs are thoroughly blended in. Add the flour, salt, and baking soda. Stir until well blended. Add the oats and continue to vigorously stir until the oats are evenly blended. Chill the dough uncovered for several hours or overnight.

When ready to bake, preheat the oven to 350°F. Roll the dough into small balls about the size of a walnut. Pour the sugar into a shallow bowl and roll each ball through it, so that it's coated completely with sugar. Place on ungreased baking sheets and bake until the edges and the tops of the cookies are golden brown, 18 to 20 minutes. The cookies will flatten while baking.

Cool the cookies on a wire rack or a plate and then put into sealed containers. These cookies will stay fresh for up to 7 days.

$250 COOKIES

Makes 10 dozen cookies

This recipe uses a lot of oatmeal and nuts, and nuts, especially, have traditionally been saved for special occasions because of their expense. I think this is why they're called $250 Cookies. In some churches, this recipe is also known as a Bushel of Cookies. These cookies, like the Church Cookies (page 238), are passed around in church halfway through the services for the children to have a snack. Usually there are four or five different kinds of cookies to choose from after church. Oatmeal, chocolate chip, sugar, and molasses cookies are among the most popular. But there is usually a cookie like this among the mix.

1 pound butter

2 cups granulated sugar

2 cups packed brown sugar

4 large eggs

2 teaspoons vanilla extract

4 cups all-purpose flour

5 cups quick-cooking rolled oats

1 teaspoon salt

1 teaspoon baking soda

1 teaspoon baking powder

1 (12-ounce) package semisweet chocolate chips

3 cups chopped nuts of your choice

1 (8-ounce) milk chocolate bar, grated

Preheat the oven to 375°F.

In a large bowl, cream together the butter and sugars. Stir in the eggs and vanilla. Mix in the flour, oats, salt, baking soda, and baking powder until the oats are evenly mixed. Add the chocolate chips, nuts, and grated chocolate bar and mix to combine. Roll the dough into balls and place 2 inches apart on ungreased baking sheets. Bake them until the edges of the cookies are golden, 8 to 10 minutes.

Cool the cookies on a wire rack or a plate and then put into sealed containers. These cookies will stay fresh for up to 7 days.

MAKING WHOOPIE PIES

Whoopie pies are the delicious dessert most closely identified with the Amish. The actual origins, however, are in some dispute among non-Amish. One group of food historians claims the cookie concoction is a Pennsylvania Dutch or Pennsylvania Amish creation. Some others farther north in Maine believe the whoopie pie originated there.

To the Amish, it doesn't really matter either way. We have simply embraced them as one of our favorite, most universally enjoyed, sweets. Whoopie pies can be found in Amish-owned bakeries and home kitchens across the country. Amish bakers have experimented with making the cookies in a variety of flavors, including pumpkin, peanut butter, chocolate, and spice.

The cookie's name also has its share of stories, and one of the most popularly told among the Amish is that children would shout "Whoopie!" if they found one of these in their lunch pails. That's also the story I like best because my children do love to shout "Whoopie!" when I make these cookies.

OATMEAL WHOOPIE PIE COOKIES

Makes 24 whoopie pies

It would be a real treat when we came home from school to discover Mom had made whoopie pies. After most people prepare them, they then wrap the cookies in plastic individually. This keeps them fresher and makes them easier to hand out to family and friends for lunches or as treats.

COOKIES

¾ cup (1½ sticks) butter, softened

2 cups packed brown sugar

2 large eggs

½ teaspoon salt

2 cups all-purpose flour

1 teaspoon baking powder

1 teaspoon ground cinnamon

2 cups quick-cooking rolled oats

2 teaspoons baking soda

3 tablespoons boiling water

FILLING

1 large egg white

1 tablespoon vanilla extract

2 tablespoons milk

2 cups powdered sugar

¼ cup shortening, softened

Preheat the oven to 425°F. Lightly grease a baking sheet and set aside.

Make the cookies: Cream the butter, sugar, and eggs in a large bowl. In a separate bowl, sift together the salt, flour, and baking powder. Add to the creamed mixture. Add the cinnamon and oats. Mix well. In a small dish, add the baking soda to the boiling water, and then stir the mixture into the rest of the batter. Mix well.

Drop by the tablespoon onto the baking sheets about 2 inches apart and bake until the cookies are firm and just starting to turn golden around the edges, 10 to 15 minutes. Cool the cookies on a wire rack or a plate.

Make the filling: Combine the egg white, vanilla, milk, and 1 cup of the powdered sugar. Cream well. Add the remaining 1 cup of sugar and the shortening and beat until smooth. Spread 1 tablespoon of filling (more if desired) on one cookie, and then top with a second cookie.

Wrap each whoopie pie cookie in plastic wrap and then put into sealed containers. These cookies will stay fresh for up to 5 days.

APPLE COOKIES

Makes 4 dozen cookies

While I was growing up we had three apple trees in our front yard. My dad would always keep the trees pruned. And instead of spraying the trees for bugs, he would combine equal amounts of lime, wood ash, and Epsom salts to put around the trunks of the trees. This mixture would keep bugs off the apples in an organic way with no spray. We like to make cookies like this with organically grown apples.

¾ cup shortening, softened

1½ cups packed brown sugar

3 large eggs

1 teaspoon vanilla extract

2⅔ cups all-purpose flour

½ teaspoon salt

¾ teaspoon baking powder

¾ teaspoon baking soda

¾ teaspoon ground cinnamon

1½ cups quick-cooking rolled oats

2 medium McIntosh apples, peeled and chopped

¾ cup raisins

⅔ cup walnuts

Preheat the oven to 350°F. Grease baking sheets and set aside.

In a large bowl, cream together the shortening and brown sugar. Then add the eggs and vanilla and beat the mixture until it's fluffy. Sift together 2 cups of the flour, the salt, baking powder, baking soda, and cinnamon. Add the sifted ingredients and the oats to the creamed mixture. Blend well.

In a separate bowl, stir together the remaining ⅔ cup flour, apples, raisins, and walnuts. Fold this mixture in with the rest of the batter. Drop by the teaspoon 2 inches apart onto the prepared baking sheets. Bake until the edges are golden, about 12 minutes.

Cool the cookies on a wire rack or a plate and then put into sealed containers. These cookies will stay fresh for up to 5 days.

PINEAPPLE COOKIES

Makes 3 dozen cookies

My children enjoy the taste of pineapple, either by itself or when it's baked into something like these cookies. Mom would always have some pineapple on hand. Pineapple was first used a lot in different salads, but Amish bakers have found use for the fruit in a lot of different dishes, including breads and cookies.

1 cup packed brown sugar

1 cup granulated sugar

2 large eggs

1 cup crushed pineapple, drained

1 teaspoon salt

3 teaspoons baking soda

1 teaspoon baking powder

4 cups all-purpose flour

Preheat the oven to 350°F.

In a large bowl, combine all of the ingredients together until smooth. Drop by the tablespoon 2 inches apart onto ungreased baking sheets and bake until the edges are golden brown, 15 to 20 minutes.

Cool the cookies on a wire rack or a plate and then put into sealed containers. These cookies will stay fresh for up to 3 days.

FROSTED RHUBARB COOKIES

Makes 4 dozen cookies

This is a soft cookie with a subtle rhubarb flavor. It goes great with a cup of afternoon coffee. Rhubarb is commonly used in cakes and pies in Amish settlements across the United States. Rhubarb cookies are a little less common, but no less delicious.

1 cup (2 sticks) butter or shortening

1½ cups firmly packed light brown sugar

2 large eggs, beaten

3 cups all-purpose flour

1 teaspoon baking soda

½ teaspoon salt

¾ cup flaked sweetened coconut

1½ cups diced fresh rhubarb

FROSTING

3 ounces cream cheese, softened

1 tablespoon butter, softened

1 tablespoon vanilla extract

1½ cups powdered sugar

Preheat the oven to 350°F.

In a medium mixing bowl, cream the butter and brown sugar until smooth. Add the eggs one at a time, stirring until well combined. In another large bowl, sift together the flour, baking soda, and salt. Add this mixture to the batter, and beat until smooth. Fold in the coconut and rhubarb until the ingredients are evenly combined.

Drop the batter by tablespoons onto an ungreased baking sheet. Bake until lightly browned, 12 to 13 minutes. Using a spatula, remove the cookies one by one from the cookie sheet and place on a wire rack to cool completely.

Make the frosting: In a small bowl, beat together the cream cheese, butter, and vanilla until smooth. Gradually add the powdered sugar until the frosting has the consistency that you prefer. Frost the cookies.

PUMPKIN COOKIES

Makes 2 dozen cookies

Pumpkin cookies are a favorite snack to prepare for the gathering after church. They look almost like a sugar cookie but are the brownish color of pumpkin. This is a soft cookie that tastes very good with icing. The kids really like them.

1 cup vegetable shortening

2 cups sugar

4 cups all-purpose flour

2 teaspoons baking soda

2 teaspoons baking powder

2 teaspoons ground cinnamon

½ teaspoon salt

2 cups homemade pumpkin puree, or
   1 (15-ounce) can pumpkin puree

2 eggs, beaten

1 cup chocolate chips

½ cup milk

2 tablespoons butter

½ cup packed brown sugar

¾ teaspoon vanilla extract

½ cup powdered sugar

Preheat the oven to 350°F. Grease two baking sheets.

Combine the shortening and sugar in a large bowl and stir until smooth. Combine the flour, baking soda, baking powder, cinnamon, and salt in a medium bowl. Stir with a whisk to blend. Stir the dry ingredients into the wet ingredients, then stir in the pumpkin and eggs until smooth. Stir in the chocolate chips. Drop by the teaspoonful 2 inches apart on the prepared sheets. Bake until the cookies become firm and the edges begin to brown, about 8 to 10 minutes. Remove from the oven and let cool on the pans for 5 minutes. Transfer the cookies to wire racks to cool completely.

Make the icing: Combine the milk, butter, brown sugar, and vanilla in a small saucepan. Stir over low heat until the sugar is dissolved and the butter is melted. Remove from the heat and let cool completely. Stir in the powdered sugar. Spread the icing on the cookies and let stand until the icing is set.

DOUBLE-TREAT COOKIES

Makes 8 dozen cookies

In some Amish communities these are known as "Triple-Treat Cookies" because bakers add butterscotch chips to them. The treats in this cookie are peanuts and chocolate chips, but you can add a "triple" to this recipe with another sweet tidbit of your choosing.

2 cups all-purpose flour

2 teaspoons baking soda

¼ teaspoon salt

1 cup shortening, softened

1 cup granulated sugar, plus more for shaping

1 cup packed brown sugar

2 large eggs

1 teaspoon vanilla extract

1 cup creamy peanut butter

1 cup chopped salted peanuts

1 (6-ounce package) semisweet chocolate chips

Preheat the oven to 350°F.

In a medium bowl, sift together the flour, baking soda, and salt. In a large bowl, beat together the shortening, sugars, eggs, and vanilla until fluffy. Blend in the peanut butter, and then add the dry ingredients. Stir in the peanuts and chocolate chips. Shape into small balls (about 1⅓ inches in diameter) and place 3 inches apart on ungreased baking sheets. Flatten with a glass dipped in granulated sugar and bake them until browned, about 8 minutes. Let the cookies cool on the baking sheet before transferring to a plate.

Cool the cookies on a wire rack or a plate and then put into sealed containers. These cookies will stay fresh for up to 5 days.

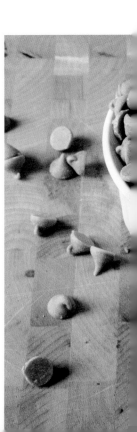

CRYBABY COOKIES

Makes about 3 dozen cookies

Joe and I both like to drink coffee on occasion, although we try not to drink too much of it. Sometimes you wonder what to do with leftover coffee. I never like to just throw anything away. If you have leftover coffee, then this is a good recipe to use it up. These cookies have a good coffee flavor. I'm not sure why they are called "crybabies," but it's a funny name.

¾ cup shortening, softened

1 cup sugar

2 large eggs, beaten

1 cup molasses

4 cups all-purpose flour

¾ cup strong cold coffee

1 teaspoon salt

1 teaspoon baking soda

2 teaspoons ground cinnamon

2 teaspoons ground ginger

½ teaspoon ground cloves

Preheat the oven to 350°F. Grease baking sheets.

In a large bowl, mix all of the ingredients together until the dough forms a very thick batter. (This does not lend itself well to an electric mixer because it is so thick.) Stir this vigorously with a wooden spoon. Use the spoon to mash the mixture against the side of the bowl if there are any bits of shortening not dissolved into the batter. Then resume stirring until all is mixed evenly. Drop by the teaspoon 2 inches apart onto the baking sheets. Bake until the edges are firm and slightly darker than the rest of the cookie, 10 to 15 minutes.

Cool the cookies on a wire rack or a plate and then put into sealed containers. These cookies will stay fresh for up to 3 days.

SOUR CREAM CUTOUT COOKIES

Makes about 18 cookies, depending on shapes

This is an easy cookie the kids like to cut out and decorate. It takes a lot longer when they help, but they enjoy it. Sometimes I have to watch the younger children, as they like to eat the dough. But with the raw eggs in there, I don't let them.

1 cup (2 sticks) butter, softened	FROSTING
1½ cups sugar	⅓ cup shortening
3 large eggs, beaten	1 teaspoon vanilla
1 cup sour cream	4 cups powdered sugar
2 tablespoons vanilla extract	½ cup milk
3½ to 4 cups all-purpose flour	Food coloring (optional)
2 teaspoons baking powder	Colored sprinkles, for decorating (optional)
1 teaspoon baking soda	Chocolate chips, for decorating (optional)

Preheat the oven to 350°F. Lightly grease a baking sheet.

Cream the butter and sugar together in a large bowl. Stir in the eggs, sour cream, and vanilla. Combine the flour, baking powder, and baking soda in a medium bowl and stir with a whisk to blend. Add the dry ingredients to the wet ingredients and stir until a soft, firm dough is formed. Roll the dough out to a ½-inch thickness on a floured surface. Use your favorite shaped cookie cutters to cut out the dough. Place the shapes on the prepared pan.

Bake until golden brown around the edges, about 10 minutes. Remove from the oven and let cool on the pan for 5 minutes, then transfer to wire racks to cool completely.

Make the frosting: Cream the shortening with the vanilla and 1 cup of the powdered sugar. Gradually add the milk and the rest of the powdered sugar, beating constantly. More powdered sugar can be added to give you your desired thickness. Food coloring can also be added if you like. Spread the frosting on the cookies and decorate with colored sprinkles or chocolate chips, if you like. Let the frosting set before storing.

MONSTER COOKIES

Makes 6 dozen cookies

My children like these cookies because of the M&Ms. If these are in the pan when cookies are passed around at church, the children will grab these first because they see the M&Ms. Mom would make these sometimes, not too often, because it was difficult to keep the M&Ms on hand.

1 cup (2 sticks) butter, softened

1 cup granulated sugar

1 cup packed brown sugar

3 large eggs

½ teaspoon vanilla extract

½ teaspoon corn syrup

2 teaspoons baking soda

1½ cups creamy peanut butter

4½ cups quick-cooking rolled oats

2 cups chocolate chips

2 cups plain M&Ms

Preheat the oven to 350°F.

In a large bowl, cream the butter and sugars. Add the eggs, one at a time and mixing between each addition, and the vanilla, corn syrup, baking soda, and peanut butter. Mix well until smooth. Add the oats and mix well, scraping the sides of the bowl. Add the chocolate chips and mix until they are evenly distributed throughout the batter. Then add the M&Ms and mix well.

Drop the batter by the tablespoon 2 inches apart onto ungreased baking sheets. Bake until the edges are golden brown, 10 to 12 minutes. Let cool on baking sheets for about 3 minutes before transferring to cooling racks.

Cool the cookies on a wire rack or a plate and then put into sealed containers. These cookies will stay fresh for up to 5 days.

BASIC BROWNIES

Makes 2 dozen brownies

This is another great recipe to use to teach children to bake. The ingredients are simple ones and the batter takes just a few minutes to mix. The result is a sweet and chewy chocolate brownie, the type of snack that doesn't last very long around here!

1½ cups all-purpose flour

2 cups sugar

½ cup unsweetened cocoa powder

½ teaspoon salt

1 cup vegetable oil

4 large eggs

2 teaspoons vanilla extract

½ cup chopped walnuts (optional)

Preheat the oven to 350°F. Grease a 9 by 13-inch pan.

In a large bowl, combine all the ingredients. Stir vigorously for about 3 minutes, until the batter is well blended and creamy. Pour into the prepared pan. Bake until a knife inserted into the center comes out clean, about 30 minutes.

Store the brownies in a sealed container or cake safe, if you have one. These will stay fresh for 3 to 4 days.

CHOCOLATE CHIP OATMEAL BROWNIES

Makes 2 dozen brownies

This is a favorite of the children's. It makes a great after-school snack with a cold glass of milk! This is also a fun recipe to experiment with by using peanut butter or butterscotch chips instead of chocolate chips.

1 cup (2 sticks) butter, softened

$\frac{2}{3}$ cup granulated sugar

$\frac{2}{3}$ cup packed dark brown sugar

2 large eggs

$\frac{1}{2}$ teaspoon vanilla extract

1 cup all-purpose flour

1 teaspoon baking powder

$\frac{1}{4}$ teaspoon ground nutmeg

1 teaspoon ground cinnamon

2 cups quick-cooking rolled oats

2 cups semisweet chocolate chips

Preheat the oven to 350°F. Lightly grease a 9 by 13-inch pan and set aside.

In a large bowl, beat the butter, sugars, and eggs until fluffy. Stir in the vanilla. Then blend in the flour, baking powder, nutmeg, cinnamon, and oats with a wooden spoon. Blend in 1 cup of the chocolate chips. The batter will be thick. Electric mixers are not recommended for mixing the batter. Once the mixture is well blended, spread with a spoon into the prepared pan. Sprinkle the top with the remaining 1 cup of chocolate chips. Bake until a butter knife inserted in the center comes out clean, about 30 minutes.

Store the brownies in a sealed container or cake safe. These will stay fresh for 3 to 4 days.

COOKIE DOUGH BROWNIES

Makes 2 dozen brownies

The children like this dessert because, as you can tell by the name, it tastes like cookie dough, but it's a brownie. So it is sort of like having two desserts in one because it is as close to cookie dough as I'll let my children eat. I don't let them eat uncooked cookie dough because it often contains raw eggs.

BROWNIES

2 cups granulated sugar

½ cup unsweetened cocoa powder

1½ cups all-purpose flour

½ teaspoon salt

1 cup vegetable oil

4 large eggs

2 teaspoons vanilla extract

½ cup chopped walnuts (optional)

FILLING

½ cup (1 stick) butter, softened

½ cup packed brown sugar

¼ cup granulated sugar

2 tablespoons milk

1 teaspoon vanilla extract

1 cup all-purpose flour

GLAZE

1 cup chocolate chips

1 tablespoon shortening

¾ cup chopped walnuts (optional)

Preheat the oven to 350°F. Grease a 9 by 13-inch baking pan.

Make the brownies: In a bowl, combine the sugar, cocoa, flour, and salt. Add the oil, eggs, and vanilla. Combine the ingredients until well blended. Stir in walnuts if desired. Spread into the prepared pan. Bake until a toothpick inserted in the center comes out clean, about 30 minutes. Let the brownies cool while preparing the filling.

Make the filling: Cream the butter and sugars together, and then add the milk and vanilla. Stir in the flour until the filling resembles cookie dough. Spread the filling evenly over the entire pan of cooled brownies. Place in the refrigerator for 15 to 20 minutes, or until firm to the touch. While the brownies are refrigerated, prepare the glaze.

Make the glaze: In a small saucepan, melt the chocolate chips and shortening over low heat. Quickly spread the glaze over the filling, as the filling will soften from the heat of the glaze. Sprinkle and press the walnuts on top, if using. Place the brownies back in the refrigerator until the glaze has set up.

Store the brownies in a sealed container or cake safe. These will stay fresh for 3 to 4 days.

BUTTERSCOTCH BROWNIES

Makes 20 brownies

Homemade butterscotch has been a favorite among the Amish for as long as I can remember. It's an economical and easy sweet treat to make. It's a good alternative to using chocolate in a dessert.

4 tablespoons (½ stick) butter

1 cup packed brown sugar

1 large egg, beaten

1 teaspoon vanilla extract

1 cup all-purpose flour

½ teaspoon salt

1 teaspoon baking powder

½ cup walnuts, chopped

Powdered sugar for topping

Preheat the oven to 350°F. Grease a 9 by 13-inch pan and set aside.

In a medium saucepan, melt the butter over medium heat. Add the brown sugar and stir for 1 to 2 minutes, until it has a thick, peanut butter–like consistency. Remove from the heat, and then stir in the beaten egg and vanilla, followed by the flour, salt, and baking powder. Once combined, stir in the nuts. Spread the batter into the prepared pan and bake until the edges begin to brown and a toothpick inserted in the center comes out clean, 25 to 30 minutes. Cut into 2 by 2-inch squares while warm and sprinkle with powdered sugar. Store in an airtight container.

DELICIOUS PECAN BROWNIES

Makes 2 dozen brownies

Never use a glass pan for this recipe, because the brownies just seem to get too hard. But the brownies are delicious and chewy every time when I make these using a stainless steel or aluminum pan.

BROWNIES

1 cup (2 sticks) butter, softened

2 cups granulated sugar

4 large eggs

1 cup semisweet chocolate chips, melted

2 teaspoons vanilla extract

1 cup all-purpose flour

1 cup chopped pecans

FROSTING

3 cups powdered sugar

⅓ cup butter, softened

2 ounces semisweet chocolate chips, melted

3 to 4 tablespoons milk

1 teaspoon vanilla extract

Preheat the oven to 350°F. Grease a 9 by 13-inch pan.

Make the brownies: In a large bowl, cream the butter and sugar. Beat in the eggs until the mixture is smooth and creamy. Then blend in the melted chocolate and vanilla. Stir in the flour and nuts. Pour into the prepared pan. Bake for 30 minutes. Remove from the oven and allow the brownies to cool to room temperature.

Make the frosting: Mix the powdered sugar, butter, melted chocolate, milk, and vanilla until smooth and creamy. Apply the frosting to the cooled brownies with a butter knife or the back of a spoon.

Store the brownies in a sealed container or cake safe. These will stay fresh for 7 days.

BUTTERMILK BROWNIES

Makes 2 dozen brownies

This recipe provides another way to use leftover buttermilk. Buttermilk always makes baked goods taste very moist. This is more like a cake than a brownie.

2 cups sugar

2 cups all-purpose flour

¼ cup unsweetened cocoa powder

1 cup cold water

½ cup (1 stick) butter, softened

½ cup vegetable oil

½ cup buttermilk

1 teaspoon baking soda

2 large eggs

1 teaspoon vanilla extract

Dash of salt

Preheat the oven to 400°F. Lightly grease a 9 by 13-inch pan.

In a large bowl, sift together the sugar, flour, and cocoa. In a small saucepan, bring the water, butter, and oil to a boil over low heat. Remove from the heat after the mixture has boiled for 1 full minute. Pour the hot mixture over the dry ingredients and beat until smooth and creamy. Add the buttermilk, baking soda, eggs, vanilla, and salt. Stir thoroughly. Spoon the mixture into the prepared pan and bake until a butter knife inserted in the center comes out clean, about 20 minutes.

Store the brownies in a sealed container or cake safe, if you have one. These will stay fresh for 3 to 4 days.

CHOCOLATE CHIP BARS

Makes 20 bars

These are good with or without icing. My daughter Elizabeth likes to make these for her brothers and sisters.

$\frac{1}{2}$ teaspoon salt

$\frac{1}{2}$ teaspoon baking soda

1 cup packed brown sugar

1 large egg

$\frac{1}{2}$ cup shortening, softened

1 teaspoon vinegar

$\frac{1}{2}$ cup sour milk

1 teaspoon vanilla extract

$1\frac{3}{4}$ cups all-purpose flour

1 cup chocolate chips

Preheat the oven to 350°F. Grease a 10 by 15-inch baking sheet.

Mix the salt, baking soda, brown sugar, egg, shortening, vinegar, sour milk, and vanilla in a large bowl. Then stir in the flour, followed by the chocolate chips. Spread the batter evenly into the prepared pan. Bake until the edges are golden brown and the chips are melted, 20 minutes. Let cool, and then cut into bars.

Store the bars in a sealed container or cake safe. These will stay fresh for 3 to 4 days.

HONEY BARS

Makes 2 dozen bars

Some Amish keep bees so that they can make and sell their own honey. Pure homemade honey tastes delicious. I often use honey in place of molasses in recipes because we prefer the taste. This bar is delicious and has a rich taste of honey.

1 cup granulated sugar

2 cups all-purpose flour

1 teaspoon baking soda

1¼ teaspoons ground cinnamon

1 large egg, lightly beaten

¾ cup vegetable oil

¼ cup honey

1 cup walnuts, chopped

GLAZE

1 cup powdered sugar

1 teaspoon vanilla extract

1 tablespoon water

2 tablespoons mayonnaise

Preheat the oven to 350°F.

In a large bowl, stir the sugar, flour, baking soda, and cinnamon until evenly mixed. Then add in the egg, vegetable oil, honey, and nuts. Stir until the mixture is smooth. Spoon into an ungreased jelly-roll pan or a 9 by 13-inch pan. Bake until a toothpick inserted in the center comes out clean, about 20 minutes.

Make the glaze: In a small bowl, stir together the powdered sugar, vanilla, water, and mayonnaise until smooth and creamy. Spread onto the honey bars while they are still warm.

Store the bars in a sealed container or cake safe. These will stay fresh for 3 to 4 days.

PECAN PIE BARS

Makes 20 bars

These were always a favorite of mine when they were served after church. The bars will keep well for several days.

CRUST

2 cups all-purpose flour

1 cup packed brown sugar

1 cup butter, softened

FILLING

5 large eggs

1 cup light corn syrup

1 cup packed brown sugar

¾ cup granulated sugar

Dash of salt

1 teaspoon vanilla extract

1 cup pecan pieces

Preheat the oven to 350°F. Lightly grease a 9 by 13-inch pan and set aside.

Make the crust: In a large bowl, combine the flour and brown sugar. Dice the butter into little cubes and cut it into the flour mixture. Using your fingertips, blend until the mixture resembles coarse crumbs. Do not use an electric mixer. Press the flour mixture into the prepared pan and bake for 10 minutes.

Make the filling: While the crust is baking, combine the eggs, corn syrup, sugars, salt, and vanilla in a large bowl. Blend well until the mixture is the color of butterscotch. Stir in the pecan pieces. Remove the crust from the oven and pour the filling over the hot crust. Lower the oven temperature to 275°F and bake until the center is set, about 50 minutes. Cool in the pan or on a wire rack before cutting into bars.

Store the bars in a sealed container or cake safe. These will stay fresh for 3 to 4 days.

DELICIOUS PEANUT BUTTER SWIRL BARS

Makes 2 dozen bars

These bars are very pretty with their dark chocolate swirls throughout. The dessert is a sweet treat to add to any lunch-bucket meal!

1 cup creamy peanut butter

⅔ cup butter, softened

1½ cups packed brown sugar

1½ cups granulated sugar

4 large eggs

4 teaspoons vanilla extract

2 cups all-purpose flour

2 teaspoons baking powder

½ teaspoon salt

1 (12-ounce) package semisweet chocolate chips

Preheat the oven to 325°F. Grease a 9 by 13-inch pan and set aside.

In a large bowl, cream together the peanut butter, butter, and sugars until well blended and smooth. Make sure any lumps of brown sugar are dissolved. Then add the eggs and vanilla. Mix until smooth and creamy and thoroughly blended. Add the flour, baking powder, and salt. Mix thoroughly until the batter is once again smooth and creamy. Spoon the batter into the prepared pan. Sprinkle the chocolate chips over the batter and put into the oven for 5 minutes.

Remove from the oven and, using a butter knife, swirl the chocolate chips through the dough. Return to the oven and bake until a butter knife inserted into the center comes out clean (some chocolate may stick to the knife), about 40 minutes. Let cool for 1 hour and cut into bars.

Store the bars in a sealed container or cake safe. These will stay fresh for 3 to 4 days.

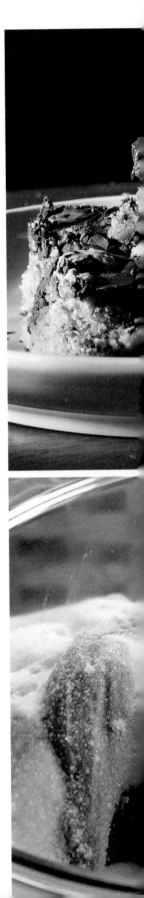

10-MINUTE COOKIE BARS

Makes 2 dozen bars

This is another good teaching recipe. Children as young as seven or eight can easily mix up the batter and frosting for this recipe. It's good to start giving them experience baking at an early age.

BROWNIES

1 cup packed brown sugar

4 cups quick-cooking rolled oats

1 cup (2 sticks) butter, softened

FROSTING

1 cup chocolate chips

½ cup creamy peanut butter

Preheat the oven to 400°F.

Make the brownies: Combine the brown sugar and oats in a large bowl. Melt the butter in a small saucepan, then pour into a large bowl. Pour over the brown sugar and oats, and mix well. Press the mixture into an ungreased 9 by 13 by 2-inch baking pan. Bake for 10 minutes.

Make the frosting: Melt the chocolate chips and peanut butter together in a saucepan. Spread the frosting over the baked layer and chill.

Store the bars in a sealed container or cake safe. These will stay fresh for 3 to 4 days.

AFTER-SCHOOL NO-BAKE CHOCOLATE–PEANUT BUTTER CORNFLAKE BARS

Makes 16 to 20 bars

My mother chose this age-appropriate, kid-friendly recipe to accompany her first column. This is a delicious, easy bar for kids to make!

½ cup sugar

½ cup light corn syrup

5 tablespoons cocoa powder

1 cup creamy peanut butter

5 cups cornflakes

Lightly grease a 9 by 13-inch pan and set aside.

In a small saucepan, combine the sugar, corn syrup, and cocoa powder. Heat over medium heat, stirring frequently, until the mixture reaches a boil. Immediately remove it from the heat. Add the peanut butter and stir until the mixture is very smooth.

Put the cornflakes in a large bowl. Pour the peanut butter mixture over the cornflakes and stir until evenly coated. Transfer the cookie mixture to the prepared pan and spread evenly. After the mixture has cooled completely, use a knife to cut it into bars.

APPLE BARS

Makes 25 to 30 bars

My sister Susan likes to make these apple bars. These are almost like brownies, and are always a hit. You can see the little apple pieces on the top, and they taste really good warmed.

3 large eggs

1 cup vegetable oil

1¾ cups sugar

2 cups all-purpose flour

1 teaspoon baking soda

½ teaspoon salt

½ teaspoon ground cinnamon

2 cups peeled, cored, and chopped apples

1 cup walnuts, chopped

Preheat the oven to 350°F. Grease a 9 by 13-inch baking pan.

Beat the eggs, oil, and sugar together in a large bowl. In a medium bowl, combine the flour, baking soda, salt, and cinnamon. Stir with a whisk to blend. Stir the dry ingredients into the wet ingredients until blended. Stir in the apples and walnuts. Pour into the prepared pan and smooth the top. Bake until firmly set, like a brownie, 35 to 40 minutes. Remove from the oven and let cool. Cut into bars.

RHUBARB DREAM BARS

Makes 15 bars

The sugar in this recipe takes the tartness out of the rhubarb, so even people who don't usually like it usually like this!

CRUST

1½ cups all-purpose flour

⅔ cup powdered sugar

¼ cup margarine or butter, softened

FILLING

3 large eggs, beaten

2 cups sugar

½ cup all-purpose flour

½ teaspoon salt

3 cups chopped rhubarb

Preheat the oven to 350°F. Butter the bottom and sides of a 9 by 13-inch cake pan.

Make the crust: In a medium bowl, mix the flour, sugar, and margarine until the mixture resembles coarse crumbs. Press evenly across the bottom of the cake pan. Bake for 15 minutes. Remove from the oven, leaving the oven on, and let stand while making the filling.

Make the filling: Combine the eggs, sugar, flour, and salt in a medium bowl. Stir to make a batter. Stir in the rhubarb until incorporated. Pour into the crust. Bake until the bars are firm when you shake the pan a little, about 35 minutes. Remove from the oven and let stand until completely cool. Cut into bars to serve.

ZUCCHINI BARS

Makes 40 bars

This is a favorite in some Amish homes around here. Our children like brownies or any kind of bars, so these seem to go over well in our home!

2½ cups all-purpose flour

1 cup whole wheat flour

2 teaspoons baking soda

1½ teaspoons salt

2 teaspoons ground cinnamon

2 cups sugar

1 cup vegetable oil

4 eggs, beaten

⅔ cup water

2 cups peeled and grated zucchini

1 (12-ounce) package chocolate chips

1 (12-ounce) package butterscotch chips

1 cup chopped walnuts (optional)

Preheat the oven to 350°F. Grease two 9 by 13-inch baking pans or one 12 by 17-inch baking pan.

Combine the flours, baking soda, salt, cinnamon, and sugar in a large bowl and stir with a whisk to blend. Add the oil, eggs, and water and stir until smooth. Stir in all the remaining ingredients. Stir for about 5 minutes, until everything is very evenly blended. Then pour the batter into the prepared pan(s). Bake for 35 minutes, or until firm. Remove from the oven, let cool, and cut into squares.

HALFWAY BARS

Makes 2 dozen bars

I still remember the first time I made these. I was helping out at my brother Amos's house when they were remodeling. There was a crew there working on their house. My sister-in-law had me mix this recipe together, and I really liked them. I asked her if I could have the recipe, and now we really make these a lot. They are halfway between a bar and a cookie, which is how they got their name. They taste a bit like a cookie, but you cut them like bars. I made these several times when we had the crew working on our house, too; they were something warm to take out to the guys when they were working. They thought it was a real treat.

1 cup (2 sticks) butter, softened	2 egg yolks
½ cup packed brown sugar	1 teaspoon water
½ cup granulated sugar	2½ cups all-purpose flour
1 teaspoon vanilla extract	1 cup chocolate chips
¼ teaspoon salt	GLAZE
¼ teaspoon baking soda	2 egg whites
1 teaspoon baking powder	1 cup brown sugar

Preheat the oven to 350°F. Grease a 9 by 13-inch baking pan.

In a small saucepan, melt the butter. Pour the melted butter into a large bowl. Add the sugars, vanilla, salt, baking soda, baking powder, egg yolks, water, and flour to form a stiff dough. Spread the dough into the prepared baking pan. Spread the chocolate chips evenly over the dough.

Make the glaze: In a small bowl, beat the egg whites into the brown sugar. Pour the glaze over the bars. Bake until a toothpick inserted in the center comes out clean, about 35 minutes.

Store the bars in a sealed container or cake safe. These will stay fresh for 3 to 4 days.

SUSAN'S CARROT BARS

Makes 20 bars

The children enjoy eating carrots just as a snack, but this is another way to get them to eat and enjoy them. You can use any kind of frosting that you like for these, but I like to use a cream cheese icing. My daughter Susan especially enjoys preparing these bars.

1 cup sugar

¾ cup vegetable oil

2 eggs, beaten

1 cup all-purpose flour

1 teaspoon baking soda

1 teaspoon ground cinnamon

½ teaspoon salt

1 cup shredded carrots

½ cup walnuts (optional)

FROSTING

(use Carrot Cake frosting, page 364)

Preheat the oven to 350°F. Grease a 9 by 13-inch baking pan.

Stir the sugar, oil, and eggs together in a large bowl until blended. Combine the flour, baking soda, cinnamon, and salt in a medium bowl and stir with a whisk to blend. Add the dry ingredients to the wet ingredients and stir to blend. Add the carrots and nuts and stir until you have a smooth batter.

Pour the batter into the prepared pan and smooth the top. Bake until a toothpick inserted in the center of the cake comes out clean, 35 to 40 minutes. Frost.

OATMEAL BARS

Makes 2 dozen bars

I always have quick-cooking oatmeal in my pantry, and it is just so handy for making a quick snack for the children. Oatmeal can be used for cookies, bars, and cakes in a pinch. This is a surprisingly chewy and moist snack.

1¼ cups boiling water

1 cup quick-cooking rolled oats

½ cup (1 stick) butter, softened

1 cup granulated sugar

2 large eggs

1½ cups all-purpose flour

1 teaspoon baking soda

½ teaspoon salt

1 teaspoon vanilla extract

ICING

6 tablespoons butter

1 cup packed brown sugar

¼ cup milk or cream

1 cup powdered sugar

Preheat the oven to 350°F.

In a medium bowl, pour the boiling water over the oats and butter. Let set until room temperature. In a large bowl, cream together the sugar, eggs, flour, baking soda, salt, and vanilla. Add the oat mixture and stir to blend. Pour the mixture onto a 10 by 15-inch baking sheet. Bake until browned, 20 to 30 minutes. Let cool before frosting.

Make the icing: In a small saucepan, bring the butter, brown sugar, and milk to a boil over low heat. Let boil for 2 minutes, and then remove from the heat. Add the powdered sugar and stir to blend and dissolve. Spread the icing over the cooled bars.

Store the bars in a sealed container or cake safe. These will stay fresh for 3 to 4 days.

GROWING RHUBARB

If you want to start your own rhubarb patch, plant the rhubarb one year and then don't touch it until the second year, no matter how good the stalks look. You don't use newly planted rhubarb for a year so the plants have time to develop strong roots. This is key to having a healthy patch that comes back year after year. I plant my rhubarb in full sun, because the plants do not do as well, or grow as abundantly, in the shade. Rhubarb grown right is always one of the first goodies ready to be harvested in the spring, and will continue to produce throughout the season.

RHUBARB SQUARES

Makes 2 dozen squares

Rhubarb finds its way into so many baked goods. It just adds a nice, tart taste to everything. Mom baked with her homegrown rhubarb often, and she never had trouble growing rhubarb.

FILLING

4 cups rhubarb cut into ¼–inch pieces

2 cups water

1 cup granulated sugar

3 tablespoons cornstarch

½ teaspoon almond extract

CRUST

¾ cup shortening, softened

1 cup packed brown sugar

1 teaspoon baking soda

1 teaspoon vanilla extract

1 cup all-purpose flour

1 cup quick-cooking rolled oats

1 teaspoon ground cinnamon

Preheat the oven to 350°F. Lightly grease a 9 by 13-inch pan and set aside.

Make the filling: In a medium saucepan over low heat, cook the rhubarb, water, and sugar until bubbling. Then add the cornstarch and stir until the cornstarch is mixed throughout and the mixture has thickened. Add the almond flavoring and stir. Keep on the stove over low heat.

Make the crust: In a large bowl, combine the shortening, sugar, baking soda, vanilla, flour, oats, and cinnamon until the mixture forms coarse crumbs. Take half of the crumbs and pat them into the bottom of the prepared pan. Remove the filling from the heat and pour over the bottom crust, spreading it evenly. Then crumble the remaining half of the crumbs evenly over the filling. Bake until the crust is golden and a toothpick inserted in the center comes out clean, about 40 minutes.

Store the brownies in a sealed container or cake safe. These will stay fresh for 3 to 4 days.

TOFFEE NUT BARS

Makes 2 dozen bars

This is a favorite dessert because it's a sweet treat that is a change from choco-late. Before chocolate became popular among the Amish, desserts like this one (and also desserts with molasses) were more common.

CRUST

½ cup (1 stick) butter, softened

½ cup packed brown sugar

1 cup all-purpose flour

TOPPING

2 large eggs

1 cup packed brown sugar

1 teaspoon vanilla extract

2 tablespoons all-purpose flour

1 teaspoon baking powder

½ teaspoon salt

1 cup shredded coconut, unsweetened

1 cup almonds, slivered

Preheat the oven to 350°F.

Make the crust: In a small bowl, stir together the butter, brown sugar, and flour until the ingredients are evenly mixed. Press and flatten by hand into the bottom of an ungreased 9 by 13-inch pan. Bake for 10 to 12 minutes, checking for firmness at 10 minutes.

Make the topping: While the crust is baking, in a large bowl, beat the eggs and then stir in the brown sugar, vanilla, flour, baking powder, salt, coconut, and almonds. Remove the crust from the oven and spread the topping evenly over the crust. Be careful not to tear the crust. Return to the oven and bake until the topping is golden brown, 23 to 25 minutes. Watch carefully, as the top will easily burn. Cut while warm.

Store the bars in a sealed container or cake safe. These will stay fresh for 3 to 4 days.

LEMON SQUARES

Makes 16 squares

Lemon makes for a nice, light dessert during the summer months. Sometimes after an exhausting day's work outside, a snack sounds good, but not something heavy like pound cake or cookies. These lemon squares with their light, fluffy filling are a great treat!

CRUST

1¼ cups powdered sugar

Pinch of salt

½ cup all-purpose flour

½ cup (1 stick) plus 1 tablespoon butter
   or margarine

FILLING

1 cup granulated sugar

¼ cup fresh lemon juice

½ teaspoon baking powder

2 large eggs, slightly beaten

GLAZE

¾ cup powdered sugar, sifted

2 tablespoons fresh lemon juice

1 tablespoon butter, melted

Preheat the oven to 350°F. Line an 8 by 8-inch cake pan with parchment paper. Make sure an inch of paper overlaps the edges so that the bars can be lifted out when they are done.

Make the crust: In a large bowl, combine the sugar, salt, flour, and butter together until dry, coarse crumbs form. Press firmly into the prepared pan. Bake for 15 minutes. Let cool for a few minutes before adding the filling.

Make the filling: Whisk together the sugar, lemon juice, baking powder, and eggs in a bowl until the sugar has completely dissolved. Pour over the crust. Bake until the filling is nearly set but still jiggles a little, 25 to 30 minutes. Let cool completely.

Make the glaze: In a small bowl, mix the powdered sugar, lemon juice, and butter until evenly blended. Pour over the cooled filling. Let set until room temperature. Lift from the pan and cut into bars.

Store the squares in a sealed container or cake safe. These will stay fresh for 3 to 4 days.

FROSTY STRAWBERRY SQUARES

Makes 10 to 12 squares

Scorching summer days call for cool, refreshing desserts. With our bountiful crop of fresh strawberries, this frozen dessert becomes a seasonal favorite in the Eicher household.

2 egg whites	2 cups fresh strawberries, crushed
1 cup sugar	1 cup whipping cream

In a large bowl, combine the egg whites and the sugar. Beat with a whisk about 10 minutes, or until the mixture has tripled in size. Gently stir the crushed strawberries into the beaten egg mixture. In a separate bowl, beat the whipping cream until stiff peaks form. Carefully fold the whipped cream into the strawberry mixture until well blended. Pour into a 9 by 13-inch rectangular cake pan. Freeze until firm, at least 6 hours. Cut into squares and serve.

FRUIT-FILLED OATMEAL SQUARES

Makes 2 dozen squares

I like to use homemade pie filling for this recipe, but you can use store-bought, too. You can experiment with this recipe using whatever fruit filling you choose.

½ cup (1 stick) butter, softened	1½ cups quick-cooking rolled oats
¼ cup all-purpose flour	1 (21-ounce) can apple pie filling
1 cup packed brown sugar	

Preheat the oven to 325°F.

In a large bowl, combine the butter, flour, brown sugar, and oats until mixed evenly and the texture resembles coarse crumbs. Press two-thirds of the mixture into an ungreased 9 by 9-inch pan. Pour the pie filling over the crumbs in the pan. Then sprinkle the remaining crumbs on top. Bake until the oatmeal topping begins to turn golden brown, about 25 minutes. Cool completely and cut into squares.

Store the squares in a sealed container or cake safe. These will stay fresh for 3 to 4 days.

RHUBARB COBBLER

Serves 6

This dish looks really nice when it is done and tastes great served with a scoop of ice cream! Try it with the Homemade Vanilla Ice Cream, page 386.

TOPPING

1 cup all-purpose flour

2 tablespoons sugar

1½ teaspoons baking powder

¼ teaspoon salt

¼ cup margarine or butter

¼ cup milk

1 large egg, lightly beaten

FILLING

1 cup sugar

2 tablespoons cornstarch

¼ teaspoon ground cinnamon

4 cups rhubarb, chopped into 1-inch pieces

1 tablespoon water

1 tablespoon margarine or butter

Preheat the oven to 400°F. Butter the bottom and sides of an 8 by 8-inch baking dish.

Make the topping: Whisk the flour, sugar, baking powder, and salt in a medium bowl to blend. Rub in the margarine using your fingertips or cut it in with a pastry cutter until the mixture resembles coarse crumbs. Add the milk and egg, stirring just until incorporated.

Make the filling: Whisk the sugar, cornstarch, and cinnamon together in a medium saucepan. Stir in the rhubarb and water. Cook, stirring constantly, over medium heat until the mixture boils. Cook and stir 1 minute more.

Pour the filling into the prepared baking dish. Dot with the margarine. Immediately spoon the topping on the filling in six small mounds. Bake until the topping is golden brown, 20 to 25 minutes. Remove from the oven and serve warm.

PUMPKIN ROLL

Serves 10

Powdered sugar, for dusting

3 eggs

1 cup sugar

1 teaspoon lemon juice

$\frac{2}{3}$ cup pumpkin

$\frac{3}{4}$ cup all-purpose flour

1 teaspoon baking powder

2 teaspoons cinnamon

$\frac{1}{2}$ teaspoon salt

$\frac{1}{2}$ teaspoon nutmeg

FILLING

8 ounces cream cheese, softened

2 cups powdered sugar

4 tablespoons butter, softened

$\frac{1}{2}$ teaspoon vanilla extract

Preheat the oven to 375°F.

Line a jelly-roll pan with waxed paper and set it aside. On a clean surface, lay out a clean, lint-free dish towel that is slightly larger than the jelly-roll pan. Sift powdered sugar over the surface of the towel.

In a large bowl, beat the eggs well. Then add the sugar, lemon juice, and pumpkin and beat well. Then add the flour, baking powder, cinnamon, salt, and nutmeg and beat well until smooth in consistency. Pour the pumpkin mixture into the waxed paper–lined jelly-roll pan and bake for 15 minutes, or until set. Remove the pan from the oven and, while it is still hot, flip it over onto the powdered sugar–covered dish towel. Peel off the waxed paper and roll the towel and cake together as if rolling up a jelly roll and place it in the refrigerator for 45 minutes to 1 hour, until the towel doesn't feel warm any longer.

Make the filling: While the pumpkin cake is chilling, beat together the cream cheese, powdered sugar, butter, and vanilla until smooth. When the pumpkin roll is cool, unroll it and remove the towel. Spread filling over the pumpkin cake, then roll it up and refrigerate at least an hour before slicing and serving.

POPCORN BALLS

Makes 12 to 18 popcorn balls

My mom always put red food coloring in these to make them pink for a festive touch. Most of the time we ate them so quickly that there weren't any leftovers to store. But if you have leftovers, you can do what Mom did and just put them in a plastic container.

1 cup sugar

¾ cup water

¼ teaspoon salt

¼ cup light corn syrup

½ teaspoon vanilla extract

½ teaspoon distilled white vinegar

10 cups popped corn (about ½ cup popcorn kernels)

Combine the sugar, water, salt, and syrup in a small saucepan. Bring to a boil over high heat and cook, stirring constantly, to the hard-ball stage, when the mixture forms a firm ball, at around 255°F on a candy thermometer. Add the vanilla and vinegar and continue cooking to the soft-crack stage, when the mixture begins to separate into firm but still flexible strings, at about 270°F on a candy thermometer.

Put the popcorn in a large bowl and pour the sugar mixture slowly over the popcorn. Stir well to coat every kernel. When the mixture has cooled enough to handle, press it into baseball-size balls with your buttered hands.

BUTTER TARTS

Makes approximately 20 tarts

Tarts are a quintessentially Canadian confection. Only recently have you been able to find these sweet treats on Amish menus south of the Canadian border—and it's for good reason they've migrated south. They're delicious! The texture and taste resemble pecan pie. When combined with a crisp crust, the soft filling and pastry make a wonderful contrast in textures. The recipe allows for additions such as raisins or coconut, but most enjoy butter tarts without those.

1 recipe Never-Fail Pastry (page 299)

4 large eggs

½ cup firmly packed brown sugar

2 cups dark corn syrup

2 teaspoons vanilla extract

1 teaspoon white vinegar

10 tablespoons butter, softened

2 cups raisins, walnuts, or coconut (optional)

Preheat the oven to 350°F. Lightly grease a standard muffin pan.

Roll out the pastry dough on a lightly floured surface to form a 12-inch-diameter circle. Use a glass to cut out rounds and place them into the muffin tin. Cut off any excess overhang.

In a large mixing bowl, combine the eggs, brown sugar, corn syrup, vanilla, vinegar, and butter until the mixture is creamy and thoroughly mixed.

Spoon the optional ingredients into the bottom of the unfilled crusts. Pour the combined mixture into the pastry crusts until three-quarters full. Bake until the crusts are golden and the filling is firm.

tip: brown sugar

To soften brown sugar that has hardened, put the sugar in a sealed container with a slice of bread. After a couple of hours, remove the bread and the sugar will be softened.

AN AMISH FAMILY CHRISTMAS

A visit to an Amish home around the holidays is notable because of what you *won't* see. There's no Christmas tree, no lights on the house, no hanging stockings or candles on the windowsill.

The absence of these typical holiday signs doesn't mean we aren't observing the occasion. Christ's birthday is—along with Easter—one of the most sacred events on the Amish religious calendar. We *are* busy with the holidays, but in our own quiet, more subdued way.

One of the few outward ways the Amish do cel-ebrate the season is with food. A whole host of special goodies make its way onto menus only at Christmas: rich fudges, peanut brittle, handmade candies, and iced cookies in holiday shapes (recipes follow). Often, we give these treats to friends and family as Christmas presents.

The exchanging of other gifts varies greatly depending on each local church's rules. Many Amish do exchange presents for Christmas, and they are usually handmade. A husband might make a special kitchen shelf for his wife; while a

wife might make a fine Sunday shirt for her husband.

A few Amish will venture into department stores to buy more mainstream gifts—this is especially true when it comes to purchasing gifts for children. After all, children are children, no matter what culture or creed, and a toy is always a treasure.

Some Amish parents do include secular figures such as Santa Claus in their celebrations, while others do not. This depends largely on local custom and the parents' preference.

As a general rule, though, I think Amish children tend to be less focused on gifts than on the spirit of the season. For example, when my family and I moved to our new home in Michigan, shortly after Christmas in 2006, our children cheerfully went without gifts that year so we could focus on moving to our new house—which we all agreed was more than gift enough for all.

Here are some of our favorite holiday recipes, ones we make only during the Christmas season.

CHRISTMAS HOLLY CANDY

Makes about 3 dozen candies

This candy is a common sight on Amish tables during the Christmas season. They're meant for guests, but it seems impossible for anyone in my family to walk by a bowl of them without taking one!

½ cup (1 stick) margarine

30 large marshmallows

1 teaspoon vanilla extract

2 teaspoons green food coloring

4½ cups cornflakes

1 tablespoon "red hot" cinnamon candy

In a large saucepan, melt the margarine over low heat. Add the marshmallows and stir until completely melted. Stir in the vanilla and food coloring, followed by the cornflakes. Mix until evenly combined. Drop walnut-size mounds of the mixture onto waxed paper. Decorate each mound with 3 pieces of the cinnamon candy. Allow to cool until set, about 1 hour.

NOEL COOKIES

Makes 1 giant cookie or several smaller ones

This is a colorful cookie you can decorate to look bright and inviting. The batter is baked as one large cookie and can later be cut into pieces.

1 cup (2 sticks) butter, softened

1 cup sugar

2 large eggs

1 teaspoon vanilla extract

2 cups all-purpose flour, plus more for dusting

ICING

1 cup sifted powdered sugar

2 tablespoons milk

Colored sugar, for decorating (optional)

Preheat the oven to 325°F. Grease and lightly flour a baking sheet.

Combine the butter, sugar, eggs, vanilla, and the 2 cups of flour. Beat vigorously with a wooden spoon until smooth. Spread the dough to the edges of the prepared pan. Lightly dust with flour. Bake until the center is set and the edges begin to turn golden brown, 25 to 30 minutes. Remove from the oven and let cool completely.

Make the icing: Stir the powdered sugar and milk together until smooth. Spread the icing on the cookie and sprinkle with colored sugar. Cut into squares or leave as one giant cookie.

PEANUT BRITTLE

Makes about 15 to 20 pieces

Mom would fix peanut brittle every Christmas that I can remember. My dad really likes homemade peanut brittle. I fixed this recipe the first Christmas Joe and I were married and continue to make it every year.

2 cups sugar

1 cup light corn syrup

½ cup water

2 cups unsalted raw peanuts

2½ teaspoons baking soda

1 teaspoon butter

1 teaspoon vanilla extract

Combine the sugar, corn syrup, and water in a heavy, medium saucepan. Cook over medium heat, stirring constantly, until the sugar dissolves. Cook to the soft-ball stage, 235°F. Stir in the peanuts. Cook, stirring constantly, for 7 or 8 minutes to the hard-crack stage, 300°F.

Remove from the heat and stir in the baking soda, butter, and vanilla. Stir well and pour into a shallow, greased 9 by 13-inch baking dish. Let cool completely, then break into pieces about the size of a playing card.

HOLIDAY FUDGE

Makes 64 pieces

When I was growing up, I always knew when the holidays were getting close because that's when fudge started appearing in the kitchen, including my favorite, chocolate fudge. I find that a tin full of homemade fudge is a great gift to give for Christmas.

1 cup granulated sugar

1 cup packed brown sugar

2 tablespoons cornstarch

2 ounces semisweet chocolate, chopped, or 6 tablespoons unsweetened cocoa powder

½ cup heavy cream

3 tablespoons butter

1 teaspoon vanilla extract

1 cup walnut pieces (optional)

Combine the sugars, cornstarch, chocolate, and cream in a heavy, medium saucepan. Bring to a boil over medium heat and cook for 2½ minutes. Stir in the butter and vanilla. Remove from the heat. Let cool to lukewarm and then beat with a spoon until the mixture holds its shape. Stir in the nuts. Pour into a buttered 8 by 8-inch pan and let cool. Refrigerate until set. Cut the fudge into 1-inch squares.

standalone desserts

Baking is something my mother taught me, as her mother taught her, and her mother before her. The oven plays a central role in my life—it is the means through which we bring so much joy to our families with sweet and sticky desserts developed over centuries. And it is also a fundamentally important way for our families to bond, mother to daughter, generation to generation. Whenever possible, make these extraordinary desserts with the help, and in the company, of your own family members.

MY HOMEMADE PIE DOUGH

Makes three single 9-inch crusts

No matter how good the filling of a pie, if the crust doesn't taste good the whole thing can be ruined. I have had luck with two different piecrust recipes—this one, and my Pat-a-Pan Piecrust on page 298. Don't get discouraged if you don't have success with this one the first time. Sometimes you have to try a few times to get the experience.

3 cups all-purpose flour

1 teaspoon salt

1 cup lard

1 large egg

⅓ cup cold water

1 tablespoon apple cider vinegar

In a large bowl, combine the flour and salt. Stir to blend. Add the lard and rub it into the flour with your fingertips until the mixture resembles coarse crumbs. Add the egg, water, and vinegar and stir with a fork until the dry ingredients are moistened. Form the dough into a ball and divide that into three balls. Form a ball into a disk and roll it out to a ⅛-inch thickness on a floured surface.

Fit the dough into a 9-inch pie pan and trim the edges to a 1-inch overhang. Fold the dough under and crimp the edges. If not using now, form the remaining two balls of dough into thick disks, place each in a resealable plastic bag, and freeze for up to 3 months.

tip: beating eggs

Eggs will beat up fluffier, and make your piecrust flakier, if you set them out for at least an hour prior to baking. This allows them to come up to room temperature before you beat them and gives you better pastry.

PAT-A-PAN PIECRUST

Makes one single 9-inch crust

This is a great one to teach children to make a pie dough for the first time, or just for someone who is in a hurry and doesn't have time to roll out a crust. I think this tastes very good and works for a single-crust pie. The crust is quick and needs no rolling out. You cannot double this recipe or roll out a top crust with it, for it is just too tender to transfer from a pastry board to a pie tin. I recommend this recipe especially if you think you can't make a piecrust.

1½ cups all-purpose flour

1½ teaspoons sugar

½ teaspoon salt

½ cup vegetable oil

3 tablespoons cold milk

Place the flour, sugar, and salt in a 9-inch pie pan and mix with your fingertips until evenly blended. In a measuring cup, combine the oil and milk and beat until creamy. Pour all at once over the flour mixture. Mix with a fork until the flour mixture is completely moistened. Pat the dough with your fingers, first at the sides of the plate and then across the bottom. Flute the edges.

The shell is now ready to be filled. If you are preparing a shell to fill later or your recipe requires a prebaked crust, preheat the oven to 425°F. Prick the surface of the pastry with a fork and bake until golden brown, 15 minutes. Check often and prick more if needed.

NEVER-FAIL PASTRY

Makes two 9-inch piecrusts

This is a popular piecrust recipe in many Amish settlements. This recipe is used to make a small pastry shell for the Butter Tarts on page 286, but it can also be used to make two 9-inch piecrusts for any pie recipe in this book. Butter can be substituted for the lard.

2½ cups all-purpose flour

½ teaspoon salt

½ pound lard

1 large egg

1 tablespoon vinegar

4 to 5 tablespoons very cold water

Stir the flour and salt together in a medium bowl. Cut in the lard with a pastry blender until it forms the consistency of oatmeal. In a cup, beat the egg lightly. To the egg, add the vinegar and water and stir until well beaten. Gradually add the egg mixture to the flour mixture, constantly stirring with a fork or knife until the dough holds together. The dough is ready to roll out and use for butter tarts or pies.

APPLE CRUMB PIE

Makes one 9-inch pie

My mom would get apples from her trees for homemade applesauce and apple pies. We had three apple trees on our property that were planted the year I was born. This helped my parents remember how old the trees were. When Mom would send us to go out to get apples, we had to go to certain trees. For applesauce we used Yellow Transparent and for snacking, the Jonathan. Pies got McIntosh apples. Mom never had to measure anything for her apple pie; she just knew how to make it perfect every time.

¾ cup granulated sugar

1 teaspoon ground cinnamon

6 to 7 cups sliced McIntosh apples

1 disk My Homemade Pie Dough (page 296) or Pat-a-Pan Piecrust (page 298)

½ cup (1 stick) butter, softened

½ cup packed brown sugar

1 cup all-purpose flour

Preheat the oven to 425°F.

Mix the sugar and cinnamon with the apples in a large bowl and put into the unbaked pie shell. Mix the butter, brown sugar, and flour in a medium bowl for the topping. Sprinkle over the pie. Bake for 15 minutes, then lower the oven temperature to 350°F and bake for 30 more minutes. Cool on a wire rack or windowsill until the pie is firm, about 45 minutes. Store any leftovers in a sealed container. The pie will keep for about 5 days.

SOUR CREAM APPLE PIE

Makes one 9-inch pie

This is a delicious and spectacular apple pie with a hint of crunch from its crumb topping. The recipe for the crumb topping can easily be doubled or tripled for use on additional pies.

8 to 10 medium-size apples (such as Ida Red or Golden Delicious), peeled and sliced

1 disk My Homemade Pie Dough (page 296) or Pat-a-Pan Piecrust (page 298)

4 large eggs, beaten

1½ cups sugar

¼ cup all-purpose flour

2 teaspoons vanilla extract

2 teaspoons ground cinnamon

½ teaspoon salt

2 cups sour cream

CRUMB TOPPING

¾ cup all-purpose flour

½ cup firmly packed brown sugar

⅓ cup butter, softened

Preheat the oven to 325°F.

Place the apple slices in the pie shell. Mix the eggs, sugar, flour, vanilla, cinnamon, salt, and sour cream in a large mixing bowl. Pour the mixture into the pie shell over the apple slices.

Make the crumb topping: In a small mixing bowl, mix the flour, brown sugar, and softened butter, using your fingers, until the mixture resembles coarse crumbs. Top the apple mixture with a generous layer of the crumbs. Bake for 35 to 40 minutes, until the pie is solid when jiggled.

SNITZ HALF-MOON PIES

Makes about 12 small pies

Snitz apples are a staple among the Amish. Snitz simply means "dried." Homemade dried apples can be made simply; many Amish cooks use their ovens at a low setting for an all-day drying of the apples.

3 cups water

2 quarts dried apple slices (apple snitz), preferably Cortland or Empire varieties

1½ cups brown sugar

½ teaspoon salt

½ teaspoon ground cinnamon

Pie dough for 2 (9-inch) double-crust pies (see Never-Fail Pastry, page 299)

Place the water and apple slices in a 4-quart pot. Cover and simmer for 20 to 30 minutes, until the apples are soft and look like the apple slices in a traditional apple pie. Add water to the pot if the water boils off and the apples are not yet soft enough.

Remove the apples from the heat. Strain and return to the pot. Add the brown sugar, salt, and cinnamon, and mix well with the apples.

Preheat the oven to 450°F. Roll out each portion of the pie dough, and cut out twelve 7- to 8-inch circles. Using a fork, pierce one half of each circle with a couple of small holes to allow steam to vent. Place ½ cup of the filling on the other half of each circle. Wet the circles' edges, fold over the dough so that the filling is on one side of the crease, and smooth the dough over the filling so that air pockets will not form inside the pie. Press the edges together and seal them firmly all the way around the half-moon. Be sure there are no gaps, to prevent filling from escaping.

Bake the half-moon pies on ungreased baking sheets for 15 to 20 minutes, or until the edges of the crust are golden brown and the tops of the pies are beginning to brown.

PUMPKIN PIE

Serves 6

Pumpkin pie was something Mom always fixed around Thanksgiving or whenever the big orange fruits were ready to harvest and be canned.

1 disk My Homemade Pie Dough (page 296)

4 large eggs, separated

2 cups homemade pumpkin puree, or 1 (15-ounce) can pumpkin puree

½ teaspoon pumpkin pie spice

1 teaspoon vanilla extract

1 cup sugar

Pinch of salt

2 tablespoons all-purpose flour

2 cups milk, scalded

Preheat the oven to 400°F.

Roll the disk of dough out to a ⅛-inch thickness on a floured surface. Fit the dough into a 9-inch pie pan. Trim the overhang to 1 inch. Fold the dough under and crimp the edges.

Beat the egg whites in a large bowl until soft, glossy peaks form. Beat the egg yolks in a small bowl.

In a large bowl, mix the pumpkin puree, egg yolks, pumpkin pie spice, vanilla, sugar, salt, flour, and milk together until the mixture is smooth. Fold in the egg whites. Pour the filling into the piecrust. Bake for 10 minutes. Reduce the oven temperature to 350°F and bake until the pie is set, about 40 minutes. Remove from the oven and let cool completely.

SWEET POTATO PIE

Makes three 9-inch pies

I like that this recipe makes three pies because sweet potato pie always has everyone, family and guests alike, coming back for more.

6 large sweet potatoes (about 3 pounds or 6 heaping cups)

6 tablespoons all-purpose flour

5 eggs

5½ cups milk

1½ cups sugar

½ cup brown sugar

3 teaspoons vanilla extract

¾ teaspoon salt

1 teaspoon cinnamon

3 disks My Homemade Pie Dough (page 296)

Boil the whole sweet potatoes in their skin for 40 minutes, or until soft. Run cold water over the sweet potatoes and remove the skins. Preheat the oven to 350°F.

Mash the sweet potatoes in a large bowl, sprinkling in the flour as you mash. Beat the eggs and add to the sweet potatoes, along with the remaining filling ingredients. Mix together until well blended. Pour the filling into the pie shells. Bake for 55 to 60 minutes, or until a butter knife inserted in the center comes out clean. Pies will puff up as they bake, then settle back down as they cool. Store any leftovers in a sealed container. The pies will keep for about 2 days.

GARDEN HUCKLEBERRY PIE

Makes one 9-inch pie

Unlike wild huckleberries, garden huckleberries are very tart, and most people don't like them that way. But when they're used in a pie, bread, or jam, that tartness really softens to let the berry flavor come out.

1 quart prepared garden huckleberry juice

½ cup cornstarch

½ cup sugar

1 (9-inch) prebaked pie shell

Whipped cream, for topping

Combine the huckleberry juice, cornstarch, and sugar in a small saucepan over medium heat and cook, stirring constantly, until thickened. Let cool. Pour the mixture into the baked pie shell and top with the whipped cream before serving.

OATMEAL PIE

Makes one 9-inch pie

This is an old favorite, a very sweet, rich pie that some say tastes a lot like pecan pie. It's so good my husband, Joe, and I served it at our wedding. This same oatmeal pie was the first recipe that Mom had in "The Amish Cook" column when it began back in 1991.

2 large eggs

¾ cup dark brown sugar

½ cup (1 stick) butter, softened

¾ cup dark corn syrup

1 cup quick-cooking rolled oats

1 disk My Homemade Pie Dough (page 296) or Pat-a-Pan Piecrust (page 298)

Preheat the oven to 325°F.

In a large bowl, cream together the eggs, sugar, and butter. Add the corn syrup and oats and mix until the mixture is well blended and brown in color. Pour into the unbaked pie shell. Bake until a toothpick inserted in the center comes out clean, about 1 hour. This pie can be stored in a sealed container or cake safe and will stay fresh for up to 10 days.

ORANGE SUPREME PIE

Makes one 9-inch pie

This is a delicious, citrusy pie that has become a Florida favorite among the Amish community in that state.

2 cups water

1 cup granulated sugar

1 tablespoon cornstarch

1 teaspoon orange Kool-Aid powder

3 oranges, peeled and chopped

4 ounces cream cheese, softened

2 cups powdered sugar

8 ounces Homemade Whipped Topping, plus more for serving (page 47)

1 (9-inch) prebaked pie shell

Bring 1½ cups of the water to a boil in a small saucepan. In a small mixing bowl, combine the granulated sugar, cornstarch, and Kool-Aid, stir in the remaining ½ cup of water, and mix until the ingredients are thoroughly combined. Pour the sugar mixture into the boiling water, stirring as it cooks. Remove the saucepan from the heat when the mixture begins to thicken a bit. Allow the mixture to cool, then stir in the orange pieces.

In a medium bowl, stir together the cream cheese and powdered sugar until creamy. Fold in the whipped topping until the ingredients are thoroughly combined. Spoon the cream cheese mixture into the baked piecrust. Top with the orange filling. Refrigerate until chilled and set, about 1 hour. Top with extra whipped topping, if desired.

BUMBLEBERRY PIE

Makes one 9-inch pie

This is a delicious pie for the summer months when berries are everywhere. You can substitute whatever fruits are available or in season—simply use the same amounts.

1 cup blueberries

1 cup raspberries

1 cup strawberries, chopped

1 cup chopped rhubarb

1 cup peeled and chopped McIntosh apples

1 cup sugar, plus more for topping

⅓ cup all-purpose flour

1 tablespoon fresh lemon juice

2 disks My Homemade Pie Dough (page 296)

Preheat the oven to 425°F.

In a large bowl, combine all of the filling ingredients until well blended. Spoon the fruit filling into the piecrust. Use some water to wet the rim of the bottom crust, which will help both crusts adhere together. Cover the pie with the top crust and crimp the crusts together all the way around. Make three slits in the crust. Sprinkle the top with a little sugar. Bake for 15 minutes, and then decrease the heat to 325°F and bake for another 30 minutes, until the crust is golden and the fruit filling begins to bubble out through the slits. Cool on a wire rack or windowsill until the pie is firm, about 45 minutes. Store any leftovers in a sealed container. The pie will keep for about 5 days.

A BUMBLE WHAT?

There's no such thing as a bumbleberry—it's just the name given to assorted mixed berries in pies and preserves. The term originated in Canada but has since spread all over the world, carried by the delicious recipes bearing the bumbleberry name.

GRAPEFRUIT PIE

Makes one 9-inch pie

When a group of Amish tried to establish a community in Honduras in the 1970s, local grapefruit were a regular snack. But it took numerous attempts by cooks to come up with a method to turn the plentiful fruit into a tasty pie. This is that recipe. For the pie shell, make the Never-Fail Pastry recipe (page 299) and use half. Save the other half for another use.

3 or 4 medium-size grapefruit

¾ cup sugar (add ¼ cup more for a less-tart pie)

3 tablespoons cornstarch

1¾ cups water

Pinch of salt

1 (3-ounce) box strawberry-flavored gelatin, such as Jell-O

1 (9-inch) pie shell, baked and cooled

Whipped cream

Peel the grapefruit, separate into slices, and cut away all the sour, white pith. Chop the slices into small pieces and drain in a strainer. Discard or drink any drained juice (do not use the juice for the pie).

Cook the sugar, cornstarch, water, and salt in a medium saucepan over medium heat until clear. Add the gelatin and stir until the mixture slightly thickens. Add the grapefruit pieces to the gelatin mixture. Stir well, pour into the baked 9-inch pie shell, and refrigerate until set. Top with the whipped cream.

CONCORD GRAPE STREUSEL PIE

Serves 4 to 6

This is a wonderful recipe to help me use up the juice grapes we pick at the vineyard. The chil-dren tried to eat the grapes by themselves as a snack, but didn't care for the bitter taste. In a pie, however, grapes take on an entirely new personality.

FILLING

4½ cups Concord (or similar) grapes

1 cup sugar

¼ cup all-purpose flour

2 teaspoons lemon juice

⅛ teaspoon salt

1 disk Never-Fail Pastry (page 299)

STREUSEL

½ cup old-fashioned rolled oats (not instant or quick-cooking)

4 cups packed brown sugar

¼ cup all-purpose flour

4 tablespoons butter, softened

Preheat the oven to 425°F.

Make the filling: Seed the grapes (if not using seedless), place them in a large saucepan, and cook over medium-high heat until soft, about 5 minutes. Drain off the liquid. Stir in the sugar, flour, lemon juice, and salt. Spoon the filling into the unbaked crust.

Make the streusel: Combine all the streusel ingredients in a medium bowl. Mix with your fingertips until it forms coarse crumbles. Sprinkle evenly on the top of the filled pie. Bake until the streusel and the edges of the crust are golden brown, 35 to 40 minutes.

MUSCADINE PIE

Makes one 9-inch pie

Muscadines are commonly seen in farmers' markets across the South. North Carolina has gone so far as to name them its state fruit. Once the Amish moved into the Carolinas, they made this fruit a favorite.

1 quart muscadine grapes, skins removed

1 cup sugar

1½ tablespoons fresh lemon juice

2 tablespoons all-purpose flour

⅛ teaspoon salt

¼ teaspoon ground cinnamon

1 recipe Never-Fail Pastry, page 299

Preheat the oven to 425°F.

In a small saucepan, cover the grape skins with water and boil until very tender, about 30 minutes. In another saucepan, combine the muscadine pulp and the sugar. Bring the pulp mixture to a near boil over medium heat, then reduce the heat and simmer for 15 minutes. Press the cooked pulp mixture through a sieve to remove the seeds. Drain the water from the cooked hulls and add them to the pulp.

Form a paste in a separate bowl by mixing the lemon juice, flour, and salt. Add the paste to the muscadine pulp and skins, and stir until well combined. Stir in the cinnamon.

Roll out half of the pastry dough on a lightly floured surface until it is large enough to fit into a 9-inch pie pan. Transfer the dough to the pan and gently press it in. Pour the muscadine filling into the crust. Roll out the top crust large enough to cover the filling, transfer it, trim off the excess, and crimp the edges shut. Bake the pie until the crust is golden brown, about 20 minutes.

GOOSEBERRY PIE

Makes one 9-inch pie

Gooseberries can be difficult to find if they aren't in season. You can buy them in some stores, but mostly they are found growing in woods and meadows in the Midwest. Gooseberries also make a great jam or preserve.

2 cups sugar

2 cups gooseberries

1 tablespoon all-purpose flour

Walnut-size pat of butter

2 disks My Homemade Pie Dough (page 296)

Preheat the oven to 425°F.

Put the sugar, berries, flour, and butter into a bowl and mix. Then pour into the pie shell. Use some water to wet the rim of the bottom crust, which will help both crusts adhere together. Cover the pie with the top crust, crimping the crusts together all the way around. Bake for 35 minutes, or until the crust is golden brown. Cool on a wire rack or windowsill until the pie is firm, about 45 minutes. Store any leftovers in a sealed container. The pie will keep for about 5 days.

APRICOT PIE

Makes one 9-inch pie

Dried fruits and nuts are commonly sold in Amish-owned bulk-food stores. During tighter economic times, and when fresh produce isn't available, Amish cooks often rely on the dried fruits sold in the bulk stores. This recipe has you plump up the dried apricots, which results in a very fruity pie. Many say this resembles a homemade peach pie.

2 cups dried apricots

2 cups water

½ cup sugar

1½ tablespoons cornstarch

Pinch of salt

2 disks My Homemade Pie Dough (page 296)

3 tablespoons butter, cut into pieces

Preheat the oven to 425°F.

In a small saucepan, bring the apricots and water to a boil. Cook for 10 minutes over low heat. Add the sugar and cook for another 5 minutes, stirring occasionally. Using a colander, drain the contents of the saucepan, reserving 1 cup of the juice. Set the apricots aside. Pour the reserved apricot juice into a small saucepan and add the cornstarch. Add the salt and cook over medium heat until the mixture thickens, 2 to 3 minutes, stirring frequently until the consistency is like gravy.

Arrange the drained apricots in the unbaked pie shell. Pour the thickened apricot juice over the apricots. Dot the top with the butter. Use some water to wet the rim of the bottom crust, which will help both crusts adhere together. Cover with the top crust and crimp the top and the bottom together all the way around. Slit the top three times and flute the edges. Bake for 30 minutes. Cover the edges only with foil, if needed, after 20 minutes, to prevent browning. Cool on a wire rack or windowsill until the pie is firm, about 45 minutes. Store any leftovers in a sealed container. The pie will keep for about 5 days.

LEMON PIE

Makes one 9-inch pie

In the summertime I buy a lot of lemons, and I slice them and make my own lemonade. I like to eat the lemon slices, rind and everything. I remember my mom doing that also.

3 tablespoons cornstarch

1¼ cups plus 6 tablespoons sugar

¼ cup fresh lemon juice

1 tablespoon lemon zest

3 large eggs, separated

1½ cups boiling water

1 disk My Homemade Pie Dough (page 296) or Pat-a-Pan Piecrust (page 298)

Preheat the oven to 425°F.

In a medium bowl, combine the cornstarch, 1¼ cups sugar, the lemon juice, and lemon zest. In a small bowl, beat the egg yolks. Add the egg yolks to the cornstarch mixture. Gradually add the boiling water to the mixture, stirring all the while. Pour the mixture into a small saucepan and heat to boiling over medium heat. Boil gently for 4 minutes, stirring constantly. Pour into the unbaked pie shell.

In a separate bowl, beat the egg whites until stiff, but not dry. Gradually beat in the remaining 6 tablespoons of sugar. Spread the meringue over the top of the pie. Bake for 5 to 10 minutes, or until browned. Cool on a wire rack or windowsill until the pie is firm, about 45 minutes. Store any leftovers in a sealed container. The pie will keep for about 5 days.

FRENCH RHUBARB PIE

Makes one 9-inch pie

French Rhubarb Pie is a local favorite, especially because so much rhubarb is raised and sold in our community. You often see this pie sold at local farmers' markets in the Midwest.

1 large egg

1 cup sugar

1 teaspoon vanilla extract

2 tablespoons all-purpose flour

2 cups diced rhubarb

1 (9-inch) unbaked pie shell (see Never-Fail Pastry, page 299)

TOPPING

¾ cup all-purpose flour

½ cup firmly packed brown sugar

⅓ cup butter

Preheat the oven to 400°F.

Combine the egg, sugar, vanilla, and flour in a large mixing bowl. Stir the mixture until smooth, then fold in the rhubarb. Pour the rhubarb mixture into the pie shell.

Make the topping: Mix the flour and sugar in a bowl. Cut in the butter with a pastry blender to form crumbs. Sprinkle the topping over the rhubarb mixture. Bake the pie for 10 minutes, then reduce the oven temperature to 350°F and bake until the center is set and the topping is browned, about 30 minutes.

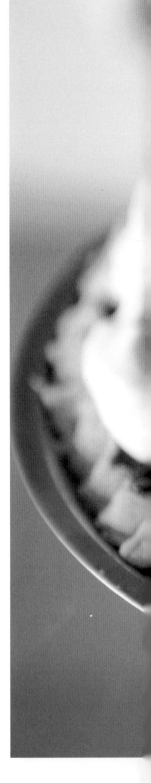

STRAWBERRY PIE

Serves 6 to 8

This recipe is one of the first cool, delicious desserts we whip up on warm days. My sister Susan is especially fond of making this, and it doesn't last very long when she brings it over!

CRUST	FILLING
1½ cups all-purpose flour	½ cup sugar
½ teaspoon salt	3 tablespoons cornstarch
½ cup vegetable oil	2 tablespoons light corn syrup
2 tablespoons milk	1 cup water
2 tablespoons sugar	3 tablespoons strawberry-flavored gelatin
	Few drops of red food coloring (optional)
	6 cups fresh strawberries, hulled and sliced

Preheat the oven to 400°F.

Make the crust: Stir together the flour, salt, oil, milk, and sugar in a medium bowl. Press the dough evenly over the bottom and up the sides of a 9-inch pie pan. Bake until golden, about 12 minutes. Remove from the oven and let cool.

Make the filling: Combine the sugar, cornstarch, corn syrup, and water in a saucepan and bring to a boil. Boil, stirring constantly, until thick, about 5 minutes. Remove from the heat. Stir in the gelatin and food coloring. Let cool until lukewarm. Add the strawberries and pour into the cooled crust. Refrigerate for 2 hours before serving. Add whipped topping and fresh berries, if desired.

tip: storing fruit pies

I always store fruit pies in the refrigerator—that way, they usually last a week to a week and a half if the fragile fruit is chilled. If you leave them out in the summer, they won't last half as long as they do left out in the wintertime.

FILLING PIES WITH FRUIT

My mother almost always made her own pie fillings, which were always delicious. She passed along many of her recipes and methods to her daughters. As a mother with a family of my own now, I have made strawberry, cherry, blueberry, and apple pie fillings from scratch. I've not tried making a peach pie filling yet, but I want to soon.

The canned store-bought pie fillings are okay in a pinch, but I like the homemade ones much better. I don't think my Grandma would have ever bought a can of pie filling in the store. Back then they didn't even consider doing that. In later years, my mom would have bought a can at the store only if she ran out of time.

The look of homemade pie filling is a little different. The ones you buy in the store probably look nicer, but homemade has none of the artificial colors and preservatives that make fruit such as cherries redder and plumper. The cherries in my homemade pie filling may seem more cooked, but the taste is so much better.

Pie fillings are best when you grow your own fruit, or have access to newly picked fruit, because the fillings can be made fresh whenever you need them. For example, my mother's homemade apple pie filling came right from the apples on her trees! It was so good.

HOMEMADE FRUIT PIE FILLING

Makes 6 quarts

This easy recipe is one of my favorite ways to make pie filling. It calls for blueberries, but you can substitute almost any firm fruit—apples, berry mixes, pears, etc. It also calls for Instant Clearjel, which is a thickener made of modified cornstarch manufactured by King Arthur Flour. It works so much better than regular cornstarch or flour, which can make fruit pie fillings watery or cloudy. You may have to ask for its location, but most grocery stores carry it. So do shops specializing in canning and preserving supplies.

6 cups sugar

2¼ cups Instant Clearjel

7 cups cold water

½ cup fresh lemon juice

6 quarts fresh or unsweetened frozen blueberries

In a large pot, combine the sugar and Instant Clearjel over medium-high heat. Add the water and stir. Cook on medium-high until the mixture thickens and begins to bubble, about 7 minutes. Add the lemon juice and boil for an additional minute, stirring constantly. Fold in the berries, and remove from the heat. If not using immediately, put into jars and cold pack, storing in a cool place.

VINEGAR PIE

Makes one 9-inch pie

This is an old recipe with roots in the Great Depression, when years were lean and times were tough. Lemons and other fruits were often in short supply during the 1930s, so Amish homemakers turned to this recipe to make something that tastes and looks like a creamy lemon pie.

½ cup (1 stick) butter, softened

1¼ cups sugar

2 tablespoons apple cider vinegar

3 large eggs

1 teaspoon vanilla extract

1 disk My Homemade Pie Dough (page 296) or Pat-a-Pan Piecrust (page 298)

Preheat the oven to 350°F.

In a large bowl, blend the butter and sugar until light and fluffy, about 2 minutes, stirring vigorously with a fork. Add the vinegar, eggs, and vanilla. Whisk vigorously for 1 full minute, until the mixture is creamy and smooth. Pour into the unbaked piecrust. Bake until a butter knife inserted in the center comes out clean, about 45 minutes. The pie will be a golden brown when done; overbaking will cause cracks in the top. Cool on a wire rack or windowsill until the pie is firm, about 45 minutes. This pie stays fresh for 3 days and should be stored in a sealed container.

HOMEMADE BUTTERMILK PIE

Makes one 9-inch pie

In the community where we now live in Michigan, Amish farmers are allowed to have bulk tanks for their milk. I was raised in a community where we kept the milk in cans. Having milkers and a bulk tank allows the Amish farmers to have many more cows. A farmer who has to milk his cows by hand can't have as many cows. There are other ways that milk can be used besides for drinking and cooking. I remember Mom making our own cottage cheese. When she would make butter, she would skim off the top layer of cream from the milk. Since we didn't have a butter churn, the children's job was to keep shaking the glass jar until the butter formed. Mom would then take out the lump of butter, and the liquid left was buttermilk. This recipe makes a warm, golden-colored pie that can be enjoyed as a dessert, with breakfast, or as a snack.

½ cup (1 stick) butter, softened

1 cup fresh buttermilk

3 large eggs

1½ cups sugar

1 tablespoon all-purpose flour

1 disk My Homemade Pie Dough (page 296) or Pat-a-Pan Piecrust (page 298)

1 teaspoon ground nutmeg

Preheat the oven to 350°F.

In a large bowl, beat together the butter, buttermilk, eggs, sugar, and flour with a whisk. Pour the filling into the unbaked piecrust. Sprinkle the top with the nutmeg. Bake until the pie turns a golden brown color and a butter knife inserted in the center comes out clean, about 35 minutes. Cool on a wire rack or windowsill until the pie is firm, about 45 minutes. Store any leftovers in a sealed container. The pie will keep for about 2 days.

VANILLA CRUMB PIE

Makes one 9-inch pie

With its crumb top, this pie has a crunchy top layer with a custardlike filling beneath. My daughter Elizabeth likes custard pie, and she says the filling of this pie reminds her of that. This is a very easy pie to make and tastes good served warm.

BOTTOM LAYER

½ cup packed brown sugar

½ cup corn syrup

1 tablespoon all-purpose flour

1 large egg

1 cup water

1 teaspoon vanilla extract

1 disk My Homemade Pie Dough (page 296) or Pat-a-Pan Piecrust (page 298)

TOP LAYER

1 cup all-purpose flour

½ cup granulated sugar

¼ cup margarine

½ teaspoon baking soda

½ teaspoon baking powder

Preheat the oven to 375°F.

Make the bottom layer: In a medium saucepan, combine the brown sugar, syrup, flour, egg, water, and vanilla and cook over low heat, stirring until thickened. Then pour into the unbaked pie shell.

Make the top layer: In a medium bowl, combine all the ingredients. Mix until coarse crumbs form. Distribute the crumbs evenly over the top of the filling. Bake until the crumbs on top get golden brown, 45 to 50 minutes. Cool on a wire rack or windowsill until the pie is firm, about 45 minutes. Store any leftovers in a sealed container. The pie will keep for about 5 days.

BUTTERSCOTCH PIE

Makes one 9-inch pie

My brother Amos loves this pie. My children also like it because they are fond of most cream pies. Homemade butterscotch isn't difficult to make, and it will last a lot longer than the instant kind.

1 cup packed brown sugar

¼ teaspoon salt

2 cups boiling water

1 teaspoon vanilla extract

4 tablespoons (½ stick) butter, softened

2 large eggs

½ cup granulated sugar

Pinch of salt

1 cup all-purpose flour

1 cup milk

1 (9-inch) prebaked pie shell

Preheat the oven to 350°F.

In a small saucepan over low heat, boil the brown sugar, salt, water, vanilla, and butter. Mix until well blended, and then stir in the eggs, granulated sugar, salt, flour, and milk. Cook, stirring, until thick, about 10 minutes. Pour into the baked piecrust and let cool to room temperature before serving.

TEARS ON MY PILLOW PIE

Makes one 9-inch pie

The origins of this pie's funny name are unknown. No one I know seems to remember where its name comes from. My column editor, Kevin Williams, tells me that if you remove the pie from the oven too early it will collapse, which could cause bakers to head to bed with tears on their pillows. He also said that someone told him that the pie tasted so soft inside that it was like a pillow.

$\frac{1}{3}$ cup butter, melted

1$\frac{1}{2}$ cups packed brown sugar

2 large eggs

1 tablespoon all-purpose flour

$\frac{1}{2}$ cup evaporated milk

1 disk My Homemade Pie Dough (page 296) or Pat-a-Pan Piecrust (page 298)

Preheat the oven to 350°F.

In a large bowl, beat together the butter, brown sugar, eggs, flour, and milk until smooth. Pour the filling into the unbaked pie shell. Bake for 25 minutes, or until the crust and filling are golden brown. Turn off the oven and leave the pie in the closed oven for 1 hour, and then remove it. This pie should be eaten within a day or two of baking.

THICK MILK PIE

Makes two 9-inch pies

This pie's name isn't very appetizing, but the pie itself definitely is—it's delicious and economical to make. This is a great pie to make if you happen to have milk that has gone sour. Surprisingly, it tastes a little like pumpkin pie. The pie will not look set when taken out of the oven. It will look like pools of liquid, but will set once it cools. Molasses can be used in place of the honey.

3 large eggs

1 cup honey

1 cup sugar

½ cup all-purpose flour

1 teaspoon baking soda

3 cups thick, sour milk

2 disks My Homemade Pie Dough (page 296) or Pat-a-Pan Piecrust (page 298)

2 teaspoons ground cinnamon

Preheat the oven to 400°F.

In a large bowl, beat the eggs and add the honey. Combine the sugar, flour, and baking soda with the egg mixture. Add the thick milk and stir until smooth. Pour into the unbaked pie shells. Sprinkle the cinnamon over the tops.

Bake for 10 minutes. Then decrease the heat to 325°F and bake for 45 to 50 more minutes, or until a toothpick inserted into the center comes out clean. Cool on a wire rack until the pie is firm, about 45 minutes. Store any leftovers in a sealed container. The pie will keep for 2 days.

tip: making sour milk

It's easy to make sour milk when any recipe calls for it. Simply put 1 tablespoon lemon juice or vinegar in a measuring cup. Fill with whole milk to make 1 cup. Let the mixture sit at room temperature for 15 minutes. When the milk becomes thick and lumpy, it's ready to use. (Since the Thick Milk Pie recipe calls for 3 cups of sour milk, you'll need to triple the amount you make.)

SAWDUST PIE

Makes one 9-inch pie

This pie's name is probably taken from the sawdustlike appearance of the pie, as sawdust is a familiar sight in Amish-owned mills and lumberyards. This is a thick pie full of coconut.

1½ cups shredded coconut

1½ cups graham cracker crumbs

1½ cups chopped pecans

1½ cups sugar

1 cup egg whites (4 to 5 egg whites)

1 disk My Homemade Pie Dough (page 296) or Pat-a-Pan Piecrust (page 298)

Preheat the oven to 350°F.

In a medium bowl, combine the coconut, graham cracker crumbs, pecans, and sugar. Mix in the egg whites (do not beat them first). Pour the filling into the unbaked pie shell. Bake for 35 to 40 minutes. Cover the edges only with foil if needed to prevent overbrowning. The middle may still look moist, but it will set upon cooling. Cool on a wire rack or windowsill until the pie is firm, about 45 minutes. Store any leftovers in a sealed container. The pie will keep for about 3 days.

BOB ANDY PIE

Makes one 9-inch pie

This favorite pie among the Amish can be best described as a sweet custard. The cinnamon and cloves add a big splash of spice flavors and contribute to a dark, rich color. The pie's unusual name has no shortage of stories about its origin. The most common tale is that an Amish farmer christened his wife's sweet concoction after their two prized geldings, named Bob and Andy.

2 cups sugar

3 heaping tablespoons all-purpose flour

½ teaspoon ground cloves

1 teaspoon ground cinnamon

3 large eggs, separated

1 tablespoon butter, melted

2 cups milk

1 disk My Homemade Pie Dough (page 296) or Pat-a-Pan Piecrust (page 298)

Preheat the oven to 350°F.

In a large bowl, mix together the sugar, flour, cloves, and cinnamon. In a small bowl, beat the egg yolks. Then add the butter, yolks, and milk to the flour mixture and stir vigorously until the filling is creamy and light colored. In another separate small bowl, beat the egg whites for 2 minutes, until stiff peaks form, and then fold into the filling mixture. Pour the pie filling into the unbaked piecrust and bake for about 1 hour, or until a butter knife inserted in the center comes out clean and the filling looks firm. Let set for about an hour before serving.

SUGAR CREAM PIE

Makes one 9-inch pie

This is an old favorite among Amish in the Midwest. The pie is made from simple staples found in most people's pantries. While there are many local variations in sugar cream pie recipes, this one is very typical of what is served most often. My children like it because it tastes kind of like a sweet pudding.

½ cup granulated sugar

⅓ cup packed brown sugar

¼ cup all-purpose flour

¼ teaspoon salt

½ cup boiling water

½ cup thin cream or half-and-half

½ teaspoon vanilla extract

¼ teaspoon ground nutmeg

1 disk My Homemade Pie Dough (page 296) or Pat-a-Pan Piecrust (page 298)

Preheat the oven to 425°F.

In a large bowl, combine the sugars, flour, and salt until well blended. Slowly add the boiling water and stir until well blended. Then add the cream, vanilla, and nutmeg and stir until the mixture is completely blended. Pour the filling into the unbaked pie shell. Bake for 20 minutes. Reduce the oven temperature to 350°F and bake for 20 to 25 minutes more, until done. The top should be lightly bubbling all over and no longer liquid, but it should still jiggle like gelatin in the center. Let cool before serving. Cool on a wire rack or windowsill until the pie is firm, about 45 minutes. Store any leftovers in a sealed container. The pie will keep for about 5 days.

COCONUT CREAM PIE

Serves 6 to 8

Historically, coconut has not been a part of Amish culinary culture. But over the past 50 years, as it's become more readily available in shops near our communities, it has become widely used. I'm thankful for that, since the result has been wonderful pies such as this one.

2 eggs

½ cup sugar

½ cup (1 stick) margarine, softened

½ cup milk

¼ cup all-purpose flour

1 cup shredded sweetened coconut

1 (8-inch) pie shell, unbaked

Preheat the oven to 350°F.

In a large bowl, whisk the eggs and the sugar until the mixture is lemon colored. Gradually stir in the margarine, milk, flour, and coconut with a spoon. Mix until well combined. Pour the mixture into the unbaked pie shell. Bake for 45 to 50 minutes, until the filling is set and the crust is golden brown. Let cool at room temperature before slicing and serving.

SOUTHERN CREAM PIE

Serves 6 to 8

Amish cooking has, over time, taken on a distinct Southern flair, as the communities in the Southern states work with local ingredients and traditions and create recipes such as this delicious pie.

²⁄₃ cup sugar

1½ tablespoons all-purpose flour

⅛ teaspoon salt

1 cup light cream

1 teaspoon vanilla extract

1 (8-inch) pie shell, unbaked

Pinch of ground cinnamon

Preheat the oven to 350°F.

In a medium bowl, combine the sugar, flour, and salt. Slowly stir the cream and vanilla into the dry ingredients. Mix until well combined and smooth. Pour the cream mixture into the unbaked pie shell. Lightly sprinkle the top of the pie with ground cinnamon. Bake for about 1 hour, until the filling is nearly set. The filling will thicken slightly as the pie cools. Let cool at room temperature before slicing and serving.

JUST-RIGHT CUSTARD PIE

Makes one 9-inch pie

This is a classic—and for good reason. It's a traditional Amish recipe that creates a light, fluffy pie. It can also be enjoyed for breakfast!

2 large eggs, separated

¾ cup sugar

2 tablespoons all-purpose flour

Pinch of salt

2 cups milk, scalded

1 teaspoon vanilla

1 (9-inch) unbaked pie shell (see Never-Fail Pastry, page 299)

Preheat the oven to 400°F.

Beat the egg yolks in a bowl, then stir in the sugar, flour, and salt. Very gradually, add the heated milk to the egg yolk mixture. In a separate bowl, beat the egg whites and vanilla until foamy. Add to the milk mixture, and stir until evenly combined. Pour the custard into the pie shell, and bake for 10 minutes. Reduce the oven temperature to 325°F and bake until nicely browned on top, about 25 minutes.

RHUBARB CUSTARD PIE

Makes one 9-inch pie

When the rhubarb begins peeping up on the first days of spring, this is a pie we often think of making first. And if someone's wedding falls during the summer, Rhubarb Custard Pie is often served. It was one of the pie flavors served at our wedding.

3 cups diced rhubarb

1 disk My Homemade Pie Dough (page 296) or Pat-a-Pan Piecrust (page 298)

½ cup sugar

2 tablespoons cornstarch

¼ teaspoon salt

1 large egg

¾ cup corn syrup

1 tablespoon butter, softened

Preheat the oven to 450°F.

Place the rhubarb in the unbaked pie shell. In a large bowl, combine the sugar, cornstarch, and salt. Add the egg and beat well. Then add the corn syrup and butter. Beat until smooth, and pour over the rhubarb. Bake for 15 minutes. Then decrease the heat to 350°F and bake for 30 more minutes, or until the rhubarb is tender. Cool on a wire rack or windowsill until the pie is firm, about 45 minutes. Store any leftovers in a sealed container. The pie will keep for about 5 days.

ELDERBERRY CUSTARD PIE

Makes one 9-inch pie

Elderberries are typically harvested in late summer in the northeastern United States. Some Amish claim medicinal benefits from elderberries.

1 cup elderberry juice

¼ cup all-purpose flour

1 cup sugar

¼ teaspoon salt

1 large egg, separated

1 cup milk

1 disk My Homemade Pie Dough (page 296) or Pat-a-Pan Piecrust (page 298)

Preheat the oven to 350°F.

Bring the juice to a boil over medium heat in a medium saucepan. While it's heating, combine the flour, sugar, and salt in a small mixing bowl, and gradually add the egg yolk and milk. Add the boiling juice and stir until thickened. Remove the mixture from the heat.

Beat the egg white with a whisk or hand mixer in a medium mixing bowl until stiff peaks form. Fold the beaten egg white into the elderberry mixture until evenly combined. Pour the filling into the pie shell. Bake for 20 to 30 minutes, until the center is bubbly.

SWISS CUSTARD PEACH PIE

Makes one 9-inch pie

Fresh peaches are always a hit in my household. We like to use them in pies or sometimes in homemade preserves. This is an easy pie to make that is both pretty and tasty!

5 fresh peaches, sliced, or 1 pint sliced peaches, drained

1 disk My Homemade Pie Dough (page 296) or Pat-a-Pan Piecrust (page 298)

2 large eggs

½ cup sugar

¼ teaspoon salt

2 tablespoons butter, melted

1 (14-ounce) can sweetened condensed milk

Preheat the oven to 375°F.

Place the peaches in the unbaked piecrust. Mix the eggs with the sugar, salt, and butter. Beat until well blended. Add the condensed milk. Beat once more until well blended. Pour the mixture over the peaches in the shell. Bake for 15 minutes. Decrease the heat to 300°F and bake for 40 to 50 minutes longer, until the custard is firm and no longer jiggles in the middle. Cool on a wire rack or windowsill until the pie is firm, about 45 minutes. Store any leftovers in a sealed container. The pie will keep for about 3 days.

A STORY OF SHOOFLY PIE

I walked into an Amish restaurant in Indiana a few years ago to have lunch. When dessert was offered, I asked, "Do you have any shoofly pie?" In return, I got a puzzled expression.

I am generally very knowledgeable about Amish culture, but I was astonished to learn that even this most famous of Amish pies isn't universally known or baked among Amish cooks, unlike such standards as whoopie pies and pickled beets. What I didn't entirely realize then—and what many non-Amish don't know—is that Amish cooking is very different in different areas. One Amish cook's shoofly pie is another's muscadine pie (recipe on page 314).

This book is full of examples of regional favorites known primarily to the Amish in those particular areas. There's Elderberry Custard Pie (page 338) from Upstate New York, and Grilled Moose Steaks (page 205) developed by Amish cooks in Rexford, Montana, and Florida Orange Rice (page 65), created by Amish in, you guessed it, Pinecraft, Florida.

Some traditional foods take root in one settlement but don't catch on elsewhere. Or the same foods are popular, but for different reasons. For instance, in some Indiana settlements, homemade raisin pie is a popular wedding offering. Yet among the Amish in Pennsylvania, raisin pie is served so often at funerals that it's called Funeral Pie (recipe on page 221).

The fact is, if they're not forced to move by land shortages, most Amish generally don't stray far from the settlements they were born in. So they tend to be raised on the same foods and recipes for generations. One very important recipe that has been passed down in Lovina's family for as long as anyone can remember is shoofly pie. Here is her recipe for the traditional dessert, in the hope that you can always find a slice, no matter where you may be.

—by Kevin Williams

WHERE DOES THE NAME COME FROM?

I'm told that the origin of shoofly pie's unusual name has been debated by food historians for almost a century. That may be, but I like the simplest explanation best, one that I first heard: Amish cooks usually cool their pies on a windowsill. So the shoofly name comes from the flies that are attracted to the pools of molasses that sometimes form on top of the pie as it cools.

MY SHOOFLY PIE

Makes one 9-inch pie

There are many baked goods we in the Amish communities are credited with either concocting or co-opting, but none probably so widely known as shoofly pie. This is the recipe that has been handed down in my family.

1 cup molasses

⅔ cup boiling water

1 teaspoon baking soda

1 disk My Homemade Pie Dough (page 296) or Pat-a-Pan Piecrust (page 298)

TOPPING

3½ cups all-purpose flour

1 cup sugar

¾ cup shortening, softened

Dash of salt

Preheat the oven to 350°F.

In a large bowl, combine the molasses, boiling water, and baking soda. Pour the mixture into the unbaked pie shell.

Make the topping: In a large bowl, mix the flour with the sugar, shortening, and salt. Spread this on top of the molasses mixture in the pie shell. Bake until the center of the pie is set, about 45 minutes. Cool on a wire rack or windowsill until the pie is firm, about 45 minutes. Store any leftovers in a sealed container. The pie will keep for about 5 days.

CHOCOLATE CHIP PIE

Makes one 9-inch pie

If your children like chocolate chip cookies, then they'll love this pie. The dessert looks like a pie from the top, but when you cut into it, the inside resembles a chocolate chip cookie. A glass of cold milk goes great with a slice of this pie.

1 cup sugar

½ cup all-purpose flour

2 large eggs

½ cup melted butter

1½ cups semisweet chocolate chips

1 teaspoon vanilla extract

1 disk My Homemade Pie Dough (page 296) or Pat-a-Pan Piecrust (page 298)

Preheat the oven to 350°F.

In a large bowl, combine the sugar and flour; stir in the eggs and butter until the batter is well blended and smooth. Add the chocolate chips and vanilla; mix until smooth and the chocolate chips are evenly distributed. Pour the mixture into the unbaked pie shell. Bake until golden brown, 40 to 45 minutes. Cool on a wire rack until the pie is firm, about 45 minutes. Store any leftovers in a sealed container. The pie will keep for about 5 days.

CHOCOLATE NUT PIE

Makes one 9-inch pie

Most of the time my children don't like nuts in dessert, but this pie is an exception. When I make this pie, it doesn't last very long around here! My daughter Susan is my "pie eater," because she seems to like pie more than the other children, and she gave this pie her absolute approval.

½ cup margarine

¾ cup semisweet chocolate chips

3 large eggs

1 cup sugar

1 teaspoon vanilla extract

¾ cup walnuts

1 disk My Homemade Pie Dough (page 296) or Pat-a-Pan Piecrust (page 298)

Preheat the oven to 350°F.

Melt the margarine in a small saucepan over low heat. Add the chocolate chips to the margarine, stirring until melted. Remove from the heat and transfer to a large bowl. In a small bowl, beat the eggs lightly with a fork. Then stir the sugar, eggs, vanilla, and nuts into the chocolate mixture. Pour into the unbaked pie shell. Bake until the center is firm, about 45 minutes. While it bakes, the nuts will rise to the top. Cool on a wire rack or windowsill until the pie is firm, about 45 minutes. Store any leftovers in a sealed container. The pie will keep for about 5 days.

PECAN PIE

Makes one 9-inch pie

This is one of my husband's favorite pies—and mine, too—so we make it a lot. I usually buy the pecans at the bulk-food store if I can. Some people leave their pecans whole, but I prefer mine chopped up, and so does Joe. I think it tastes better to have the pecans in smaller bites. Pecan is a very rich pie, so you can't have too much at once. I do know some people who will use walnuts, and they call it a poor man's pecan pie. I tried it once with walnuts and it was true, it was hard to tell the difference.

3 large eggs

¼ teaspoon salt

1 cup sugar

¾ cup light corn syrup

2 teaspoons margarine, melted

¾ cup pecans, chopped

1 disk My Homemade Pie Dough (page 296) or Pat-a-Pan Piecrust (page 298)

Preheat the oven to 350°F.

In a large bowl, beat the eggs well. Add the salt, sugar, corn syrup, and margarine. Place the pecans in the unbaked pie shell. Pour the mixture over the pecans and bake until golden brown, about 1 hour. Cool on a wire rack or windowsill until the pie is firm, about 45 minutes. Store any leftovers in a sealed container. The pie will keep for about 7 days.

BAKING EQUALS BONDING

Among the Amish, a loaf of homemade bread or a plate of homemade cookies can be the equivalent of a handshake or a hug. The Amish, true to their religious tenets of plainness, simplicity, and stoicism, have comparatively few outward ways in which to show affection. Enthusiastic embraces or rowdy greetings just aren't considered seemly.

One of the few ways in which the Amish display affection is through food. And baked goods occupy a central role in this Amish culinary and cultural emotional expression. Amish baking is by its very definition simple, self-sufficient, and often sweet and sticky. There's a calming comfort passed on as many hands shape dough; serenity and patience are conveyed when multiple generations watch bread balloon into a billowy golden pillow in a wood-fired oven.

Through centuries of religious persecution in Europe and often harsh settlement conditions in the United States and Canada, the Amish have turned to their hands to feed themselves: men to plant and harvest, women to bake and cook. This insular self-sufficiency has elevated the Amish into legendary creators of cakes, pies, rolls, and doughnuts out of the basic building blocks of baking: flour, eggs, butter, vanilla, oatmeal, seasonal fruits, cinnamon, and molasses.

Baking is considered by many to be a science, but among the Amish it's more art. And art is subjective, inexact, and beholden to the artist's definition of beauty. Amish bakers aren't schooled in methodology driven by the knowledge of how long yeast takes to ferment, exact water temperatures, and precise instructions. They instead are driven by intuition and experience and success, all passed between the generations.

BASIC FROSTING

Makes 2 cups

I use this recipe for anything that needs frosting: cakes, cinnamon rolls, Long John Rolls (page 76), and even cookies. If you want a really white frosting, use shortening instead of butter. And if you want a certain color icing, just add a few drops of whatever food coloring you want.

⅓ cup butter, softened

1 teaspoon vanilla extract

4 cups powdered sugar

½ cup milk

In a medium bowl, cream the butter with the vanilla and 1 cup of the powdered sugar. Gradually add the milk and the remaining powdered sugar and stir until smooth.

BASIC CAKE MIX

Serves 15

This is an easy mix for a basic cake. I remember one spring, I bought a horseshoe-shaped cake pan at a garage sale. The children were eager to see how a cake shaped like a horseshoe would look, so my daughter Elizabeth made one, frosted it, and lined the edges with chocolate chips. Needless to say, the children were all excited to see it and eat it. All we had that summer were horseshoe-shaped cakes, often made with this mix.

9½ cups all-purpose flour

6 cups sugar

¼ cup baking powder

1 tablespoon salt

2½ cups shortening, softened

In a large bowl, sift together the flour, sugar, baking powder, and salt and add the softened shortening. Cut in until the mixture resembles very fine crumbs. Divide the mix into four equal portions of 4½ cups each. Place in airtight containers and store in a cool, dry place for up to 2 months. Or place in freezer containers and freeze for up to 6 months.

Before use: *Allow the mix to come to room temperature.*

FOUR-IN-ONE CAKE FROM MIX

Serves 4

This basic mix makes yellow cake when prepared as is, or follow the instructions below for white cake, chocolate cake, or spice cake.

4½ cups Basic Cake Mix (page 349)

1 cup milk

1 teaspoon vanilla extract

2 large eggs

Preheat the oven to 350°F. Grease and flour a 9 by 13-inch pan and set aside.

In a bowl, combine all the ingredients. Beat until moistened, 1 to 2 minutes. Pour into the prepared pan and bake until a toothpick inserted in the center comes out clean, about 25 minutes.

Make white cake from mix: Prepare the batter as for the yellow cake, but use 3 egg whites instead of 2 whole eggs.

Make chocolate cake from mix: Follow the ingredients as for the yellow cake, but add ¼ cup unsweetened cocoa powder.

Make spice cake from mix: Follow the recipe as for a yellow cake, except add 1 teaspoon ground cinnamon, ¼ teaspoon ground allspice, and ¼ teaspoon ground cloves.

LAZY WOMAN'S CAKE

Serves 6 to 8

This also makes good cupcakes. The cake has a funny name, but if you have a houseful of children like I do, sometimes a lazy cake is just the answer when dessert is needed in a pinch!

2 cups sugar

3 cups all-purpose flour

1 teaspoon salt

5 tablespoons unsweetened cocoa powder

2 heaping teaspoons baking soda

1 cup vegetable oil

1 tablespoon vanilla extract

2 tablespoons vinegar

2 cups cold water

Preheat the oven to 350°F.

In a large bowl, combine all the ingredients. Mix until the batter is creamy and smooth. Pour into an ungreased 9 by 13-inch pan and bake until a toothpick inserted in the center comes out clean, about 30 minutes. Let the cake cool completely and store in a sealed container. This cake will stay fresh for 3 to 4 days.

EGGLESS CAKE

Serves 6 to 8

Often eggs are needed when baking a cake, especially if you want it to be nice and moist. This is a recipe (Lazy Woman's Cake, page 351, is another) that doesn't require eggs and still makes a nice, moist chocolate cake.

2 cups granulated sugar

½ cup vegetable oil

1 cup buttermilk

1 teaspoon vanilla extract

Dash of salt

3 tablespoons unsweetened cocoa powder

2¾ cups all-purpose flour

1 cup water

2 teaspoons baking soda

CARAMEL ICING

4 tablespoons (½ stick) butter

½ cup packed brown sugar

2 tablespoons milk

1¾ cups powdered sugar

Preheat the oven to 350°F. Grease and flour a 9 by 13-inch pan and set aside.

In a large bowl, mix the sugar, oil, buttermilk, vanilla, salt, cocoa, and flour until evenly mixed. In a small saucepan, heat the water to boiling. Remove from the heat and add the baking soda. Pour the mixture into the batter and mix until smooth. Then pour into the prepared pan and bake until a toothpick inserted in the center comes out clean, about 35 minutes.

Make the icing: Stir together the butter and brown sugar in a small saucepan, and bring to a boil over low heat. Remove from the heat and add the milk and powdered sugar. Stir until smooth and spread onto the cake. Let the cake cool completely and store in a sealed container or cake safe. This cake will stay fresh for 3 to 4 days.

CHOCOLATE SHEET CAKE

Serves 25 to 30

This is a really moist cake and very easy for children to make (and eat!). Our daughter Elizabeth usually makes this cake for us. One year, she made it for Joe to take to work on his birthday. This cake works well for us because of its large size—when our family gets together with Jacob and Emma's family to celebrate a birthday, a 9 by 13-inch cake isn't big enough anymore!

2 cups all-purpose flour

2 cups sugar

1 teaspoon baking soda

1 teaspoon salt

½ cup (1 stick) margarine or butter

1 cup water

¼ cup unsweetened cocoa powder

2 large eggs, beaten

½ cup sour cream

½ cup milk

1 teaspoon vanilla extract

ICING

½ cup (1 stick) margarine or butter

6 teaspoons milk

¼ cup unsweetened cocoa powder

1 pound powdered sugar, sifted

1 teaspoon vanilla extract

½ cup chopped walnuts (optional)

Preheat the oven to 350°F. Grease a 10 by 15-inch baking pan.

Combine the flour, sugar, baking soda, and salt in a large bowl. Stir with a whisk to blend. Combine the margarine, water, and cocoa in a medium saucepan and bring to a boil over medium heat. Add the hot mixture to the dry ingredients and stir well. Add the eggs and beat well, then add the sour cream, milk, and vanilla.

Pour the batter into the pan and bake until a toothpick inserted in the center comes out clean, 20 to 25 minutes. Remove from the oven and let cool completely.

Make the icing: Combine the margarine, milk, and cocoa in a large bowl. Gradually stir in the powdered sugar until smooth; stir in the vanilla until blended. Spread the icing over the cooled cake and sprinkle with the nuts.

HOT FUDGE SUNDAE CAKE

Serves 8 to 10

This is good served warm with ice cream or milk. The dessert is cakelike on top, with a nice, warm, syrupy layer beneath.

2 cups all-purpose flour

1½ cups granulated sugar

¾ cup unsweetened cocoa powder

4 teaspoons baking powder

1 teaspoon salt

1 cup milk

¼ cup vegetable oil

2 teaspoons vanilla extract

1 cup walnuts, chopped

1½ cups firmly packed brown sugar

3½ cups boiling water

Preheat the oven to 350°F. Grease a 10 by 15-inch baking pan and set aside.

Sift together the flour, sugar, ½ cup of the cocoa powder, the baking powder, and salt in a large bowl. Add the milk, vegetable oil, and vanilla, and stir until smooth and well combined. Fold in the nuts until evenly incorporated. Pour the batter into the prepared baking pan, then sprinkle the brown sugar and the remaining ¼ cup of cocoa powder on top. Pour the boiling water on top of everything. Bake until the top looks dry, about 40 minutes.

MOIST CHOCOLATE CAKE

Serves 14 to 16

This is an easy chocolate cake, typical of many Amish "from the pantry" desserts. It goes great with a scoop of vanilla ice cream.

3 cups all-purpose flour

2 cups sugar

¼ cup unsweetened cocoa powder

2 teaspoons baking soda

1 teaspoon salt

1 cup vegetable oil

2 tablespoons vinegar

1 teaspoon vanilla extract

2 cups water

Preheat the oven to 350°F.

Sift together the flour, sugar, cocoa, baking soda, and salt in a large bowl. Add the oil, vinegar, vanilla, and water and stir to form a smooth batter. Pour the batter into a greased 9 by 13-inch baking pan and bake until a toothpick inserted in the center comes out clean, 30 to 40 minutes.

MARBLE CAKE

Serves 6 to 8

Cakes are needed for so many different occasions around here that sometimes it is nice to bring something to a gathering that is a little different. This is a good, moist cake and a nice change from a plain chocolate cake. More chocolate added, though, makes it more "marbled/gooey" and can be done if that is your preference. If you like, sprinkle powdered sugar over the cake and serve warm, or let it cool and ice it with chocolate frosting.

2½ cups all-purpose flour	1 cup semisweet chocolate chips, melted
1½ teaspoons baking powder	2 tablespoons hot water
1¾ teaspoons baking soda	¾ cup shortening, softened
1 teaspoon salt	1 cup sour milk or buttermilk
1⅔ cups plus 1 tablespoon sugar	2 large eggs

Preheat the oven to 350°F. Grease a 9 by 13-inch pan and set aside.

In a bowl, mix together the flour, baking powder, 1½ teaspoons of the baking soda, the salt, and 1⅔ cups of the sugar. Set aside. In another bowl, combine the melted chocolate, hot water, the remaining ¼ teaspoon of baking soda, and the remaining 1 tablespoon of sugar. Mix well and set aside.

In a large bowl, put the softened shortening. Add the flour mixture and sour milk into the shortening alternately, stirring after each addition. Add the eggs and mix well. The batter will be slightly thick.

Remove about one-quarter of the batter (1¼ cups), add to the chocolate mixture, and mix well. Alternately spoon the plain and chocolate batters into the prepared pan. Then, with a knife, cut through the batter in a wide zigzag course until the desired marbling is reached.

Bake until a toothpick inserted 1 inch from the center comes out clean, 35 to 40 minutes. Cover with aluminum foil after 20 minutes of baking to prevent the top from over-browning. Let the cake cool completely and store in a sealed container or cake safe. This cake will stay fresh for 3 to 4 days.

RHUBARB CAKE

Serves 8 to 12

We love using fresh rhubarb in this cake recipe when the first tart stalks are ready in the spring. But this same recipe can be made using apples, strawberries, or whatever fruit is in season. This cake is also very good when served with an icing drizzled over it or topped with whipped cream.

1¼ cups packed brown sugar

½ cup shortening, softened

1 large egg

2 cups all-purpose flour

½ teaspoon baking soda

½ teaspoon salt

1 cup buttermilk

1½ cups chopped fresh rhubarb

Whipped cream for serving (optional)

Preheat the oven to 350°F. Grease a 9 by 13-inch pan and set aside.

In a large bowl, combine the brown sugar, shortening, and egg. Beat until light and fluffy. In a separate bowl, blend the flour, baking soda, and salt. Add to the shortening mixture alternately with the buttermilk. Fold in the rhubarb. Spoon into the prepared pan and bake until a toothpick inserted into the center comes out clean, about 35 minutes. Let the cake cool completely and store in a sealed container or cake safe. This cake will stay fresh for 3 to 4 days. Top slices with the whipped cream, if desired, when serving.

APPLESAUCE CAKE

Serves 8 to 12

We had a Yellow Transparent tree in our front yard when I was growing up. We also had a McIntosh and a Jonathan tree. The Jonathan is a good eating apple, while the McIntosh is good for cooking and baking. But with the yellow apples, Mom always used to make applesauce, and I would always get my apples for applesauce off my mom and dad's tree if I needed more. My children like applesauce with cake or cookies, so this recipe is a big hit in our house.

1 cup sugar

1 cup Miracle Whip salad dressing (not mayo)

½ cup milk

2 cups unsweetened applesauce

1 teaspoon vanilla extract

3 cups all-purpose flour

2 teaspoons baking soda

2 teaspoons ground cinnamon

½ teaspoon ground nutmeg

½ teaspoon ground allspice

½ teaspoon salt

Preheat the oven to 350°F. Grease and flour a 9 by 13-inch pan and set aside.

In a large bowl, cream together the sugar, salad dressing, and milk. Beat in the applesauce and vanilla. In a separate bowl, combine the flour, baking soda, cinnamon, nutmeg, allspice, and salt. Add the dry ingredients, a little at a time, to the wet mixture. The batter will be thick and slightly lumpy. Pour into the prepared pan and bake until a toothpick inserted in the center comes out clean, 35 to 40 minutes. Let the cake cool completely and store in a sealed container or cake safe. This cake will stay fresh for 3 days.

PEANUT BUTTER CAKE

Serves 8 to 12

Everyone in my family likes peanut butter: peanut butter spread, peanut butter cookies, and so on. My children will eat just plain peanut butter on bread or on celery sticks.

CAKE

¼ cup margarine, softened

¾ cup creamy peanut butter

1½ cups packed brown sugar

2 large eggs

½ cup warm water

1 cup buttermilk

2 cups all-purpose flour

1 teaspoon salt

1 teaspoon baking soda

PEANUT BUTTER FROSTING

1 cup semisweet chocolate chips, melted

2 tablespoons margarine, softened

5 tablespoons creamy peanut butter

2 cups powdered sugar

½ teaspoon vanilla extract

3 to 4 tablespoons milk

Preheat the oven to 350°F. Grease and flour a 9 by 13-inch pan and set aside.

Make the cake: In a large bowl, blend the margarine, peanut butter, and brown sugar until thick and creamy in consistency. Add the eggs, water, buttermilk, flour, salt, and baking soda. Mix until creamy and thoroughly blended. Spoon into the prepared pan and bake until a toothpick comes out clean, 25 to 30 minutes. Let the cake cool completely and store in a sealed container or cake safe. This cake will stay fresh for 3 to 4 days.

Make the frosting: Blend together all the frosting ingredients in a medium bowl until thick and creamy. Spread on the cooled cake.

tools

Amish kitchens aren't equipped with microwave ovens, blenders, high-powered food processors, or electric mixers. Without the electricity that non-Amish homes so freely utilize, those pieces of equipment would be as useful as old tree stumps. Instead, Amish kitchens hold an abundance of heavy-duty hand tools and pots and pans that are often passed down from mother to daughter. A typical countertop looks like this:

Wooden spoons

Spatulas

Rolling pin

Measuring cups and spoons

Cookie scoops

Hand-cranked egg beater

All-in-one apple corer, slicer, peeler

tips

"Thinking big" is a common theme in Amish kitchens because so often a homemaker is called upon to serve voluminous quantities of food. In the event of a church service, wedding, funeral, barn raising, or quilting bee, hundreds of people may need to be fed. And no Amish hostess worth her salt and pepper shakers (handmade, of course) wants to be caught short.

Spending so much time in the kitchen gives Amish women an array of culinary know-how. The following collection of tips is just an example of what most Amish cooks carry right in their heads.

STORAGE TIP: COOKIES

Store cookies in a sealed jar, and add a slice of bread to the container. It helps keep the cookies softer, longer. Do not mix one kind of cookie with another because chocolate chip, for example, will draw moisture from sugar cookies if stored together, leaving the sugar cookies hard and dried out.

BAKING TIP: ROLLING COOKIE DOUGH

When rolling out cookie dough, sprinkle the surface with powdered sugar instead of flour. Too much flour can make the dough heavy and dry.

BAKING TIP: CHILLING DOUGH

Any cookie dough works better if chilled for an hour or two before baking. If dough is too sticky, chilling it makes it easier to handle. Cookie dough for slicing will cut more easily and neatly.

BAKING TIP: FLAWLESS BREAD

Perfect bread requires perfect mixing. For best results, put all liquid ingredients in a chilled bowl first, then mix in flour very slowly and thoroughly ¼ to ½ cup at a time so it blends uniformly. For a tender crust, rub a thin coat of olive or vegetable oil on the top and bottom of the dough before letting it rise. Bread slices if you let it rest overnight.

BAKING TIP: GREASING CAKE PAN

To avoid getting messy hands when greasing a cake pan, put your hand in a plastic sandwich bag or take a folded paper towel or napkin to spread the grease.

BAKING TIP: CUPCAKES

If you want more cupcakes than you have muffin pans, try using canning jar rings to hold the papers in place on a baking sheet.

BAKING TIP: DRY OR FALLEN CAKES

If a cake cracks on top, it is usually because your oven is too hot or because the cake has too much flour added. Dry, crumbly cakes often come from overbaking, overbeating, or too much flour. A fallen cake can often be from underbaking or a too-low oven temperature.

HOW-TO TIP: MAKING BAKING POWDER

If you run out of baking powder, make more by the teaspoon: Simply mix ⅓ teaspoon baking soda with ½ teaspoon cream of tartar.

HOW-TO TIP: MAKING CREAM

If a recipe calls for cream and you don't have any, whisk together ¾ cup milk with 4 tablespoons melted butter to make 1 cup of substitute cream.

HOW-TO TIP: MAKING CAKE FLOUR

Sometimes, recipes call for cake flour, which most cooks don't keep on hand. To make 1 cup, put 2 tablespoons cornstarch in a cup measure and fill the rest with all-purpose flour. Mix before using.

HOW-TO TIP: SUBSTITUTING BROWN SUGAR

Instead of 1 cup of brown sugar, you can use 1 cup granulated sugar plus 2 tablespoons dark corn syrup or molasses.

CARROT CAKE

Serves 6

This sweet treat is probably a child's favorite way of all to eat carrots. Many adults like it, too—my sister Susan is a big fan of carrot cake.

2 cups sugar

1½ cups vegetable oil

4 large eggs, beaten

2 cups all-purpose flour

2 teaspoons baking soda

2 teaspoons ground cinnamon

1 teaspoon salt

3 cups peeled and grated carrots

⅓ cup chopped walnuts

1 cup raisins

CREAM CHEESE FROSTING

1 pound powdered sugar, sifted

1 (8-ounce) package cream cheese, softened

4 tablespoons margarine or butter, softened

1 teaspoon vanilla extract

½ cup chopped walnuts

Preheat the oven to 350°F. Grease a 9 by 13-inch cake pan and set aside.

Mix the sugar, oil, and eggs together in a large bowl. Combine the flour, baking soda, cinnamon, and salt in a medium bowl. Stir with a whisk to blend. Stir the dry ingredients into the wet ingredients. Add the carrots, nuts, and raisins and stir to blend. Pour the batter into the pan and smooth the top. Bake until a toothpick inserted in the center of the cake comes out clean, 35 to 40 minutes. Remove from the oven and let cool completely.

Make the frosting: Cream the sugar, cream cheese, and margarine together in a medium bowl. Stir in the vanilla and walnuts. Spread on the cooled cake.

CHOCOLATE CHIP CAKE

Serves 10

This is a moist, classic chocolate cake that can be used to celebrate birthdays or a child's accomplishments at school. Be sure to spread the chocolate chips evenly over the top of the batter.

1¾ cups flour

1 teaspoon baking soda

1 teaspoon salt

2 tablespoons unsweetened cocoa powder

1 cup shortening

1 cup sugar

2 large eggs, beaten

1 teaspoon vanilla extract

1 cup boiling water

6 ounces chocolate chips

Preheat the oven to 350°F. Lightly grease a 9 by 13-inch pan and set aside.

In a large bowl, sift together the flour, baking soda, salt, and cocoa. Set aside. In a separate large bowl, cream together the shortening and sugar. Add the eggs and vanilla to the shortening mixture. Beat thoroughly. Add the boiling water and the flour mixture alternately to the shortening mixture, mixing the batter until smooth after each addition. The mixture will be smooth and creamy.

Spoon and spread into the prepared pan. Sprinkle the batter evenly with the chocolate chips. Bake until the cake is firm, about 45 minutes. Let the cake cool completely and store in a sealed container or cake safe. This cake will stay fresh for 3 to 4 days.

PLUM CAKE

Serves 8 to 12

Mom would often order a bushel of plums. A truck would come to an Amish farm nearby and he would deliver peaches, apples, plums, or any fruit you wanted. Mom would order a bushel and can them. We'd open a can of plums just like we would a can of peaches or cherries, and that would be another fruit for us to experience. We would eat them with cake or cookies and mix the fruits all together. With peaches the pits were out already, but with the plums they were not, so we had to be careful when we ate them.

CAKE

1 cup vegetable oil

1½ cups sugar

3 large eggs

2 cups all-purpose flour

1 teaspoon baking powder

1 teaspoon baking soda

½ teaspoon salt

1 teaspoon ground cinnamon

½ teaspoon ground nutmeg

½ teaspoon ground allspice

1 cup thick sour milk or buttermilk

1 cup cooked, chopped plums, drained

¾ cup chopped walnuts

GLAZE

½ cup sugar

¼ cup thick sour milk or butter

1 tablespoon light corn syrup

2 tablespoons butter

½ teaspoon baking soda

½ teaspoon vanilla extract

Preheat the oven to 350°F. Grease and flour a 9 by 13-inch pan and set aside.

Make the cake: In a large bowl, combine the vegetable oil, sugar, eggs, flour, baking powder, and baking soda until the mixture is smooth and creamy. Then stir in the salt, cinnamon, nutmeg, allspice, sour milk, plums, and walnuts. Stir until the fruits and nuts are evenly distributed throughout the batter. Pour into the prepared pan and bake until a toothpick inserted in the center comes out clean, 35 to 40 minutes.

Make the glaze: Combine the sugar, sour milk, corn syrup, butter, baking soda, and vanilla in a small saucepan and cook over medium heat, stirring constantly until the mixture boils. Turn the heat to low and boil for 5 minutes, stirring occasionally. Remove from the heat. Cool the cake for 5 minutes, and then make deep holes in it with a fork so that the glaze will soak into the cake. Pour the glaze over the hot cake. Let the cake cool completely and store in a sealed container or cake safe. This cake will stay fresh for 3 to 4 days.

PEACH UPSIDE-DOWN CAKE

Serves 6 to 8

My children eat and enjoy home-canned peaches. While we don't have a peach tree in our yard, we do make sure we get plenty of peaches each year when they are in season. A lady in church will usually have a truck unload them at her place, and everyone has to go pick up their bushels of peaches from there. I ordered several bushels one year. I like to order at least one bushel every year, but if prices aren't too bad I order more. The children like to also just eat peaches fresh. Peaches can also be enjoyed in jams and baked goods like this upside-down cake. Most around here would use homegrown, home-canned peaches. But you can use store-bought for this recipe.

1 quart canned sliced peaches

6 tablespoons margarine or butter

1 cup packed brown sugar

$\frac{2}{3}$ cup vegetable shortening

1 cup granulated sugar

2 large eggs

2 teaspoons vanilla extract

2$\frac{1}{2}$ teaspoons baking powder

1 teaspoon salt

2 cups all-purpose flour

Preheat the oven to 350°F. Grease a 9 by 13-inch cake pan and set aside.

Drain the peaches and reserve the syrup. Melt the margarine in a large skillet. Add the brown sugar, 2 tablespoons of the peach syrup, and the drained peaches to the skillet. Let simmer over low heat. Add enough water to the remaining peach syrup to make 1 cup, and set aside.

In a large bowl, cream together the shortening and granulated sugar until light and crumbly. Add the eggs and vanilla. Beat until fluffy. In a separate medium bowl, sift together the baking powder, salt, and flour. Add the dry mixture and the 1 cup of syrup alternately to the creamed mixture, stirring after each addition until smooth. The batter will be thick, a bit heavier than a cake batter.

Remove the skillet from the heat and, using a slotted spoon, remove the peaches from the skillet and spread the fruit in the bottom of the prepared cake pan. Spread the batter evenly over the peaches and bake until the top is brown and a toothpick inserted in the center comes out clean, 35 to 40 minutes. Let the cake cool completely and store in a sealed container or cake safe. This cake will stay fresh for 3 to 4 days.

OLD-FASHIONED BLUEBERRY CAKE

Serves 6 to 8

We have several blueberry "U-pick" patches around. My sister Emma and her husband, Jacob, and their children usually go every year and bring me some fresh blueberries. You can freeze blueberries well as long as you don't wash them before freezing. They shouldn't have any water on them when going into the freezer or they deteriorate.

1 pint blueberries (2 cups fresh or frozen)	¾ teaspoon baking soda
1 cup plus 2 tablespoons sugar	¼ teaspoon ground cinnamon
1½ cups plus 1 tablespoon all-purpose flour	Dash of salt
	2 large eggs, at room temperature
Grated lemon zest from 2 lemons	½ teaspoon vanilla extract
9 tablespoons butter, softened	⅔ cup sour cream
¾ teaspoon baking powder	Pinch of ground nutmeg

Preheat the oven to 350°F. Grease a 2-quart ovenproof casserole dish or a 9 by 9-inch pan.

In a large bowl, combine the blueberries with ½ cup of the sugar, 1 tablespoon of the flour, and 2 teaspoons of the lemon zest and place in the prepared casserole dish. Cut in 2 tablespoons of the butter and toss. Bake for 10 minutes. Stir gently after removing from the oven.

While the berries are baking, sift together the remaining 1½ cups of flour, the baking powder, baking soda, cinnamon, salt, and 1 tablespoon of the lemon zest. Set aside.

In a separate bowl, cream 6 tablespoons of the butter with ½ cup of the sugar. Add the eggs one at a time and beat until well blended. Blend in 1 teaspoon of the lemon zest and the vanilla. Add the flour mixture and the sour cream alternately to the egg mixture, starting with the flour and ending with the sour cream and combining after each addition.

Drop the batter by spoonfuls over the baked berries, spreading evenly. Combine the remaining 2 tablespoons of sugar, the nutmeg, ¼ teaspoon lemon zest, and the remaining 1 tablespoon of butter. Crumble over the top of the batter. Bake until a toothpick inserted in the center of the cake comes out clean, about 35 minutes. Let the cake cool completely and store in a sealed container or cake safe. This cake will stay fresh for 3 to 4 days.

HOT MILK SPONGE CAKE

Serves 6 to 8

This is an old recipe that is simple and easy to make. It has a good, sweet taste that goes over well in this household!

2 cups cake flour

2 teaspoons baking powder

½ teaspoon salt

4 large eggs

2 teaspoons vanilla extract

2 cups sugar

1 cup milk

1 tablespoon butter

Preheat the oven to 350°F. Grease a 9 by 13-inch pan, flour only the bottom, and set aside.

In a large bowl, sift together the flour, baking powder, and salt. In another large bowl, beat the eggs and vanilla together. Then gradually add the sugar and continue beating until the mixture becomes light and lemon colored. Blend the dry ingredients into the creamed mixture. Bring the milk and butter to the boiling point, then quickly stir into the batter and blend well. Pour quickly into the prepared baking pan. Bake until the cake is set, 35 to 40 minutes. Let the cake cool completely and store in a sealed container or cake safe. This cake will stay fresh for 3 to 4 days.

SOUR CREAM SPICE CAKE

Serves 6 to 8

Mom didn't ever buy sour cream. We had a plentiful supply of sour milk and buttermilk, which could be used in recipes like these. Her homemade sour cream also tasted so good and added a lot of flavor to a cake like this. Since most people wouldn't make their own, you can use store-bought for this cake and it'll still taste nice and moist.

½ cup shortening, softened

2 cups packed brown sugar

1 cup sour cream

1¾ cups all-purpose flour

3 large eggs, separated

1 tablespoon baking soda

1 tablespoon cloves, crushed

1 teaspoon ground allspice

½ teaspoon salt

1 teaspoon vanilla extract

Preheat the oven to 350°F. Lightly grease a 5 by 9-inch loaf pan and set aside.

In a large bowl, cream together the shortening and sugar. Add the sour cream and mix well. Then add the flour, egg yolks, baking soda, cloves, allspice, and salt. Stir in the vanilla. Beat the egg whites until stiff and then fold them into the mixture. Bake in the prepared pan until a toothpick inserted in the center comes out clean, about 30 minutes. Let the cake cool completely and store in a sealed container or cake safe. This cake will stay fresh for 3 to 4 days.

AMISH ANGEL FOOD CAKE

Serves 12

Angel food cakes are a great light dessert during the hot summer months, which is when our family really enjoys them. Also, angel food cakes are often prepared for weddings around here and put on the guests' tables. Pie filling is often drizzled on the cake. You could also serve it with fruit and whipped cream, or drizzled with icing. I really like angel food cake, and I would go for that before other flavors of cake.

1¼ cups cake flour

1¾ cups sugar

1½ cups egg whites (from 8 to 11 eggs, depending on size)

1½ teaspoons cream of tartar

1 teaspoon vanilla extract

¼ teaspoon salt

Preheat the oven to 375°F.

Mix together the flour and ¾ cup of the sugar. Divide into four equal parts and set aside.

In a large bowl, beat the egg whites, cream of tartar, vanilla, and salt until foamy. It would be best to use a rotary hand mixer (or an electric mixer, if accessible). Beat in the remaining 1 cup of sugar, 2 tablespoons at a time. Stir vigorously for several minutes until the meringue holds stiff peaks that are glossy and moist. With a rubber spatula, gently fold each of the four portions of the flour mixture into the meringue, gently folding after each addition until the flour and sugar mixture disappears.

Scrape the batter into an ungreased 10-inch tube pan. Gently cut through the batter once with a spatula to remove air bubbles. Do not lift the spatula out of the batter while doing this. Bake until the cake springs back when lightly touched with a finger and a long wooden toothpick inserted halfway between the sides comes out clean, 35 to 40 minutes. Invert the pan over a cooling rack and let the cake cool before removing. Let the cake cool completely and store in a sealed container or cake safe. This cake will stay fresh for 3 to 4 days.

RED BEET CHOCOLATE SHEET CAKE

Serves 8 to 12

I was reluctant to try this cake, as I had a hard time associating red beets with chocolate. I love pickled red beets, but other than that I am not too fond of beets. But when I took my first bite of this cake, I was amazed by the taste. It is a very moist cake, and you cannot taste the beets. Neither can you taste the chocolate chips that were added. My daughter Elizabeth doesn't care for red beets at all either, and she agreed you couldn't taste the beets. She said this is probably the only way she could eat red beets. I gave my youngest children a piece, and they really went for it. This is not a cake to eat warm, so let it cool completely before serving.

1¾ cups all-purpose flour

½ teaspoon salt

½ teaspoon baking soda

1½ cups granulated sugar

3 large eggs

1 cup vegetable oil

1½ cups cooked and pureed fresh beets

1 cup semisweet chocolate chips, melted

1 teaspoon vanilla extract

Sifted powdered sugar for sprinkling

Preheat the oven to 350°F. Butter a 9 by 13-inch cake pan and set aside.

Mix together the flour, salt, and baking soda and set aside. Combine the sugar, eggs, and oil in a large bowl. Stir vigorously (those who use electric mixers can use one here on medium speed for 2 minutes). Beat in the beets, melted chocolate, and vanilla. Gradually add the dry ingredients to the beet mixture, beating well after each addition. Pour into the prepared pan. Bake until a toothpick inserted into the center of the cake comes out clean, 40 to 45 minutes. Cool in the pan. Cover and let stand overnight to improve the flavor. Sprinkle with powdered sugar. Let the cake cool completely and store in a sealed container or cake safe. This cake will stay fresh for 3 to 4 days.

BEETS: A UNIVERSAL LANGUAGE

What many outsiders don't understand is that Amish cooking is very different in different areas. Amish cooks are the original locavores, using local ingredients in local recipes. Some Amish don't make shoofly pie, or even know what it is! But beets are different. Pickled beets, along with a few other standards, such as whoopie pies, can universally be found in Amish homes.

HOMEMADE BLACKBERRY CAKE

Serves 10 to 12

This is a favorite recipe in Amish settlements across Virginia and North Carolina, where wild blackberries are plentiful. This is a very moist cake that tastes great frosted. You'll want to have the icing cooked and ready to put on the cake as soon as it is done, while both are still warm.

CAKE

2 cups granulated sugar

4 cups all-purpose flour

½ cup (1 stick) butter

2 cups blackberry jam

1 cup walnuts

2 teaspoons ground cinnamon

2 teaspoons ground cloves

2 teaspoons ground nutmeg

2 teaspoons ground allspice

2 teaspoons baking soda, dissolved in 1 cup buttermilk

6 large eggs

ICING

2 cups granulated sugar

1 cup milk

½ cup (1 stick) butter

Preheat the oven to 300°F. Lightly grease a 9 by 13-inch baking pan and set aside.

Make the cake: Thoroughly mix all of the ingredients in a large mixing bowl until smooth and lump free. Pour into the prepared pan and bake for 1 hour, or until the cake is firm in the center and a toothpick comes out clean.

Make the icing: During the final 20 minutes of baking, make the icing. Place all the ingredients in a small saucepan over medium heat. Cook, stirring often, until thick. Keep warm until ready to use.

Remove the cake from the oven and pour the icing over it while both are still hot. Let cool completely before serving.

SWEET POTATO SURPRISE CAKE

Serves 10 to 12

This recipe sweetens the sweet potatoes, hence the name "surprise cake." If you're expecting supper when preparing this, think dessert instead!

1½ cups vegetable oil

2 cups sugar

4 large eggs, separated

¼ cup hot water

2½ cups all-purpose flour

1 tablespoon baking powder

¼ teaspoon salt

1 teaspoon ground cinnamon

1 teaspoon ground nutmeg

1½ cups grated raw sweet potatoes

1 cup walnuts, chopped

1 teaspoon vanilla extract

FROSTING

1 (12-ounce) can evaporated milk

1 cup sugar

½ cup (1 stick) butter

3 large egg yolks

1 teaspoon vanilla extract

1⅓ cups shredded coconut

Preheat the oven to 350°F. Grease and flour three 9-inch round cake pans and set aside.

Combine the vegetable oil and sugar in a large mixing bowl and mix well. Add the egg yolks, beating until smooth in consistency. Stir in the hot water, then add the flour, baking powder, salt, cinnamon, and nutmeg. Mix well to form a smooth batter. Stir in the grated sweet potatoes, nuts, and vanilla until the ingredients are thoroughly mixed.

In a separate bowl, beat the egg whites until stiff peaks are formed, and fold the egg whites into the sweet potato mixture. Pour the batter into the prepared cake pans and bake for 25 to 30 minutes, or until the center is cooked through. Let cool completely.

Make the frosting: Combine the evaporated milk, sugar, butter, egg yolks, and vanilla in a medium saucepan. Cook over medium heat, stirring constantly, for 12 minutes, or until the mixture thickens. Stir in the coconut. Spread the frosting between the layers of the cooled cake and on the outside of the cake.

PINEAPPLE SHEET CAKE

Serves 12

This is an easy, sweet cake that will appeal to pineapple lovers. Sometimes it is served with the other desserts after Sunday church services.

CAKE

1 (20-ounce) can crushed pineapple, drained

2 teaspoons baking soda

¼ cup water

1 teaspoon vanilla extract

2 large eggs, beaten

2 cups granulated sugar

2 cups all-purpose flour

FROSTING

½ cup margarine, softened

1 (8-ounce) package cream cheese

1 teaspoon vanilla extract

2 cups powdered sugar

Preheat the oven to 350°F. Grease a 10 by 15-inch sheet cake pan and set aside.

Make the cake: In a large bowl, stir the pineapple, baking soda, water, and vanilla until the ingredients are well blended. Add the eggs and mix until blended. Slowly add the sugar and flour, scraping down the sides of the bowl when necessary to ensure the mixture is evenly blended. The batter will be a medium yellow color and slightly bubbly. Spoon the batter into the prepared pan. Bake until the cake pulls away from the edges of the pan and is golden brown, about 30 minutes. A knife inserted in the center will come out clean. Remove from the oven and let cool.

Make the frosting: Stir the softened margarine in a small bowl for about a minute until smooth, and then add the cream cheese. Blend together for several minutes, and then add the vanilla. After the vanilla is thoroughly mixed in, add the powdered sugar, ½ cup at a time, scraping down the sides of the bowl frequently and mixing until the frosting is smooth. Spread evenly over the warm cake. Let the cake cool completely and store in a sealed container or cake safe. This cake will stay fresh for 3 to 4 days.

MOLASSES CAKE

Serves 12

Molasses always reminds me of honey. I'm not sure if it is because they are both sticky to handle. If a recipe calls for molasses and I don't have any, I'll substitute honey, and vice versa. This cake can be enjoyed with Basic Frosting (see page 348) or without.

2 cups all-purpose flour

¾ cup molasses

¼ cup sugar

2 teaspoons baking soda

1 large egg

½ cup buttermilk or sour milk

½ cup hot water

Preheat the oven to 350°F. Lightly grease a 9 by 13-inch pan and set aside.

In a large bowl, combine all the ingredients. Mix thoroughly. Spoon into the prepared pan. Bake until the cake is firm and a toothpick inserted into the center comes out clean, about 40 minutes. Let the cake cool completely and store in a sealed container or cake safe. This cake will stay fresh for 3 to 4 days.

PEAR CAKE

Serves 6 to 8

At my parents' house there used to be a pear tree out by the garden. That is how I learned to like pears. If any of us children were hungry for an afternoon snack, we'd just go out to the pear tree and grab one, take it to the water pump to wash it, and then just eat it. We had a little shed right next to the pear tree where we had our dolls and playhouse, so I have good memories of pears. Most people I know would use home-canned pears for this recipe, but the recipe has been changed to use store-bought canned pears. This is delicious served with a scoop of vanilla ice cream.

CAKE

1½ cups vegetable oil

2 cups sugar

3 large eggs

3 cups all-purpose flour

1 teaspoon salt

1 teaspoon ground cinnamon

1 teaspoon baking soda

1 teaspoon vanilla extract

1 cup pecans, finely chopped

2 cups pears (15¼-ounce can in heavy syrup), chopped and drained (reserve syrup)

GLAZE

1 tablespoon butter, softened

1½ cups powdered sugar

3 tablespoons syrup from the pears

Preheat the oven to 325°F. Grease a Bundt or tube pan.

Make the cake: In a large bowl, combine the oil, sugar, and eggs. Beat until creamy. In a medium bowl, sift together the flour, salt, cinnamon, and baking soda. Stir the dry ingredients into the creamed mixture until smooth. Add the vanilla. Fold in the pecans and pears. Pour the mixture into the prepared pan. Bake until a toothpick inserted into the center comes out clean, about 1 hour and 15 minutes.

Make the glaze: Blend the butter and sugar. Add the pear syrup and stir until well mixed and slightly runny. Drizzle over the cake. Let the cake cool completely and store in a sealed container or cake safe. This cake will stay fresh for 3 to 4 days.

PUMPKIN SHEET CAKE

Serves 12

Pumpkin is something we grow in the garden some years. When my son Benjamin saved seeds from a pumpkin one year, he wrapped them in paper towels to dry out and then put them in one of my kitchen drawers. He'd keep asking me, "When is it time to plant the seeds in the garden?" When planting season came around, he didn't forget, and he was there with his seeds. We did get a few little pumpkins from the seeds, of which he was very proud. Basic Frosting (page 348) can be added if desired, or it is tasty plain. I use a home-canned pumpkin for this, but store-bought works fine, too.

2 cups sugar

4 large eggs

1 cup vegetable oil

2 cups all-purpose flour

1 cup nuts of your choice

2 cups pureed pumpkin

$\frac{1}{2}$ teaspoon salt

1 teaspoon baking soda

2 teaspoons baking powder

2 teaspoons ground cinnamon or pumpkin pie spice

Preheat the oven to 350°F.

In a large bowl, combine all the ingredients until the mixture is evenly and thoroughly mixed. Spoon into a 10 by 15-inch pan. Bake until a toothpick inserted in the center comes out clean, about 30 minutes. Let the cake cool completely and store in a sealed container or cake safe. This cake will stay fresh for 3 to 4 days.

APPLE PUDDING CAKE

Serves 14 to 16

This cake can be served immediately or after cooling, and it's good plain or with vanilla ice cream. Any variety of apple works fine, but slightly tart apples lend more flavor to the cake.

2 large eggs, beaten

1½ cups vegetable oil

3 cups all-purpose flour

2 cups sugar

½ teaspoon salt

1 teaspoon baking soda

1½ teaspoons ground cinnamon

3 cups diced apples

½ cup raisins (optional)

Preheat the oven to 350°F. Grease and flour a 9 by 13-inch pan and set aside.

Mix together the eggs, oil, flour, sugar, salt, baking soda, and cinnamon in a large bowl until well blended. Add the apples and raisins. The batter will be doughlike, and it may be necessary to knead in the apples and raisins to fully incorporate them. Spread the batter evenly into the prepared pan. Bake for 1 hour, or until the top is golden brown and the edges are firm.

RHUBARB CAKE DESSERT

Serves 4 to 6

This recipe reminds me of a rhubarb pie, just without the pie dough. This layered dessert is something that I usually make as a treat for the children in the spring. They seem to really like it.

CRUST

1 cup margarine or butter, softened

2 cups all-purpose flour

2 tablespoons sugar

FILLING

6 large egg yolks

2 cups sugar

¼ cup all-purpose flour

¼ teaspoon salt

1 cup heavy cream or whole milk

5 cups rhubarb, cut into ½-inch pieces

TOPPING

6 large egg whites

Pinch of salt

¾ cup sugar

2 tablespoons vanilla extract

Preheat the oven to 350°F. Butter the bottom and sides of a 9 by 13-inch cake pan.

Make the crust: Combine the margarine, flour, and sugar in a bowl and work until the mixture resembles coarse crumbs. Press evenly across the bottom of the cake pan.

Make the filling: Combine the egg yolks, sugar, flour, salt, and cream in a bowl. Stir until blended. Add the rhubarb and stir to incorporate. Pour the filling onto the crust. Bake until the filling is firm when you shake the pan a little, about 30 minutes. Remove from the oven, leaving the oven on, and let stand while making the topping.

Make the topping: Beat the egg whites and salt in a large bowl until soft peaks form. Gradually beat in the sugar until stiff, glossy peaks form. Fold in the vanilla until blended. Spread the topping evenly over the cake. Return to the oven and bake until lightly browned, about 15 minutes. Remove from the oven and spoon into bowls or onto plates to serve.

RHUBARB SHORTCAKE

Serves 6 to 8

When I was growing up, we would have rhubarb shortcake a lot of times right out of the oven for supper in the evenings. We would sprinkle sugar and cold milk on top. We never had it for break-fast unless it was left over. My dad wouldn't put milk on it; he would just eat it warm. I have fixed rhubarb shortcake for my children many times, and some like it more than others. If we have ice cream in the freezer, they would prefer that ice cream be served with it. We never had that choice growing up. They don't act like they care for the milk on the rhubarb like I did when I was younger. The children do really like rhubarb juice and jam.

4 cups all-purpose flour

1 teaspoon baking soda

2 teaspoons baking powder

Pinch of salt

3 cups sour milk

2 cups chopped rhubarb

1 cup sugar

Preheat the oven to 350°F.

In a large bowl, combine the flour, baking soda, baking powder, and salt. Then gradually add the sour milk until a really soft dough forms. Spread a layer of this dough in a 9 by 13-inch cake pan, and then add a thick layer of rhubarb. Put the sugar on the rhubarb. Put the rest of the dough on the top and bake until the rhubarb is tender, about 45 minutes.

TRUSTY APPLE DESSERT

Serves 12 to 14

This dessert is delicious served warm with Homemade Vanilla Ice Cream (page 386). Or let it cool before covering it with a creamy topping. This is a good eggless dessert to serve. And if you like crunch, add walnut pieces.

2 medium-size apples (Red Delicious or Gala), peeled and shredded

1 cup sugar

2 tablespoons butter, softened

2 cups all-purpose flour

1 cup milk

2 rounded teaspoons baking powder

1 tablespoon ground cinnamon

1 teaspoon vanilla extract

Pinch of salt

SYRUP

1½ cups firmly packed brown sugar

1½ cups water

2 tablespoons butter, melted

1 tablespoon imitation maple flavoring

Preheat the oven to 350°F.

Place the shredded apples in the bottom of a 9 by 9-inch baking pan. Combine the sugar, butter, flour, milk, baking powder, cinnamon, vanilla, and salt in a large bowl. Mix until smooth and well combined. Pour the dough mixture on top of the grated apples.

Make the syrup: In another bowl, combine the brown sugar, water, butter, and maple flavoring. Pour the syrup mixture over the top of the dough. Bake for 35 to 40 minutes, until bubbly and the center is set.

APPLE CRISP

Serves 4 to 6

I fix this a lot. It looks a little like a pie, but there's no dough. We like to eat it with a scoop of ice cream when it's warm. For this recipe, you can really use any apple, but I like Golden Delicious apples. Honey Crisp is another good cooking apple that goes well in this recipe.

5 large apples, peeled, cored, and thinly sliced (6 cups)

1 cup granulated sugar

TOPPING

1 cup (2 sticks) butter, slightly softened

1½ teaspoons ground cinnamon

1½ cups old-fashioned rolled oats

1 cup packed brown sugar

1 cup all-purpose flour

Preheat the oven to 350°F. Lightly grease a 9 by 13-inch pan.

Put the apple slices in the pan and sprinkle with the granulated sugar. Gently toss with your fingers to mix.

Make the topping: Combine the butter, cinnamon, oats, brown sugar, and flour in a medium bowl and mix with your fingertips until the mixture is coarse and crumbly. Spoon evenly over the apples. Bake until golden brown, about 45 minutes.

HOMEMADE VANILLA ICE CREAM

Makes 1 gallon

This cool classic is a Southern staple in Amish settlements, assuming an icehouse is on the premises. Otherwise homemade ice cream has to wait until winter, when Mother Nature supplies the ice. This recipe has been adapted for an ice-cream maker; Amish-made ice creams are simpler and don't usually call for overnight freezing.

6 large eggs

2 cups sugar

½ teaspoon salt

1 tablespoon vanilla extract (or other flavoring of your choice)

1 quart heavy cream

1 quart whole milk

Beat the eggs in a large mixing bowl and gradually add the sugar, beating until the mixture is light in color. Add the salt, vanilla, cream, and milk, and mix until thoroughly combined and creamy. Pour into a 1-gallon ice-cream maker and follow the manufacturer's directions. When done, let sit in the freezer for 2 hours before serving.

SHLICK AND QUICK STRAWBERRY ICE CREAM

Serves 6

Shlick is a Pennsylvania Dutch term for "simple" or "easy," and on a scorching summer day this refreshing dessert is an amazing antidote to the heat. This unpreserved homemade ice cream will melt faster than commercially sold brands and does not require an ice-cream maker—just stir and freeze.

2 cups granulated sugar

¾ cup firmly packed brown sugar

¾ cup instant Clear Jel

½ teaspoon salt

2 to 3 cups heavy cream

2 teaspoons vanilla extract

1 quart frozen, chopped strawberries

2 to 3 cups milk

Stir the sugars, Clear Jel, and salt in a large mixing bowl. Add the cream, and stir vigorously. Add the vanilla, strawberries, and milk and mix well. Transfer to a freezer-safe container, seal tightly, and freeze until firm.

FINDING CLEAR JEL

This recipe calls for a product called Clear Jel, which acts as a thickening agent. Clear Jel can be purchased in most bulk-food and baking stores or online at sites such as Amazon.com. It is a very popular baking and canning ingredient among Amish cooks.

METRIC CONVERSION FORMULAS

TO CONVERT	MULTIPLY
Ounces to grams	Ounces by 28.35
Pounds to kilograms	Pounds by 0.454
Teaspoons to milliliters	Teaspoons by 4.93
Tablespoons to milliliters	Tablespoons by 14.79
Fluid ounces to milliliters	Fluid ounces by 29.57
Cups to milliliters	Cups by 236.59
Cups to liters	Cups by 0.236
Pints to liters	Pints by 0.473
Quarts to liters	Quarts by 0.946
Gallons to liters	Gallons by 3.785
Inches to centimeters	Inches by 2.54

METRIC EQUIVALENTS

LENGTH

$\frac{1}{8}$ inch	3 millimeters
$\frac{1}{4}$ inch	6 millimeters
$\frac{1}{2}$ inch	1.25 centimeters
1 inch	2.5 centimeters
2 inches	5 centimeters
$2\frac{1}{2}$ inches	6 centimeters
4 inches	10 centimeters
5 inches	13 centimeters
6 inches	15.25 centimeters
12 inches (1 foot)	30 centimeters

VOLUME

$\frac{1}{4}$ teaspoon	1 milliliter
$\frac{1}{2}$ teaspoon	2.5 milliliters
$\frac{3}{4}$ teaspoon	4 milliliters
1 teaspoon	5 milliliters
$1\frac{1}{4}$ teaspoons	6 milliliters
$1\frac{1}{2}$ teaspoons	7.5 milliliters
$1\frac{3}{4}$ teaspoons	8.5 milliliters
2 teaspoons	10 milliliters
1 tablespoon ($\frac{1}{2}$ fluid ounce)	15 milliliters
2 tablespoons (1 fluid ounce)	30 milliliters
$\frac{1}{4}$ cup	60 milliliters
$\frac{1}{3}$ cup	80 milliliters
$\frac{1}{2}$ cup (4 fluid ounces)	120 milliliters
$\frac{2}{3}$ cup	160 milliliters
$\frac{3}{4}$ cup	180 milliliters
1 cup (8 fluid ounces)	240 milliliters
$1\frac{1}{4}$ cups	300 milliliters
$1\frac{1}{2}$ cups (12 fluid ounces)	360 milliliters
$1\frac{2}{3}$ cups	400 milliliters
2 cups (1 pint)	460 milliliters
3 cups	700 milliliters
4 cups (1 quart)	0.95 liter
1 quart plus $\frac{1}{4}$ cup	1 liter
4 quarts (1 gallon)	3.8 liters

WEIGHT	
¼ ounce	7 grams
½ ounce	14 grams
¾ ounce	21 grams
1 ounce	28 grams
1¼ ounces	35 grams
1½ ounces	42.5 grams
1⅔ ounces	45 grams
2 ounces	57 grams
3 ounces	85 grams
4 ounces (¼ pound)	113 grams
5 ounces	142 grams
6 ounces	170 grams
7 ounces	198 grams
8 ounces (½ pound)	227 grams
16 ounces (1 pound)	454 grams
35.25 ounces (2.2 pounds)	1 kilogram

COMMON INGREDIENTS AND THEIR EQUIVALENTS

1 cup uncooked rice = 225 grams

1 cup all-purpose flour = 140 grams

1 stick butter (4 ounces • ½ cup • 8 tablespoons) = 110 grams

1 cup butter (8 ounces • 2 sticks • 16 tablespoons) = 220 grams

1 cup brown sugar, firmly packed = 225 grams

1 cup granulated sugar = 200 grams

OVEN TEMPERATURE
To convert Fahrenheit to Celsius, subtract 32 from the Fahrenheit temperature, multiply the result by 5, then divide by 9.

INDEX

Underscored page references indicate boxed text and sidebars. **Boldface** references indicate photographs.

Beseech Thee, beloved and merciful Father, that Thou wouldst let Thy Word, which we have heard and received, be powerful and genuine in the heart of each one of us, and be fruitful, bearing fruit that remains until eternal life. May we through it be not only born again, but completely turned about, changed, and renewed.

—*An Amish Prayer*